P9-EEE-554

TAX-FREE WEALTH

HOW TO BUILD MASSIVE WEALTH BY PERMANENTLY LOWERING YOUR TAXES

SECOND EDITION

TOM WHEELWRIGHT, CPA

FOREWORD BY ROBERT KIYOSAKI

...SOR BOOK

TAX-FREE WEALTH

HOW TO BUILD MASSIVE WEALTH BY PERMANENTLY LOWERING YOUR TAXES

SECOND EDITION

TOM WHEELWRIGHT, CPA

FOREWORD BY ROBERT KIYOSAKI

RDA
PRESS

This publication is designed to provide competent and reliable information regarding the subject matter covered. However, it is sold with the understanding that the author and publisher are not engaged in rendering legal, financial, or other professional advice. Laws and practices often vary from state to state and country to country and if legal or other expert assistance is required, the services of a professional should be sought. The author and publisher specifically disclaim any liability that is incurred from the use or application of the contents of this book.

Published by RDA Press, LLC

Rich Dad Advisors, B-I Triangle, CASHFLOW Quadrant and other Rich Dad marks are registered trademarks of CASHFLOW Technologies, Inc.

RDA Press LLC
15170 N. Hayden Road
Scottsdale, AZ 85260
480-998-5400
Visit our Web sites: RDAPress.com and RichDadAdvisors.com

Printed in the United States of America

First Edition: March 2012
Second Edition: April 2018

ISBN: 978-1-947588-05-9

012021

After 31 years...

Major Tax Reform
and what it means to you

True overhaul of the tax law only happens about once every 30 years. In the past 75 years, the U.S. tax law has only seen three major revisions; one in 1954, the next in 1986 and most recently at the end of 2017. I have been fortunate as a tax professional to be heavily involved in the last two reforms.

In 1986, I was a manager in the National Tax Department (NTD) of Ernst & Whinney (now Ernst Young). My primary responsibility during my three years there was to create, teach and administer tax courses to the Firm's U.S. tax professionals. Just as I arrived in the summer of 1985, I discovered that much of NTD's resources were being devoted to following the tax reform bill that had been introduced that year.

This gave me, as a young tax professional, some amazing insight into the legislative process as well as the horse trading for tax reform. President Reagan wanted two things; simplicity (the 1985 act was called the Tax Simplification Act of 1985) and he wanted it to be revenue neutral (no net increase to the deficit). It took another year before bill was finally passed as the Tax Reform Act of 1986. (Simplicity took a back seat to other goals of the reform.)

In 1986 the big winners from tax reform were individuals, with significantly lower tax rates, insurance companies (who got by relatively unscathed) and businesses. The big loser was real estate investors (the passive loss rules were used as a last-ditch effort to make a "revenue-neutral" bill. The result a few years later was the Savings and Loan debacle accompanied by a massive real estate depression and the government bailing out real estate through the RTC (Resolution Trust Corporation).

Fast forward 31 years to 2017. President Trump had promised economic stimulus and had stumbled out of the blocks with the failure to repeal ObamaCare. Everyone thought tax reform would take two years to complete like it had in 1985-1986. Instead, the Republican-controlled Congress was able to use slick procedural rules to pass major tax reform in record time (less than three months from start to finish).

The result was a bill the consequences of which and application of which are still largely unknown. Known are the clear winners and losers. Losers include employees with lost deductions for moving, investment expenses and reductions in home mortgage interest and state income tax deductions. Winners include big corporations, with a major tax reduction from 35% to

21%, small businesses, with a 20% net income deduction, and real estate, with major depreciation incentives and the 20% net income deduction given to other small businesses.

The key to remember is that very few people had the chance to influence this legislation. Everyone has the same chance to take advantage of the windfalls given to the winners. Employees can choose to be independent contractors and receive the 20% small business deduction. Service professionals who were left out of the 20% deduction can now become C corporations and reduce their tax rate to 21%. Investors who received tax benefits from the costs of investing in the stock market can either begin investing in real estate, with its massive tax benefits, or invest through their Roth IRA or Roth 401(k) and avoid tax altogether on the income and gains from their investments.

Tax-Free Wealth is about using the tax law the way it's meant to be used – as a series of incentives to do what the government wants you to do. This Second Edition incorporates some ideas of how to use the new incentives. The reality is that the incentives don't really change that much. The government still wants businesses to hire employees, so businesses receive tax benefits for doing so. The government still wants investors to provide housing for renters (even more so now), so real estate investors receive large tax breaks for following through on the government's goals. Energy is still favored, both traditional energy (oil & gas and coal) and renewable energy (wind, solar and hydroelectric).

For U.S. taxpayers, you will find helpful tips in this new edition to help you apply the new tax incentives to your situation. As a bonus, I have included information and a link to a free eBook that you can download detailing the Top Ten Tax Benefits from the Trump Tax Reform. For you who live outside the United States, and no matter what country you live in, this edition should help you look for ways to apply your government's incentives. You may even decide that now is the time to do business in the United States as that country. is, to some degree, a tax haven.

You can take advantage of the tax incentives offered by your government only if you understand how the tax law works. Every day, you have the opportunity to reduce your taxes. Once you have digested this book, take it to your tax advisor and have them read it (or better yet, buy them their own copy). Then your tax advisor, who is responsible for understanding all of the technical details of the law, can help you apply them to your specific situation.

Enjoy this book and let me know what you think. You can always reach me at team@wealthability.com. Here is to your Tax-Free Wealth.

Get my FREE eBook!

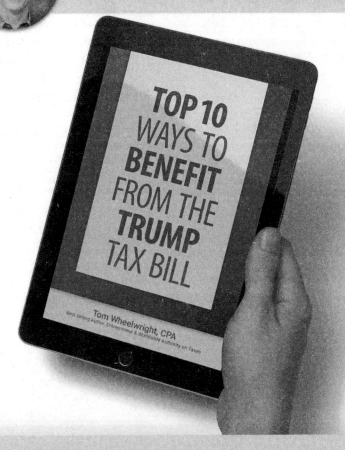

Dedication

This book is dedicated to my mother,
Deborah Ann Coulam Wheelwright,
who taught me that all problems are simply
challenges to overcome and that solutions
come from many sources and directions.

Acknowledgments

I would like to acknowledge the many hands and inspirations that allowed me to write this book. Of course, my editors, Jake Johnson and Mona Gambetta, without whom this book would sound like an accountant wrote it. My business partner and Systems Wiz, Ann Mathis, and our Executive Ambassador, Clarissa Urquidez, who made sure any inaccuracies were addressed and corrected, and who gave me constant encouragement throughout the writing and editing process. My other business partner, Karen Manahan, who manages my CPA firm, allowing me the luxury of time for writing and speaking about how to do what we teach our clients to do.

Then there are my inspirations early in my career. Thank you to Dr. Haney, my first tax professor, who truly loved the tax law and instilled this love into his students. My professors at the University of Texas, especially Sally Jones, who loved teaching the tax law and inspired me to teach others. My mother, to whom this book is dedicated, who was my inspiration in all things when I was young, and who, as the controller for my father's printing company where I worked as an accounting clerk through high school, was my first accounting supervisor.

Thanks also to Robert and Kim Kiyosaki for introducing me to the seminar and publishing world and for allowing me to be their tax advisor. Sometimes, I'm not sure who is really advising whom. They constantly get me to think about money and business differently, even while I am teaching them new ways to think about taxes.

Last but certainly not least, thanks to my adorable wife, Louanne and my children, Max and Sam. They have always supported my career. Louanne has long been a source for inspiration; long before she was my sweetheart and was simply my friend. I always knew I could trust her opinion and that she would give me sound counsel. My sons, Max and Sam, have always inspired me to reach higher and become a better person.

Contents

Part Two— Your Tax Strategy for Tax-Free Wealth

Preface

It's not easy to write a book about taxes that appeals to the average Joe. Most people are scared to death of taxes. They believe that the tax law is out to get them. For years and years, the media and so-called financial advisors have told us that the tax law is far too complex for most people to understand. What these groups are not telling you is that the tax law is actually pretty simple. Yes, there are many details, and you need a good tax advisor to help you sort them out. Still, the fundamental concepts of the tax law are easily understood by anyone with a fifth-grade education.

Of course, the tax laws were not initially intended to even include the average working man and woman. They were meant to reach only the excess earnings of the most wealthy individuals and corporations. Over the past several decades, however, they have evolved to become tools of social and economic policy making.

When the tax laws were first imposed on employees, an average employee earning the average wage was exempt from tax. Now, employees pay the highest taxes, and employers and investors pay the lowest. Why?

Economic policy makers in government discovered that people respond quickly and directly to tax incentives. So, if you want to encourage big families, you give a tax credit for each child. If you want to encourage investment in domestic oil production, you give a big tax deduction for every dollar invested in oil and gas. If you want to encourage investors to build apartments for low-income workers, you simply give them a credit for doing so. And it goes on and on.

This book is not a criticism of the world's tax laws, or even a recommendation that they change. Taxes are part of our world and will always be part of our lives. So, instead of complaining about them and hoping for parliaments and legislatures to make them fairer, let's simply understand them and put them to good use in our lives.

Taxes will either make you rich or make you poor. The tax laws of all countries are written to encourage certain activities that benefit the economy and promote social policy. It's our job to understand and take advantage of the tax laws as they are written.

This book is not about loopholes. Loopholes are unintended consequences of laws that were enacted. This book is about the consequences that lawmakers intended. Taking advantage of the intended benefits is doing what our governments ask us to do. Invest where they say to invest and you get a tax benefit. Put your time and talents into activities that produce jobs, housing, and grow the economy, and you get tax benefits. In many ways, utilizing the tax code to the fullest to save as much money in taxes as possible is one of the most patriotic things you can do.

Again, the concepts of the tax law are not difficult to understand. While this book will not make you an expert in your country's tax laws, it will teach you the fundamental principles of those laws so that you can take advantage of them in the way your government wants. And in doing so, chances are that you will become more profitable in your business and investing. After all, the tax law is really a map—a treasure map. As you follow this treasure map, your taxes go down and your profits and investment returns go up. Enjoy the treasure hunt, and you will find that you will have more money and pay less taxes.

Foreword
by Robert Kiyosaki

The old saying goes: There are two constants in life, death and taxes. I'm of the opinion that you want to do all you can to put both off as long as possible—or at least minimize the pain they cause.

To prolong my life, I eat healthy, exercise, and avoid things like drinking too much and smoking. I value my health. So, I work with experts who help me keep my body in shape and to put only good things inside my body. I put my money where my mouth is.

It didn't used to be this way. I used to love eating junk food, enjoyed my drink a little too much, and didn't exercise. And I paid the price. I was over weight, unhealthy, and had a close call with my heart.

I didn't understand the rules of my body and was breaking those rules. And that was costly. Thankfully, my health problems motivated me to get healthy. Barring the unforeseen, I've added years to my life.

When I was younger, I also didn't understand the rules of taxes. Much like you probably do, I looked at taxes as a major inconvenience that couldn't really be avoided. Thankfully, my rich dad taught me that taxes aren't unavoidable, and that, quite the contrary, they could even be used to your advantage.

My rich dad was not my real dad. He was my best friend's father. My rich dad was an entrepreneur, who owned retail stores, restaurants, and hotels. My real dad was a schoolteacher who eventually became the head of education for the State of Hawaii.

It was my rich dad that pointed out to his son and me that there are four different types of people in the world of money. He defined these four types with the diagram below, a diagram he called the "CASHFLOW Quadrant."

E stands for Employee

S stands for Self-employed or small business owner

B stands for Big business owner

I stands for Investor

As a boy, thanks to my rich dad, I knew that those in the E and S quadrants paid the highest percentage in tax. I also knew that those in the B and I quadrants paid the lowest percentage, sometimes zero in taxes. Following my rich dad's advice, I focused my life on the B and I quadrants...and have done very well financially.

All I had to know was the rules and how to play by them. My problem was finding CPAs who understood the tax laws as my rich dad did.

Over the years, I lost a lot of money to taxes simply because I had high priced, well-educated CPAs who were not the brightest matches in the box—that is until I met Tom Wheelwright. For years now, Tom has been my guiding light, allowing me to do what I do best, which is build businesses, invest, create jobs, and make money, all the while paying less and less in taxes...legally. I've encouraged Tom to write this most important book, especially at this time in history. I am glad it's here and I trust you'll enjoy and learn from it.

Today, taxes are killing many people financially. Perhaps you know what I mean. Do you look at your paycheck every month and wonder where all your money is going? I'll tell you. It's going to the people who know how to use taxes to make money rather than lose money. It's going to people like me.

As you'll find out more in this book, governments write the tax codes to incentivize investors and entrepreneurs to behave how they want. So, if a government wants more affordable housing, they'll provide some great tax incentives to motivate developers to build affordable housing.

The problem is that the governments still have to pay their bills. So whom do they tax? The middle-class. And they use those taxes to subsidize people like me who behave how they want in order to get tax breaks.

As you know, today there is a growing outcry to, "Tax the rich." Many believe the rich are tax-cheats and are ripping off the poor and middle class—and some are. As long as taxes exist, there will be tax-cheats, and not all of them are rich. The poor and middle class have their fair share of tax-cheats. We all know there is a large, underground, tax-free economy in every city of the world, all filled with tax-cheats. You probably know some of these people.

Tom Wheelwright's book will give you a different perspective on taxes. He sees taxes as government incentives and economic stimulus to keep the wheels of the economy greased and moving.

That is how my rich dad saw taxes. He simply saw himself doing what the government wanted done, and in return, the government offered him tax breaks.

Again, my problem has been, getting other people, friends, family, business associates, and yes, CPAs to see taxes from the same point of view.

Most people could not see this point of view, simply because most people are terrified of the taxman, even many CPAs. Most people live in fear of doing something wrong, which is why many people feel better just paying more and more in taxes and then protest that the rich are tax-cheats. This is not financially intelligent.

Today, I receive tax breaks because I provide jobs through my businesses, provide housing through my apartment houses, and provide energy by drilling for oil, keeping energy costs low and the economy moving.

I don't write this to rub it into your face. And I acknowledge that it doesn't even seem fair. But as not just my rich dad, but also probably every dad said, "Life isn't fair." Rather, I write this because I want you to know that you can also use the tax code to your advantage to help you make money—or at the very least, greatly reduce your tax burden.

And that's why I'm very happy that my friend and personal tax advisor, Tom Wheelwright, wrote this book. To me, there is no better person to explain how taxes work, how the tax code can help you grow richer, and who can—I'm not kidding—make taxes fun.

I think you'll find, as I have, Tom's passion for taxes—and helping you save money in taxes—to be infectious. And I know you'll find the wealth of knowledge he brings to the table to be life changing.

He brings good news: you don't have to let taxes kill you financially. The rules in the tax code, whether you know it or not, are there to help you—not harm you.

All you need is the proper knowledge and a little guidance. In this book, Tom offers both in spades.

If you believe the rich are tax-cheats and rip-off the poor and middle class, this book is not for you. You'll probably enjoy *Das Kapital* more.

If you want to earn more and pay less in taxes by doing what the government wants and needs done, however, this is the book for you.

– Robert Kiyosaki, Capitalist

Introduction

When I was a boy, I loved to argue. It didn't matter whether it was on the tennis court or playing Monopoly®. It wasn't simply that I felt I was right; it was the joy of the debate. I discovered that the more I learned about a subject, the more likely I was to win an argument. And what's the point of arguing if you don't plan on winning, right?

I also found that the more vague the question, the easier it was to argue. I grew to love studying about anything that didn't have a fixed answer. When I turned 19, I went to Paris, France, on my mission for the Mormon Church. Everybody knows how the French love to argue. And they have the right language for it. Arguing in French is one of the most enjoyable things I've ever done. It's such a beautiful language. And the French love a good argument. Unlike Americans, they don't take it personally. So you can argue with them for hours on end without anybody getting their feelings hurt. I'm convinced that the French invented the seven-course meal so that they would have plenty of time to argue without their food getting cold. (I remember more than one meal lasting over four hours.)

Maybe it was my love of a good argument that drew me to law in the first place. Although I never earned my law degree (I didn't want to hang out with lawyers—ugh), I loved the thought of practicing law.

I also enjoyed learning about money, earning money, and spending money. So when I went to college I took accounting courses and specialized in tax accounting. Being a tax accountant, I could work in the law and with money at the same time.

During my first 13 years out of college, I worked as an employee for some Big Four accounting firms and a Fortune 1000 company. I was very successful as an employee. Promotions came easily and steadily. In my first firm, Ernst & Young, they gave me the opportunity to work in the National Tax Department—a great honor for a young CPA. I did equally well at the Fortune 1000 company, making great strides in reducing their sales and property taxes. When I left them, I went back into public accounting with a different international accounting firm. One day, only seven months after I started working there, I went into my office, only to find a note on my desk from my boss that I was to come down the hall to see him as soon as I got in.

This was a little odd, as I worked in the Phoenix office and my boss worked out of the Los Angeles office and my boss had not told me previously he was coming to town. I immediately went down to the office he was in and he invited me to come in. The first thing he said to me was to please close the door. Something was up. I couldn't tell right then whether it was good or bad. Then he told me to please sit down. That couldn't be good. He proceeded to tell me that he had decided to let me go. "So you are firing me?" I asked? He nodded.

This was quite the shock for someone who had always excelled in school and work. I headed home. As I walked in the door, my wife said, "It's a little early for you to be home, isn't it? What's going on?" I told her what had happened. She had a few choice words for my then former boss. Then we started planning our future. I had always wanted to start my own business and perhaps this was the opportunity to do so. Quite a leap of faith when you consider that we were a single-income household with two young boys and that I was the sole provider.

I started with two clients. For the next nine months, I worked tirelessly to build my business, speaking to everyone I knew and even making cold calls. I was so successful that after nine months I doubled my business. That's right—I went from two to four clients. That wasn't going to pay the bills. Then one day a friend of mine, also a CPA, called me to tell me that there was an accounting firm for sale located not far from me. It turned out that I knew the CPA who was selling the firm.

The only challenge was that not only did I have no money, I was $40,000 in debt. I asked my friend for advice and he offered to lend me some of the money. The seller agreed to finance about 50% of the sales price and my parents loaned me the rest of the money. My first no-money down deal. Within a year, I was so busy I had to add a partner.

About five years later, I met Robert Kiyosaki and began studying money and business under his tutelage. I learned a completely different way to look at money and business—and education. I'd never seen teaching like Robert's before I met him and started attending his conferences.

Here I am now, writing a book in the Rich Dad Advisor series. Without Robert, I would never have written this book. In fact, I couldn't have written this book. Much of the big-picture thought process about taxes and wealth contained in this book comes from my many meetings and seminars with him.

When Robert first approached me about writing this book, he told me that it had to be about how entrepreneurs and investors could reduce their taxes. And it had to be international in scope. I did some checking in the bookstores and libraries and I couldn't find a single book on taxes with an international perspective. This presented a great challenge to me.

How could I write a book on taxes that applied to every entrepreneur and investor in every country? I know the U.S. tax law very well. I've been studying it for 35 years. But like everyone else, I thought that the tax laws of other countries would be quite different than the U.S. laws.

My research revealed something entirely different. It turns out that the tax laws in all developed countries are similar. They are so similar, in fact, that a book could be written that applies to entrepreneurs and investors around the world. This is that book.

To be sure, the details of the tax laws are different in each country. And we will look at specific tax strategies you can use in your country at the end of each chapter. But unless you are a tax professional, you, the entrepreneur and/or investor, don't need to know all of the details. You can leave those to your tax advisor. You have to know the concepts. And the concepts are the same regardless of your country of origin or the country in which you do business.

This book is about tax planning concepts. It's about how to use your country's tax laws to your benefit. In this book, I tell you how the tax laws work. And how they are designed to reduce your taxes, not to increase your taxes. Once you understand this basic principle, you no longer have to be afraid of the tax laws. They are there to help you and your business, not to hinder you.

Once you understand the basic principles of tax reduction, you can begin immediately reducing your taxes. Eventually, you may even be able to legally eliminate your income taxes and drastically reduce your other taxes. Once you do that, you can live a life of tax-free wealth.

So let's get started.

Part One

How the Tax Law Can Be
Your Best Friend

Chapter One

Taxes are Stealing Your Money, Your Time, and Your Future

"Taxes are your largest single expense."   – *Robert Kiyosaki*

Every day, taxes are stealing your life away. Income tax, sales tax, value - added tax, employment tax, and a host of other taxes are eating away at your life.

You may think they are just taking your money. If only this was all they were taking. Taxes don't just take your money—they steal your time—because money is time. People with lots of money have lots of time because they don't have to spend their life trading their time for money. Instead, they can trade their money for time..

> *Taxes don't just take your money—they steal your time—because money is time.*

The average person in a developed country spends 25 to 35 percent of their *life* working to pay taxes. That means more than two hours of every workday are dedicated to feeding your government. And three to four months out of every year are spent working solely so that you can pay your

taxes. That adds up to over 13 years in your work life and 20 years in your lifetime—20 years. That's a prison sentence.

And it's not going to get better anytime soon. As inflation eats away at the spending power of our currency, it also puts us into higher tax brackets. So we end up with even less purchasing power because a higher percentage of our income is taxed. And with the increase in the number of entitlement programs in every country, there is a higher demand for tax revenues to support them. The United States alone has over $80 trillion of unfunded social liabilities in the form of Medicare and Social Security promises to its aging population. And this number grows every day as new entitlement programs are enacted.

It hasn't always been this way. In the early years of the income tax, only the very rich were subject to the tax. It was believed that since the rich had more income than they needed in order to live comfortably, they could afford to pay some of this back to the government. And because they had earned this income under the protection of their government, certainly it was fair that, in time of war, they could pay back the government some of their excess in order to maintain their freedoms and the protection afforded by the government.

This all changed after World War II. The governments of the world found that the income tax was a useful revenue-raising tool that could be used to rebuild an economy that was ravished by war. So the governments began taxing the middle class. At first, it was only the excess earned by employees over the average cost of living that was taxed. The government provided exemptions for the first income earned so that the average person could live on their regular earnings and only pay tax on the excess that would otherwise go to investments.

As they watched the behavior of the people who were now paying income tax, the government began to tinker with the tax law to see how it would affect the activities of the taxpayers. What they found was that a minor change to the tax law could have a profound effect on the behavior of the people. If the government gave a tax incentive to invest in business, more people would invest in business. If they gave a tax benefit to those who invested in oil and gas, more people would invest in oil and gas.

And so the tax law grew from a simple revenue-raising vehicle to a vast array of laws that governed the economic activity of the land. And so it is today that the tax laws of every country are modified as the economy changes and as social policies change.

You may think that you have no choice about how much tax you pay. Everyone has to pay taxes, right? Wrong. There are millions of people who legally pay little or no tax. What's their secret? Do they know about loopholes that are in the law that allow them to get away with not paying tax? No. They simply understand how the tax law works. They understand that the tax law is not something the government uses only to raise taxes. The tax law is a tool the government uses to shape the economy and promote social, agricultural, and energy policy.

These people understand that the tax law in every developed country is now a series of incentives for entrepreneurs and investors. In the United States, over 95 percent of the tax code is intended not to raise taxes but rather to stimulate economic, agricultural and energy activities. In fact, the tax law is a map (or a code) to vast amounts of wealth. And the tax code doesn't only show you how to reduce your taxes. If you follow the tax law carefully, you will discover that the secrets to amassing huge amounts of cash flow and wealth are found within its pages.

The reason is quite simple. The government wants the economy to grow. It wants you to invest in local energy production. It wants you to invest in local agriculture. And it wants you to invest in economic activities that provide housing and jobs for the people. All of this is contained within the tax law. When

> *...the tax law is a map (or a code) to vast amounts of wealth. And the tax code doesn't only show you how to reduce your taxes. If you follow the tax law carefully, you will discover that the secrets to amassing huge amounts of cash flow and wealth are found within its pages.*

you understand the tax law of your country, you will understand what the government wants you to do with your money. And you will understand the fundamental principles for making large amounts of money.

TAX TIP:	Include tax planning in your wealth strategy. Remember that it's not just what you make that matters, it's what you keep. When you keep taxes in mind as you invest, you end up keeping more money and make better investment decisions.

Was the tax law written for the wealthy? Absolutely! The key to taking advantage of the tax law is to behave like one of the wealthy. Do those activities that the government wants you to do, and you will not only permanently reduce your taxes by 10 to 40 percent or more, you will also begin building more wealth and cash flow than you had ever imagined possible. Just look at how much faster a $10,000 investment grows without taxes.

Year	Pay Tax	No Tax
Year	With 40% Tax @ 10% Return	Without Tax @ 10% Return
1	10,616.77	11,047.13
2	11,271.59	12,203.90
3	11,966.80	13,481.81
4	12,704.89	14,893.54
5	13,488.50	16,453.08
6	14,320.44	18,175.94
7	15,203.69	20,079.20
8	16,141.42	22,181.75
9	17,136.99	24,504.47
10	18,193.96	27,070.41
11	19,316.13	29,905.04
12	20,507.50	33,036.48
13	21,772.36	36,495.84
14	23,115.23	40,317.43
15	24,540.93	44,539.19
16	26,054.56	49,203.03
17	27,661.55	54,355.23
18	29,367.65	60,046.93
19	31,178.99	66,334.63
20	33,102.04	73,280.73
21	35,143.70	80,954.18
22	37,311.29	89,431.14

23	39,612.57	98,795.75
24	42,055.78	109,140.96
25	44,649.69	120,569.45
26	47,403.59	133,194.64
27	50,327.34	147,141.86
28	53,431.42	162,549.54
29	56,726.95	179,570.60
30	60,225.75	198,373.99

The key lies in your facts. Your facts include your business activities, your investment activities, and your personal activities. They also include how you keep track of your activities. All taxes are based on your facts and circumstances. So if you want to change your tax, change your facts. It's that simple.

This book is dedicated to teaching you how to change your facts so you can lower your tax. You will also learn the principles of building wealth. The facts you must change to reduce your tax will at the same time increase your income. Start behaving like the wealthy and soon you will become one of the wealthy for whom the tax law was written.

CAUTION!

Beware of Tax Preparers who:

1. Promise they can lower your taxes and who are really tax cheats.

2. Focus on postponing or "deferring" taxes to a later year. Real tax planning is permanent so you never have to repay the taxes.

So stop letting the IRS (the U.S. Internal Revenue Service), CRA (Canada Revenue Agency), HMRC (Her Majesty's Revenue & Customs), or other government agencies steal your money. Don't let them steal your time. It's time to get out of prison. As you learn the truth about taxes, the truth will set you free. You will have the time and the money that you want so that you can live your dream of financial freedom, comfort, and security.

CHAPTER 1: KEY POINTS

1.	Become one of the wealthy and stop giving the IRS your time. Learn to trade your money for time and engage in activities the government uses to shape the economy. Remember, the tax law is a series of incentives for entrepreneurs and investors.
2.	Taxes are based on your facts and circumstances—changing your facts will change your tax.

Tax Strategy #1: Include Tax Planning in Your Wealth Strategy

Too many people ignore taxes when investing and planning their wealth strategy. They look at the return on investment as the return before they pay taxes on their investment income. This makes no sense. With taxes as your biggest expense, wouldn't you want to look at every return on every investment after taxes? When you do, you may find that you are making a lot less on some investments than you thought and are making more on others in comparison.

Let's take a couple of examples in the U.S. that we will go into in much greater detail later on in this book. First, let's look at real estate. Regularly, I hear on the news that real estate is only a moderately successful investment on average. And if you were to compare it directly to some other investment before tax and without leverage (i.e., debt), you would have to agree. Let's say you purchased a rental property for $500,000, with $100,000 of your own money and $400,000 of the bank's money. Suppose that the annual return on your investment of $100,000 is 7%. Then, let's suppose that you make a similar investment of $100,000 in the stock market that returns 10%. Which investment is a better return? It seems obvious that the stock market return of 10% is clearly better than the real estate return of 7%, right?

Not so fast. The 10% return from the stock market will get you $10,000 before taxes. You will pay capital gains tax of about 20%, counting both federal and state taxes, leaving you with an after-tax return of $8,000. The 7% return on the real estate investment will get you a before-tax return of $7,000. Due to the magic of depreciation (chapter 7), you won't pay any tax on your $7,000. Still, $7,000 is less than your after tax return of $8,000 in the stock market, so it seems you are still better off in the stock market.

Only, your real estate investment doesn't just give you tax-free cash flow. It actually reduces your taxes on your salary and/or business income, because while there is positive cash flow of $7,000, the depreciation deduction of about $27,000 gives you a tax deduction against your other income of $20,000 ($27,000 less $7,000 to offset real estate income). That $20,000 additional deduction against your other income is worth $6,000 of reduced taxes on your other income in a typical 30% ordinary income tax bracket.

So your real return from your real estate is $7,000 plus an additional $6,000 of tax refund on taxes you normally would have paid on your salary and business income for a total return of $13,000, or $5,000 more than your after-tax return from the stock investment.

This is just one example of how the tax law can have a dramatic impact on your cash flow and your wealth. If you computed your return just by looking at the cash flow before taxes, your return of $10,000 on your stock investment is way better ($3,000 better) than your return from your real estate. After taxes, though, it is the opposite. Your return from the real estate after tax benefits is $13,000 while your return from the stock market after tax is only $8,000. See why you should always consider taxes when you make your investment plans?

Chapter Two

Taxes are Fun, Easy, and Understandable

"The hardest thing in the world to understand is income taxes."
– Albert Einstein

Death and Taxes

"**D**eath" and "taxes." They're the two most dreaded words in the English language—or any language, for that matter. And it's totally understandable. You don't want to die. And you'd probably rather die than pay taxes. Perhaps we link taxes with death because they represent the death of all for which we've worked. Or maybe it's because we don't understand taxes any more than we understand death.

Worldwide, the average person pays 30 to 50 percent or more of their hard-earned income in taxes, either through income, sales, value-added, payroll, estate, or property taxes.

The reality is that taxes can kill your hopes and dreams. How? By stealing your wealth and diminishing your quality of life. That surprise vacation for your family? Gone, thanks to Uncle Sam. The improvements you need to make to your house? Kiss them goodbye come tax time. I'm sure you can relate. You're not the only one. Worldwide, the average person pays 30 to 50 percent or more of their hard-earned income in taxes, either through income, sales, value-added, payroll, estate, or property taxes. Think about that. Almost a third to one-half of the world's wealth is handed over to governments. That's bad news.

But here's the good news. Taxes don't have to kill your dreams. In fact, 90 percent of entrepreneurs and investors can reduce their taxes simply by learning the basics of tax law.

You might be saying, "Great—another book that helps entrepreneurs and investors. I'm just a regular Joe. What can I do to lower my taxes?"

To you I say, "What if you became part of this privileged class of taxpayers? What if you took the right steps and made the right preparations to not only make more money but to also pay less to the government in taxes?"

Sounds hard, right? Well, as you'll learn, it's not. And when you do take the step of becoming an entrepreneur or investor, you will easily pay 10 to 40 percent less in taxes by learning how the tax law can work for you—instead of you working for the government and paying high taxes.

TAX TIP:	Invest where you travel. Do you have a favorite destination? Consider investing in the area. It gives you a great reason to keep returning, and you turn the travel expenses you already have into deductible expenses, keeping more money in your pocket.

Anyone Can Understand Taxes

This might make you laugh, but I absolutely love taxes. Seriously. I have a passion for learning everything I can about the tax law and how it can be used to save money for my clients and me. I started learning about accounting and taxes at a young age.

In high school, I took a class on business law and loved it. And all through high school I worked in the accounting department of my father's printing company. I enjoyed working with money, and I loved learning about the law. So I decided to major in accounting and specialize in tax law. That way, I reasoned, I would get to work with money, learn about the law, and not have to spend my life with lawyers.

My first tax professor was Dr. Haney. He was a lawyer who truly had a gift for teaching and who loved tax law. I was so excited to take tax classes that I took all three that were offered in my junior year, postponing my upper-division accounting classes until my senior year.

I couldn't wait to get a job working in the tax area. During my first term of tax classes, I took out the Yellow Pages and called all of the local Certified Public Accountant (CPA) firms in town that had more than one name or had "and Associates" in the firm's name. After several days of this, I landed an interview with a firm called Francis and Company. My long and thrilling journey as a tax accountant began.

I interviewed with the senior tax manager the next day. He asked me the usual questions about my experience, education, and interests. And then he asked a really odd question. "Tom," he said. "How good is your printing?"

I was taken a bit off-guard by this question. It turns out that they prepared a lot of their tax returns by hand. They printed them in pencil and then photocopied them for their files. He wanted to make sure my handwriting was legible so that their clients and the IRS wouldn't be frustrated by not being able to make out the numbers on the tax returns. Fortunately, my handwriting was legible, because I had worked hard to learn good printing. He hired me on the spot.

That was in 1980. Since then, I have devoted my life to learning (and loving) the tax law. What I've discovered over the years is that the basic principles of the tax law are actually simple. So simple, in fact, that *anybody* can learn them, even Albert Einstein. (I'm convinced that Dr. Einstein wouldn't have been so frustrated with the tax system if he had just had someone to teach him the basic principles). The principles are so simple that by the time you finish reading this book you will know every basic principle needed to *permanently lower your taxes*. And once you know the rules, you can live a lower-tax life, which I promise is a richer life in every way. In fact, you might even be able to legally reduce your taxes to zero and enjoy tax-free wealth.

CAUTION!

Understanding Taxes Doesn't Mean Doing It Yourself	
1.	You still need a good tax advisor who understands the details of the tax law.
2.	A good tax advisor can help you create and implement sound tax strategies besides doing your tax returns.

Taxes Are Fun—Really

Anyone who knows me knows that for me, taxes are fun. Yes, I did just say "fun." I know how warped that may sound, but I love the tax law. And I firmly believe that everyone can find out just how fun, easy, and understandable taxes are with just a little basic information. Don't believe me? Well, think about this. Have you ever received a tax refund? Do you remember how happy you were when you opened that letter and saw a beautiful check? That was fun, wasn't it? In fact, did you ever notice that the word "refund" has "fun" right in the middle of it? Okay, corny joke, but you get the point.

This book is dedicated to helping get you a bigger tax refund. And we're not just talking about a one-time deal. When you apply the principles taught in this book, you'll get a nice refund *every year*. And who knows? You may even reduce your taxes to zero and enjoy the freedom that comes with tax-free wealth.

I guarantee your path to tax-free wealth is easier, simpler, and more fun than you can imagine. Think of this book as a guide to a freer financial life, a life where you get to keep more of your hard-earned money right where it belongs—in your pocket, and not the government's. Let's get started.

CHAPTER 2: KEY POINTS

1.	It's time to take action on reducing your taxes. Don't be the average person paying 30 to 50 percent or more of your hard-earned income through income, sales, value-added, payroll, estate, or property taxes—start by learning the basics of the tax law.
2.	Become part of the privileged class of taxpayers by learning how the tax law can work for you and how you can easily pay 10 to 40 percent less in taxes.

Tax Strategy #2 – Invest Where you Travel

As you will learn in Chapter 6, almost any expense can be deductible. It sounds funny to say, but one of my favorite *expenses* is travel. I love to travel and meet new people and experience new cultures. Sometimes, I just want to get away to relax and get some peace of mind.

One of my favorite places on earth is Hawaii. The people of Hawaii are so genuine and laid back. I go to Hawaii at least once a year for a couple of weeks. Of course, I also want my travel to Hawaii to be deductible—and, thankfully, it can be with proper planning.

Any travel can be deductible by making it a business or investment expense. As long as your travel has its primary purpose as business, then all of the travel expenses, including hotel, airfare and meals, will be deductible. In order for travel's primary purpose to be business, the IRS says that you have to spend more time doing business than you do in recreation. So, if you are going to Hawaii for a week, then more than half your time there has to be spent doing business. This simply means more than 4 hours of a regular 8-hour workday, meaning you need to spend four and a half hours working each day. But who wants to work while vacationing in Hawaii? What if the work is fun, interesting, and makes you lots of money? Would you do it then? What if you made Hawaiian real estate a major part of your investment strategy? When you add up the tax benefits plus add in all of the money you could make investing for four and a half hours each day, you may decide that spending that time looking at real estate and meeting with property managers isn't so bad after all. Just take a look in Chapter 5 at what this strategy did for my client who travels to New Mexico each year.

Chapter Three

The Two Most Important Rules

"Any one may so arrange his affairs so that his taxes shall be as low as possible; he is not bound to choose that pattern which will best pay the Treasury. There is not even a patriotic duty to increase one's taxes."
– Judge Learned Hand

Awhile back, one of my good friends, Guy Zanti, taught a group of people how to play *CASHFLOW*, a financial-simulation board game invented by Robert and Kim Kiyosaki. Playing the game is an excellent way to not only learn but also put into practice the Rich Dad principles on money and investing. As Guy talked about some of the tax benefits of real estate, particularly tax-free exchanges, a woman in the audience raised her hand.

> *Playing CASHFLOW 101 is an excellent way to learn the Rich Dad principles on money and investing.*

"Yes, ma'am," Guy said.

"Don't you think that it's wrong to reduce your taxes like that?," she asked. "Isn't it our responsibility to pay the taxes that we owe instead of trying to find ways to steal from the government?"

Guy was stunned. He couldn't believe what he'd just heard. He couldn't comprehend why she would think that it was wrong to reduce her tax burden. After all, doesn't everyone want to reduce taxes? But the reality is that we're trained to believe that we somehow owe the government our money. The truth is that we don't. In fact, the tax code is set up to help us reduce our tax burden—and to do so legally.

I'd say it's just the opposite of what this woman and many others think; it's wrong to *not* reduce your tax burden. Not taking advantage of the aspects of the law that are there to help you means you are stealing from yourself, your family, and your future.

> *Not taking advantage of the aspects of the law that are there to help you means you are stealing from yourself, your family, and your future.*

The simple fact is that this woman didn't understand Rule #1 when it comes to the tax law. And chances are, you may not either.

RULE #1:	**It's your money, not the government's.**

Unless you live in a dictatorship, the money you earn and the wealth that you build belongs to you. Yes, you may be required to give some of it to the government to help build roads, maintain the military, and sustain schools. But fundamentally, it's your money.

TAX TIP:	Learn how your LLC (limited liability company) can be whatever it wants to be. The LLC has become the entity of choice for asset protection purposes. But what about tax purposes? Your LLC can be whatever it wants to be—a sole proprietorship, a partnership, a C Corporation, or an S Corporation. This flexibility gives you the best of the tax and asset protection worlds. In some countries without LLCs, the LLP (limited liability partnership) may give you similar flexibility.

Judge Learned Hand, a former judge on the United States Court of Appeals for the Second Circuit and a judicial philosopher, was adamant about this principle. He went so far as to say this: "Over and over again the Courts have said that there is nothing sinister in so arranging affairs as to keep taxes as low as possible. Everyone does it, rich and poor alike, and all do right, for nobody owes any public duty to pay more than the law demands."

You may not realize this, but it's true: *The tax laws are written to reduce your taxes, not to increase them.* In the United States, for example, there are over 5,800 pages of tax law. Only about 30 pages are devoted to raising taxes. One line, Section 61(a), says, "Except as otherwise provided in this subtitle, gross income means all income from whatever source derived..." There are then several pages of tax rates and a few other miscellaneous tables. *The remaining 5,770 pages are devoted entirely to reducing your taxes.* In other words, 0.5 percent of the tax code is devoted to raising taxes, and the remaining 99.5 percent exists solely for the purpose of saving you money. So here is Rule #2.

> *You may not realize this, but it's true: The tax laws are written to reduce your taxes, not to increase them.*

RULE #2:	The tax law is written primarily to reduce your taxes.

You may not believe me about Rule #2. So go ahead and ask your own accountant how much of the tax law in your country is devoted to raising taxes. Your accountant will tell you the truth—very little. That the woman in Guy's class felt it's our patriotic duty to pay the most taxes is both ridiculous and completely wrong. In fact, as I'll show you in the next few chapters, it's actually your patriotic duty to *reduce* your taxes by all legal means.

CAUTION!

Beware of Tax Advisors Who Really Work for the Government	
1.	Many tax advisors are afraid of the tax law so they won't learn how to take advantage of the law for you.
2.	Some tax advisors are more interested in protecting themselves than reducing your taxes.

You may be wondering how I can really say that with a straight face. Well, think about it. If 99.5 percent of the tax law is written to help you reduce your taxes, then the government must really want you to do just that. If that weren't true, why would they enact so much legislation aimed at helping you do so? All of the so-called complexity of the tax law is really just aimed at reducing your taxes, not increasing them.

> *All of the so-called complexity of the tax law is really just aimed at reducing your taxes, not increasing them.*

Until you really believe and are committed to these two fundamental rules of tax law, there really is nothing you can do to limit your taxes—and this book will be worth very little to you. You will keep on unnecessarily paying 30 to 50 percent of your hard-earned income to the government. Maybe that's what you want. But I have a hunch it isn't.

Once you truly believe these two rules and have them firmly planted in your mind, you'll realize that you have the right to reduce your taxes every minute of every day. All you have to do is learn the rules of the game. And that's when this book becomes priceless.

The good news is that the tax rules are easy to understand. After all, you already understand the first two rules, right? From here on out, it's just a matter of learning who the tax laws are written for and why, and learning how to change the way you think about your money and taxes.

So if you believe that your money is yours and not the government's, and that the tax law exists to reduce your taxes, then you're ready to read on and learn how to make the tax law work for you—and not the other way around. Let's get to work.

CHAPTER 3: KEY POINTS

1.	Some of us are trained to believe we owe the government OUR money (it's just not true).
2.	The tax code is set up to help us reduce our tax burden—and to do so legally.
3.	Nearly all—99.5 percent—of the tax code exists solely for the purpose of saving you money.
4.	All of the so-called complexity of the tax law is aimed at reducing your taxes, not increasing them.

Tax Strategy # 3: Elect How Your Limited Liability Company will be Taxed

Your limited liability company (LLC) can be whatever you want it to be. The LLC has become the entity of choice for U.S. asset protection purposes. But what about for tax purposes? The good news is, your LLC can be whatever it wants to be—a sole proprietorship, a partnership, a C Corporation, or an S Corporation. This flexibility gives you the best of the tax and asset protection worlds. In some countries without LLCs, the limited liability partnership (LLP) may give you similar flexibility. The key here is that you can frequently have your cake and eat it too when it comes to the tax law. Simply by understanding that LLCs can be treated any way you want for tax purposes, you have asset protection and still get the tax advantages of the S corporation, C corporation or partnership rules. Garrett Sutton, Rich Dad Advisor for asset protection and legal services, talks in detail about the asset protection advantages of limited liability companies in his bestselling book, *Start Your Own Corporation RDA Press, 2012*. Once you decide which type of entity you want for tax purposes, be sure you make the proper entity tax election by checking the proper box on the IRS entity election form. If you don't make the election, the IRS will choose for you which tax entity you will be—a sole proprietorship for single-member LLCs or a partnership for multimember LLCs. You can make your entity election at any time during the year. This election gives you great flexibility in your tax planning. Suppose you are just starting a new business. You may want your entity to be treated as a sole proprietorship in the early years when there is a loss or not much income so you don't have to file another tax return (corporations have to file a separate income tax return from their owners). When you're ready to change to an S Corporation to reduce your employment taxes (see Chapter 11), you can check the box on the form and file the election with the IRS.

Chapter Four

Put Money Back in Your Pocket—Now

"The only difference between a tax man and a taxidermist is that the taxidermist leaves the skin."   – *Mark Twain*

As a child, I was always looking for ways to make money. I started my first business venture with a buddy of mine when we were nine years old. We noticed that the marigold flowers had died and gone to seed. Those of you who aren't green thumbs may not know this, but marigold seeds are some of the easiest things in the world to harvest. All you have to do is rip the top of the flower off and dump a whole slew of seeds into your hand. My buddy and I thought it was pretty cool how easy it was, and we came up with the brilliant idea of collecting all the seeds in the neighborhood, packaging them, and selling the seeds back to our neighbors. It worked like a charm. The same neighbors who allowed us to take the seeds from their garden in the fall bought them back from us in the spring, which proves that business isn't always about doing something other people can't do for themselves; it's doing something they haven't thought to do for themselves.

...business isn't always about doing something other people can't do for themselves; it's doing something they haven't thought to do for themselves.

And then there was the neighborhood carnival we decided to hold when we were 11 years old. We created a cupcake walk, a "fish" pond where people fished for prizes, and some other games of skill and chance. We let all of our friends know about the carnival, and we worked hard to get ready for it. In fact, looking back, it was a lot of work. When the carnival was over, we sat down to count our money. We'd made $20. Back then, that was pretty good for a couple of 11-year-olds.

Today, people come to me professionally all the time asking how they can make money. Many of them need cash right away. I'm not a believer in get-rich-quick schemes, and I steer my clients away from those types of folks. My clients are hardworking people who are looking for a better way to increase their cash flow and their wealth. I'm sure you're looking to do the same thing. And there's good news. There's one way to put cash in your pocket almost immediately, as shown in Rule #3: reducing your taxes.

RULE #3:	The fastest way to put money in your pocket is to reduce your taxes.

Think about it. By reducing your taxes, you can immediately reduce how much money comes out of your paycheck. Or, if you're an entrepreneur or investor, you can reduce your quarterly tax payments.

> *By reducing your taxes, you can immediately reduce how much money comes out of your paycheck.*

And you don't have to wait until tax time to enjoy the benefit of lower taxes. In many countries, including the United States, you can file amended returns anytime, which correct errors on returns for up to the previous three years if you learn that you paid too much in a prior year. Or you can even carry back a loss from the current year to a prior year, use the loss to offset the prior year's income, and get a refund now.

Notice what I said: you can put money in your pocket by reducing your taxes. The operative word is "you." You, and only you, have the power and the control over your money and your taxes. Nobody else. This includes your tax preparer and your tax advisor. They cannot reduce your taxes. They can only help equip you to do so.

You may say, "My tax advisor handles my taxes," but that is a myth about income taxes. Your tax advisor *cannot* handle your taxes. They can prepare your tax returns. They can give you advice about what to do in a particular situation. Quite possibly they can even tell you some rules that will help you reduce your taxes. But they cannot take the actual steps to reduce your taxes. Only you can do that.

CAUTION!

Don't Wait for Year-End to Do Tax Planning	
1.	Every day you could be reducing your taxes.
2.	Year-end tax planning is important but year-round tax planning is better.

The good news is that you *can* reduce your taxes right now. Anybody can. And you can do it every day of the week. All you have to do to change your tax is to change your facts. There are two simple principles (represented in Rule #4) that you need to keep in mind as you consider how to reduce your taxes: *Every dollar, pound, or euro you earn can increase your taxes, and every dollar, pound, or euro you spend can decrease your taxes.* And every investment or business deal you do will affect your taxes for good or for ill.

All you have to do to change your tax is change your facts.

RULE #4:	**Everything you do either increases or lowers your taxes.**

You might as well learn how to make everything you do affect your taxes for good, right? Thankfully, it's not complicated. It's simply a matter of learning the difference between bad, good, and better income—and then learning how to turn your expenses into tax deductions. And the really cool part is that every expense has the potential to reduce your taxes—really, *every expense.*

And the really cool part is that every expense has the potential to reduce your taxes – really, every expense

TAX TIP:	Eat while you work and save taxes. Business meals are a great way to spend time with employees, clients, and customers. You can discuss business and turn your meal expense into a deductible expense.

But what if you could get a 20 to 30 percent discount on all of your purchases any time of the year? That's exactly what happens when you change your expenses from a personal expense to a business deduction.

Let's face it, the best part of having money is spending it. But when you can not only spend your money but also decrease your taxes while doing so—well, then you're really cooking.

I know a lot of people who love to shop for bargains and constantly look for sales and specials. It's like a professional sport to them. You wouldn't believe the amount of time, energy, and effort that they put into finding deals and saving money. They're thrilled with a 20 to 30 percent discount on their purchases. But when it comes to doing their taxes, they don't want to take the time. I don't get it—well, actually, I do. Tax returns can be a royal pain. And most people just want to get them done and over with as quickly as possible. But what if you could get a 20 to 30 percent discount on all of your purchases any time of the year? That's exactly what happens when you change your expenses from a personal expense to a business deduction. The government essentially pays for 20 to 30 percent of your purchase in the form of a tax deduction.

I like to shop at Costco, a discount store that sells groceries and other everyday items. Costco also sells gasoline. People line up, sometimes waiting for long periods of time, in order to buy their gas at Costco because it's routinely 10 percent less than other gas stations.

I never buy my gas at Costco.

Why? Costco doesn't allow me to use my business credit card. And since most of my car use is for business, I get a deduction for the gas if I use my business credit card (plus I get frequent flyer miles). That deduction is worth 20 to 30 percent to me in lower taxes. So it's worth paying a little more at the gas station down the street in order to get the tax deduction.

It's the little decisions like these, made every day, that add up to big savings in your taxes.

By now you're probably dying to find out how you can start paying less in taxes every day.

CHAPTER 4: KEY POINTS	
1.	There is one way to put cash in your pocket almost immediately: reducing your taxes.
2.	Learn how to make everything you do decrease your taxes.
3.	Learn how to change your expenses from a personal expense to a business deduction.

Tax Strategy #4 – Deduct your Meals

Almost any expense can be deductible in the right circumstance, including food, cars, travel—even your house, if you change your facts so that the expense is a business one. What's a business expense? In the United States, the tax law requires each business deduction to meet three tests. First, the expense must have a business purpose, which means the primary reason for spending money was for your business. Take meals as an example. To be deductible, the purpose of a meal must be business. This means you need to have a conversation about business with your dining partner before, during, or after the meal. The other valid business meal would be if you were traveling away from home on business. Second, the expense must be ordinary. An expense is ordinary if it is "customary and usual." This means that within your industry, the expense should be typical of what would be spent, both in the amount of the expense and how often a person in your position would have the expense. Suppose, for example, that you go out to dinner with a business associate. In your industry, what would be the cost of a typical business meal? If you're a truck driver, the typical business meal is going to be different than if you're a movie star or professional athlete. An insurance agent might go to lunch with a client or business associate every day, while an auto parts manufacturer might only go to lunch on business once a week. The key here is that whatever is typical in your industry and your position within the industry is what the IRS will allow as ordinary.

Third, the expense must be necessary. Necessary means that the purpose of the expense is to make more money for your business. It's not enough just to go to lunch with someone and talk business simply because you are friends. Your conversation at lunch must have the intention of increasing the profits in your business. These three rules are not difficult to meet. Let's say, for example, that your business partner is your spouse. If you're like most business partners, you're always talking about business and always looking for ways to improve your business. So pretty much every opportunity you get to have a quiet meal together in a restaurant you will discuss business. Just don't be extravagant about it on a regular basis. One rule of thumb here is that "pigs get fat and hogs get slaughtered." If you are greedy and go out to expensive restaurants on a regular basis, the IRS may not look so kindly on your deductions for meals. Still, one of the most common mistakes I see is couples who are always talking about business when they go out to dinner but not paying for their meals with their business credit card.

Chapter Five

Entrepreneurs and Investors Get All the Breaks

"If you want more of something, subsidize it." – Milton Friedman

In March 1995, I started my professional accounting practice. Over the years, my partners and I have enlarged the firm through marketing and acquisitions. My most notable acquisition was that of a Phoenix-area tax practice in 2001. Earlier that year I'd been through a nasty partnership breakup with three other CPAs. Fortunately for me, about 50 percent of the clients stayed with my new partner and me, and all but one of the firm's employees stayed with us, meaning we had more workers than work.

On top of this, later in the summer one of my former graduate students came to me looking for work. She was a good student, and I thought she'd make an excellent employee. We took the advice of Jim Collins in his excellent book, *Good to Great*, to put the right people on the bus and find them seats later, and despite having more workers than work, we hired her.

The end result was that we had far more people to do work than we had actual work to do. So I started looking for a practice to acquire. One day, a card came in the mail from a business broker indicating that he had a couple of practices for sale in the Phoenix area. I called the broker and soon learned that one of the practices was a good fit for us. The practice did a lot of high-end tax planning and had some high-quality clients. One of the clients was a good friend of mine, Kim Butler. Another client was Robert Kiyosaki.

I hadn't previously heard of Robert Kiyosaki or The Rich Dad Company, but wanting to be well versed on my clients, I immediately went out and purchased his best-selling book, *Rich Dad Poor Dad*. I loved the book. Then I had lunch with my friend Kim Butler who I knew had been doing some work with Robert and asked her about him. She had nothing but good things to say about Robert and his organization. About the same time, I received a notice in the mail from one of my friends, George Duck, telling me that he had just changed jobs. Amazingly, his new job was CFO of The Rich Dad Company.

Was it a coincidence that all of these occurrences leading me to a great business relationship with Rich Dad happened at the same time? I don't really know. What I do know is that I've learned an enormous amount about teaching, money, and the economy from Robert and Kim Kiyosaki. One of the first things I learned about was the CASHFLOW Quadrant.

What I do know is that I've learned an enormous amount about teaching, money, and the economy from Robert and Kim Kiyosaki. One of the first things I learned about was the CASHFLOW Quadrant.

The CASHFLOW Quadrant separates income earners into four quadrants. On the left side are the employees (E) and the self-employed individuals (S). On the right side are big business (B) and investors (I). When I first saw the diagram, my thoughts naturally went to the tax consequences (and benefits) of being in each of the quadrants. I quickly realized that those who earned their income from the left side of the quadrant pay much higher taxes than those who earn their income from the right side of the quadrant.

Over the years, since first learning about the CASHFLOW Quadrant, I've continued to look at the tax law and apply it to the diagram. The reason why those on the B and I side of the quadrant pay so much less in tax than those on the E

The reason why those on the B and I side of the quadrant pay so much less in tax than those on the E and S side has become clear to me. It's because that's what Congress wanted.

and S side has become clear to me. It's because that's what Congress or Parliament wanted.

Think about the goals of Congress, Parliament, or any other governing body, for that matter. The government wants to encourage certain activities, and they have two ways of doing that, either by force or by policy. And, as we quoted at the beginning of the chapter, it was the great economist Milton Friedman who said, "If you want more of something, subsidize it." The easiest and most efficient way to subsidize something is through the tax law. Over the years it's not only become easier to subsidize through the tax law but it's also become *the* way a government steers the country's economic behavior, as shown in Rule #5.

RULE #5:	**The tax law is a series of incentives for entrepreneurs and investors.**

So what does the government want? First, they want to create more jobs. Who creates jobs? Entrepreneurs. Therefore, entrepreneurs get all sorts of tax breaks that act as subsidies to encourage job creation. What else does the government want? Affordable housing. Real estate investors get all sorts of tax breaks that act as subsidies to encourage building of affordable housing.

Sometimes governments make the mistake of thinking they can create jobs or build housing better than the free market. Eventually, they realize that the market does a better job. And it costs the government a lot less to give tax benefits to business owners and investors than it does to add jobs or build housing through government-sponsored programs.

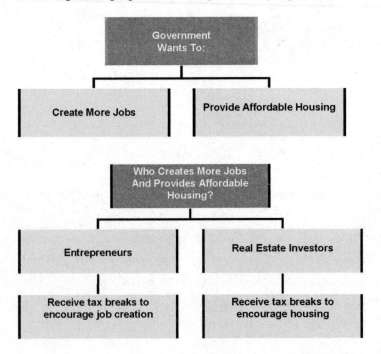

It is because of these goals that government gives entrepreneurs and investors all the tax breaks they get. Governments even get more specific about the types of investing and jobs they want the market to create by giving specific tax breaks for oil and gas investing, farming and other agriculture, green energy, and low-income housing.

CAUTION!

Don't Start a Business Just for the Tax Benefits

1.	To get tax benefits, the business must be real and intend to make a profit.
2.	Paying taxes is less expensive than failing at business. Be sure to get educated before you begin.

It's not really that those on the E and S side of the CASHFLOW Quadrant are punished. They just don't get the rewards (i.e., subsidies) that are given to those on the B and I side of the quadrant. If you want to know what the government wants to see happen in your country, take a look at the tax law. Where are all of the incentives going? That's where the government wants you to put your money and your effort. That's why I say it's more patriotic to arrange your affairs to pay less in taxes. When you do so, you're actually doing what the government wants you to do: creating jobs, building housing and other useful buildings, and producing food and energy.

> *It's not really that those on the E and S side of the CASHFLOW Quadrant are punished. They just don't get the rewards (i.e. subsidies) that are given to those on the B and I side of the quadrant.*

There is even more good news for entrepreneurs and investors. When you follow the government's rules in order to get your tax benefits, you also receive other benefits and make more money. Let me share an example of this.

A new client of mine was very anxious to reduce his income taxes. I'd already told him that any expense could be deductible, given the right situation. He and his wife were huge fans of New Mexico because of its serene beauty, and they traveled there often. Since they traveled to New Mexico so frequently, my client wanted to use their travel as a tax deduction. I explained that he had to make the travel relate to his business in order to make it deductible under the law.

He was very excited the next time I saw him. I could tell he had a story for me. He explained that he and his wife took a trip to New Mexico and that since they wanted to deduct the travel, they spent much of their time looking for real estate deals—*and they found one*. In fact, this real estate deal was so good that he expected it would net him over $1 million before taxes. While he was excited about the $3,000 in taxes he was going to save because he turned his travel into a tax-deductible business trip, he was even more excited about the $1 million he was going to make from the deal!

TAX TIP:	Put your family to work. Make your business a family business. Then when you travel for business, your family's travel is deductible. And you can shift income from your higher tax bracket to their lower tax bracket. This creates permanent *tax savings*.

Congress understands that when people spend time, money, and effort on business, those people will make money. And they understand that money produces jobs, housing, and even more tax revenue for the government. Even with good planning, the $1 million that my client makes on his real estate deal will result in $300,000 in tax revenue for the U.S. government. That deal would never have happened without the $3,000 tax incentive given for the trip—and making $300,000 on $3,000 is a good deal in anyone's book. Of course, the deal wouldn't have happened if my client hadn't understood how to turn the costs of that trip into a tax deduction.

You might be thinking, "That sounds great, but what about me? I'm on the E and S side of the CASHFLOW Quadrant." The truth is that these business deductions aren't available to you, but they can be. You just need to shift some of your income-earning activities to the B and I side of the quadrant. Thankfully, that's not difficult to do. Thousands of individuals all over the world have home-based businesses or invest in real estate, energy, or agriculture—and they all enjoy the benefits that come from saving money through the tax code.

> *You might be thinking, "That sounds great, but what about me? I'm on the E and S side of the CASHFLOW Quadrant." The truth is that these business deductions aren't available to you, but they can be.*

And you don't have to spend all of your time and money in business or investing to enjoy those benefits. You just need to get started. But before you do, you're going to want to do some planning. That's what we'll talk about next.

CHAPTER 5: KEY POINTS

1.	The CASHFLOW Quadrant is a terrific diagram that shows the four ways people earn income, which has huge implications for your taxes.
2.	Those on the E and S side of the quadrant don't experience the tax benefits of those on the B and I side unless they behave like the B and the I side.
3.	Governments steer economic behavior through the tax code. They reward desired behavior with tax breaks. That's why reducing your taxes is actually patriotic.
4.	You can easily shift the way you earn income to the B and I side of the CASHFLOW Quadrant and begin to enjoy the tax breaks.

Tax Strategy #5 – Put Your Family to Work in Your Business and Investing

One of the great tax benefits of existing on the B and the I side of the CASHFLOW Quadrant is the ability to legally shift income to your children. Children are taxpayers too, and they have their own tax brackets when it comes to earned income, which is income they work for. When they earn income through an outside job, they pay tax at their own rates.

Kids can also earn income from working in the family business or from investments. The nice thing about having your children work for you is that you get a tax deduction at your higher tax bracket for the payroll and they report the income at their lower tax bracket.

My long-time friend and client did this with his 9-year-old daughter. He put her to work doing the bookkeeping for his real estate investments. She is a very intelligent 9-year old and has no problem understanding the bookkeeping. Her mother, who is in charge of their real estate, supervises her. She gets a reasonable wage for her work as compared to other bookkeepers. In a year, she might earn $4,000. That $4,000 will be a deduction to her parents. She doesn't earn any other income and the standard deduction is more than $4,000. So, she doesn't pay any tax. In my client's 40 percent tax bracket, that $4,000 in pay to their daughter means a tax savings of $1,600.

Now, for the best part. My client's daughter is learning how to do bookkeeping and becoming part of their business. She is gaining a skill that will benefit her for her entire life, and she is beginning to understand real estate investing. No wonder Congress allows this type of planning.

In fact, Congress not only allows it but also encourages it. My friend gets a tax break on Social Security taxes as well for employing his daughter instead of employing someone else to do the bookkeeping. He doesn't have to pay any Social Security taxes on her wages.

So don't hesitate to put your children to work in your business. There are great tax benefits for you, huge educational benefits for them, and you have someone in place to take over when you are ready to retire. What an incredible exit strategy! It's one that the rich have known about for years and years. That's how they keep their money in the family, and keep the business going after they are gone.

Chapter Six

You Can Deduct Almost Anything

"I would like to electrocute everyone who uses the word "fair" in connection with income tax policies." – *William F. Buckley, Jr.*

Stop Being Average

Taxes aren't fair to the average taxpayer. Just who is the average taxpayer? The average taxpayer has a job, a family, and a mortgage or rent. The average taxpayer has little to no financial education. The average taxpayer gets his advice from CNN and H&R Block. The average taxpayer's only available tax benefits are the standard deduction or a few itemized deductions, such as home mortgage interest and charitable contributions. Oh, and, of course, a 401(k) or IRA in the U.S. or RRSP in Canada to postpone a portion of their tax burden until retirement.

The reality is that average taxpayers have average tax benefits. Average taxpayers come to me from time to time asking for my advice. They ask how they can reduce their taxes. Should they put more into their 401(k)? Should they buy a bigger house? While they're at it, should they have more children?

The reality is that average taxpayers have average tax benefits.

My answer to these folks is that as long as they're living the life of an average taxpayer, there's nothing much I can do for them. The solution is to *stop being average*. Instead, become an above-average or super taxpayer.

Start doing what Congress or Parliament wants you to do by contributing more to the economy. The good news is that you're on your way to becoming a far better than average taxpayer just by reading this book. You're gaining financial intelligence with each page you read. When you apply the concepts you learn here, you'll really take off.

My answer to these folks is that as long as they're living the life of an average taxpayer, there's nothing much I can do for them. The solution is to stop being average.

Like most professionals, I started advising people on what to do regarding their taxes long before I followed my own advice. Even before finishing graduate school, I gave people tax advice. I told business owners how to reduce their taxes even though I didn't own a business. I told real estate investors how to increase their deductions long before I owned any real estate of my own. Was the advice good? Sure. I was a smart kid who'd applied himself at school and learned the law. Was the advice great? No.

How could I possibly give great advice to other people when I'd never applied what I'd learned in school to my own situation? It wasn't until I started my own business and later began investing in real estate that I really began giving great advice to business owners and investors. Once I applied my knowledge in my own life, I finally understood my clients' businesses and gave them top-notch advice. The more I personally applied my knowledge, the better I became at giving advice to others.

The same will be true for you. Once you start applying the concepts of this book in your own life, you'll start to see how it all works. Once you begin reaping the rewards of lower taxes and more cash flow, you'll better understand what you've learned while at the same time reaping all the benefits of your knowledge. That's called wisdom.

So what's the first step to becoming a super taxpayer? Understanding rule #6.

RULE #6:	**You can deduct almost anything given the right circumstance.**

It's true. Almost any expense can be deductible from your income given the right situation. How can that be possible? It's how the law works. Remember when I said that the tax laws favor entrepreneurs and investors? That's because entrepreneurs and investors generally put money into the economy to produce rather than consume. The key to making an expense deductible is to make it a business or investment expense. *As long as the purpose of the expense is to produce more income, it can be deductible.*

> *If the purpose of the expense is to produce more income, it can be deductible.*

And yes, this principle applies worldwide. All income taxes in developed countries are based on net income, which is simply income after deductions. And deductions come from expenses. Business expenses are the best kind of deductions. Real estate expenses are the next best. Depending on your country, chances are that expenses relating to energy are good as well. Even expenses related to investing in the stock market may be partially deductible, though these are the least deductible because they aren't active investments.

Your first step to increasing your deductible expenses is to become an entrepreneur or investor. Until you take this step, you'll always be an average taxpayer and the tax laws will be stacked against you. The good news is that you don't have to quit your job. You just have to start acting like an entrepreneur or an investor. That means the first thing you need to do is to increase your financial intelligence by investing in financial education. Starting a business or investing in a deal without financial education is the riskiest action you can take with respect to your money.

Become an Entrepreneur

Here's my advice whenever starting out: Start small. Take a course in real estate or some other type of investing. Take a course in entrepreneurship. Start a home-based business—preferably dealing with something you know about.

That's how I got started. Many years ago, after I'd left public accounting and became the in-house tax advisor for a Fortune 1000 company, I decided to go back into public accounting. I missed the clients, and I missed the challenge. But in that transition I made a bad decision and took the wrong job with the wrong company. Seven months later, I was fired. For the first time in my life, I'd failed at a job, and a job had failed me. It turned out to be one of the best days of my life.

I suddenly realized that not having a job freed me up to do what I'd always wanted to do—start my own business. I had a master's degree and 13 years of experience as a tax advisor. It was time to start my own firm. With the encouragement of my wife and two young sons, I did just that, starting my firm out of my house. I worked 10 hours a day to make contacts and build my practice. It took me nine months just to get my first four clients. Since then, I've never looked back. I've never been happier in my work. And I've never paid less in taxes.

I'm not suggesting you get fired or quit your job. But I am suggesting that you probably have a set of marketable skills that you could use to start your own business. Start part-time. Set aside a room in your house for your business. Don't spend money on a nice office and lots of advertising. Just start small and think big. Think about the freedom that will come when you can devote most, if not all, of your time to your business, your investments, and your family.

And it all starts with good tax planning. When you start a business, your options for deductible expenses skyrocket. And making most of your expenses deductible is easy—make sure that when you spend money your intention is to make even more money. The U.S. tax law calls this having a business purpose for your expenses.

Then, be careful with your money. Don't spend money on stupid stuff. Spend it on things that will likely grow your business. Spend it on things that other people in your business might buy. This is called making expenditures

> *When you start a business, your options for deductible expenses skyrocket. And making most of your expenses deductible is easy—make sure that when you spend money your intention is to make even more money.*

that are ordinary in your line of business. Make your expenses count. Make them work for you. When you do that, your expenses become necessary. And when your expenses are necessary, voilà, they're deductible.

Become an Active Investor

Now let's suppose that you don't want to start a business but you still want to be a super taxpayer. What do you do? You become an investor. Remember that the right side of the CASHFLOW Quadrant includes both business owners *and* investors. But there's one catch; you can't be a typical investor if you're going to enjoy the tax benefits of investing. You have to become an *active investor*. That means you have to be an investor who actively invests for passive income, not earned income. Very simply, passive income is income that comes from dividends, rents, and business. It's taxed at a much lower rate than earned income, which comes from appreciation and capital gains, or from your paycheck. In order to become a super investor, you must find good, cash-flowing investments that produce passive income. A great book to read on this topic is the book Robert Kiyosaki and I wrote together, *Why the Rich Are Getting Richer*. (Plata Publishing, 2017)

You might be thinking that becoming an active investor sounds hard. It's not. Becoming an active investor is actually quite simple. Just as with becoming an entrepreneur, it all starts with your financial education. You don't need a four-year degree in finance. You don't even need a two-year degree, but you do need to take some courses in the type of investing you think you might enjoy. Don't know what you might like? Take a variety of courses on a variety of investments. Take a course in real estate.

> *Becoming an active investor is actually quite simple. Just as with becoming an entrepreneur, it all starts with your financial education.*

Take a course in stock investing. And take a course in business investing. You never know what you'll like until you learn about it. A great resource for becoming an active investor is educational programs offered by The Rich Dad Company. Learn more at www.WealthAbility.com.

Once you have an idea of what type of investing you want to do, find a mentor or coach to help you with your investing. Then simply start investing. Just as I advised with starting a business, start small. Do one small real estate deal, a couple of small stock market trades, or make a small investment in a private company. You don't have to risk a lot of time and money. And along the way, so long as you keep track of all of your education and investment expenses, and your tax preparer reports them properly, you should be able to deduct some or all of these expenses on your tax return.

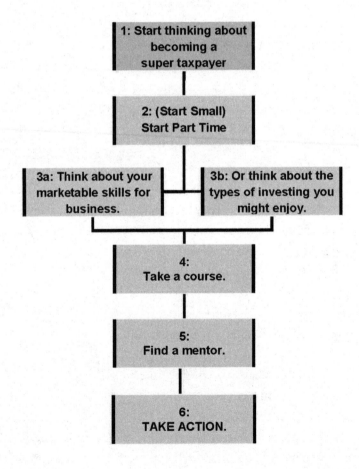

The Passive Investor

There is one other type of super taxpayer. That's the passive investor. And no, I'm not talking about the typical investor who invests in the stock market through a mutual fund or an exchange-traded fund (ETF). I'm talking about someone who invests their money with an active investor who is working directly in a business, real estate, agriculture or energy—the *tax-preferred* types of investments. Passive investors also enjoy the benefit of deducting many of their expenses. With the right tax strategy, they can even deduct losses from the investment against income they earn from other sources.

The key to good passive investing is a good team. You need a great investment advisor and a stellar tax advisor, as well as a good lawyer and a knowledgeable banker. All of these team members need to work together to make sure your best interests are met. I've found the best way to get team members to work well together is to hire a wealth strategist. This can be one of the advisors on the team or a separate strategist altogether. The strategist can work to maintain the relationships between you and the other team members.

> *The key to good passive investing is a good team.*

In many countries, only certain individuals are allowed to be passive investors. In the United States, these individuals are called "accredited investors." Accredited investors meet certain minimum wealth and earning guidelines set up by the government. In Australia these are called "sophisticated investors" or "professional investors." There are always minimum wealth requirements and in some countries, there are additional certification rules. The thinking is that if you have enough money, you either have a high enough financial education to properly evaluate a deal or you can afford to lose some of your money. Either way, you qualify under the government guidelines for becoming a passive investor.

While the losses and expenses of a passive investor can be deductible, the rules can be a little tricky. If you're thinking of going this route, be sure to sit down with your tax advisor and let him or her know what you are planning so that he or she can explain the rules to you and make sure you get the benefit of your expenses and losses.

Don't Be Cheap with Your Team Members	
1.	You often get what you pay for with team members.
2.	Low fees don't translate into a good deal when it comes to advisors. A good team member is worth their weight in gold.

Document Everything

The last key to becoming a super taxpayer is excellent documentation. All good tax planning also leads to sound business and investment decisions. One of the best business or investment decisions you can make is to keep good documentation of your income and expenses. This means that you

keep accurate books and records. Make sure
your bookkeeping is up to date at least once
each week. The more thorough and accurate
your accounting, the better business and
investment decisions you'll make, and the
less likelihood you will have difficulties in an audit.

*The last key to becoming
a super taxpayer is
documentation.*

TAX TIP: Document. Document. Document. The IRS, Revenue Canada, the HMRC, ATO, and other tax collectors love documentation. Remember that if you pretend to document a deduction, you get a pretend deduction.

If you decide to start a business, even though you are starting small (as advised earlier in this chapter), think about your business as if it were one of the big dogs, such as IBM or Microsoft. Think about all of the good reporting they need to do in order to stay in business and to keep investors, bankers and management informed about what's going on. You can do the same with your small, start-up business that you run out of your home office. When you do, chances are the IRS, CRA, or other tax officials will be in and out of your life quickly and painlessly if you're ever audited. You'll also have accurate financial information to help you to make wise and informed business and investment decisions. Best of all, your expenses will be deductible, and you won't have to worry about whether the government will allow them. Why? Because you've followed the law exactly as it was meant to be applied.

The result will be lower taxes and less stress. So now you know what I mean when I say that almost every expense can be deductible under the right circumstances. Every time you spend money you can also reduce your taxes, whether it's filling up your car at the gas station, going out to dinner with your spouse and business partner, or even going to New Mexico to look at real estate.

The basic difference between an average taxpayer and a super taxpayer is how serious they are about increasing their wealth. An average taxpayer turns his or her money over to someone else and hopes and prays that their investments go up in value. The super taxpayer is actively involved in creating wealth, either through actively investing in a business, real estate or the stock market or through actively seeking out active investors who will do that for them. Super taxpayers also build a great team of advisors, mentors and other relationships who actively help them build their wealth and reduce their taxes. Here's a chart illustrating the basic difference between an average taxpayer and a super taxpayer. Pretty simple, isn't it?

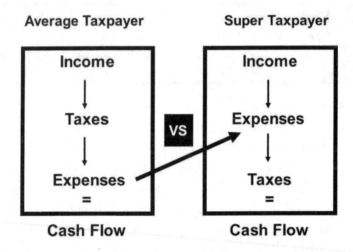

Next, we're going to look at the king of all deductions, *depreciation*.

CHAPTER 6: KEY POINTS

1.	Most people are average taxpayers who only experience average tax benefits.
2.	The key to saving more in taxes is becoming a super taxpayer and enjoying the benefits of deductible expenses.
3.	The best way to enjoy deductible expenses is to start a business or to start investing for passive income. You don't have to quit your job. Just start small.
4.	One of the best business and investing practices is to document your income and expenses, and to document them well.

Tax Strategy #6 – Document, Document, Document

Being able to immediately provide documentation upon request during an audit is always an impressive tactic. If your activities and expenses are properly documented, then the tax collector will have a hard time making a case for any changes. Plus, having your documentation in place reduces the amount of time your CPA bills you for an audit. Documentation is a successful defense strategy that enables you to always be ready for an audit and reduces the associated costs. Documentation of receipts has been made a lot easier with computers. Now, you can scan your receipts into your computer. This way, you don't have to have a file drawer just for receipts and you don't have to worry about them fading over time. Have you ever pulled out a credit card receipt that was a year or two old, only to find a blank piece of paper? This happens all the time. What if you were being audited and went to pull those receipts only to find they were all just blank pieces of paper. Be sure to scan the receipts into a file on your computer. The IRS loves it when they can just look at scanned receipts instead of going through faded paper receipts.

You will learn more about documentation in Chapter 22 when we talk about IRS audits. Just remember that this is one tax strategy you can do every day, and it doesn't take much time or effort.

Chapter Seven

Depreciation: The King of All Deductions

"The avoidance of taxes is the only intellectual pursuit that carries any reward." — *John Maynard Keynes*

The Magic of Depreciation

Several years ago, not long after I met him, Robert Kiyosaki asked me to come with him to an interview at the *Arizona Republic*. The topic was investing. The journalist was interested in Robert's claim that anyone could earn 30 to 40 percent on their investments. Robert wanted me there as backup. I think it was the first time in history that an accountant had been brought along as the "muscle."

After the interview, Robert and I walked over to the Arizona Center to have lunch. On the way, he asked me, "What do you think about depreciation?"

"Depreciation is like magic," I told him. "You get a deduction for something that doesn't cost you any money. You create money out of thin air."

And that really is the magic of depreciation. When you buy an asset that produces income, you can deduct a portion of it each year you own it. If it's a physical asset, such as real estate or equipment, the deduction is called *depreciation*. If it's an intangible asset (one you can't feel or touch, such as a customer list or computer software), the deduction is called amortization. But in the end, the benefit is the same.

Types of Deductions For Income-Producing Assets	
Type	Examples
Depreciation =	Tangible Assets: Such as real estate or equipment
Amortization =	Intangible Assets: Such as customer lists or computer software

Chez Pierre

Let me explain. Let's say, for instance, that my friend, Pierre, buys a commercial building in which to house his restaurant, Chez Pierre. Due to the magic of depreciation, he gets to take a deduction for a portion of the cost of that building every year for a set number of years. How many years depends on the type of building he's purchased and the country in which he lives. He gets to do this even though the building may not wear out for hundreds of years and may actually increase in value. That's why I call depreciation magic. You get a deduction that really hasn't cost you anything.

Sure, Pierre paid for the building. But the building isn't going down in value. In fact, over the long term, in most cases, it will go up in value. And if Pierre is a smart investor, the building costs are covered by the cash flow the building generates. So Pierre isn't really paying anything out of pocket for this expense—and he might even be making money. Despite all this, Pierre still gets to take advantage of depreciation, a deduction that was created specifically to encourage people to buy and construct buildings and equipment.

You might be asking, "Why would the government want to encourage this type of investment?" It's simple. Remember that Congress/Parliament want industry that creates jobs. And they also want the market to create housing and commercial buildings. Depreciation is one of the major catalysts for businesses and investors to do just that. Let's get back to our example of my friend Pierre and his restaurant.

Let's say Pierre pays $1 million for his building, including the land. The land by itself is worth $220,000. Because even the government understands that land doesn't wear out, there isn't a depreciation deduction for the portion of the price that relates to the land. Still, that leaves $780,000 to depreciate. That means that every year Pierre will get a deduction equal to a set portion of the $780,000.

How much Pierre gets to deduct depends on how fast the government will let Pierre depreciate the building. In the United States, for instance, commercial buildings are currently depreciated over 39 years. That means that Pierre would get a deduction each year of $20,000 for 39 years ($780,000 ÷ 39). That's about 2.5 percent per year. In Canada, the depreciation rate, or capital cost allowance, is almost double that of the United States at 5 percent (and even higher in some cases). Imagine a deduction of $40,000 per year that doesn't cost you anything out of pocket.

Sure, you may have interest expense for the loan or certain out-of-pocket expenses associated with maintenance, but those expenses are also deductible. The actual building cost is a non-cash expense (an expense that doesn't reduce your cash flow) that gives you a deduction. Even better, you not only get a deduction for the money you put into the building but you also get a deduction for the money the bank puts into the building. That's right, you get a depreciation deduction for the entire cost of the building, even if you borrowed all the cash to pay for it from someone else. Now that's what I call magic.

And believe it or not, it gets even more amazing. When Pierre bought the land and the building he also bought what was inside the building and the landscaping and other improvements outside of the building (such as the fencing or the parking lot). He bought all of the floor coverings, the window coverings, the cabinetry, and more. So a portion of the $780,000 price tag for the building really applies to these other items. This is important because these other items can be depreciated faster than the building, putting more money into his pocket faster.

One of the keys to taking full advantage of depreciation is to quickly get as much of your deduction as you can. The more deductions you can get today, the more money you can put in your pocket. And the more money you have in your pocket today, the more money you have to invest back into your business or into other investments.

One of the keys to taking full advantage of depreciation is to quickly get as much of your deduction as you can.

Let's say that of the $780,000 price tag for the building, $100,000 really belongs to the cabinets, floor coverings, window coverings, and other things that came with the building but aren't really a part of it. This $100,000 is depreciated much faster than the building. Instead of getting a 2.5 to 5 percent deduction each year, Pierre will get a 20 percent or more deduction each year for this portion of his purchase. That's another $20,000 each year in deductions.

In total, Pierre gets a deduction each year of about $37,500 [($680,000 ÷ 39 years) + ($100,000 x 20%)], which means that $37,500 of his restaurant income won't be taxable. And this can pay off in a big way.

TAX TIP: Avoid the tax collector's traps. The trick is to properly document the values of all the items you depreciate in a cost segregation or chattel appraisal—even better, have a tax professional or engineer document them for you. Without it, the tax collector can make your tax savings from depreciation disappear. Protect your tax savings with good documentation.

Pick Your Bracket

Let's say Pierre is in a tax bracket where his income is taxed at 40 percent. The depreciation deductions save him $15,000 that he can put back into his business or invest somewhere else *every year*. Or he could use the money to take a very nice vacation. After all, he's been working hard in the restaurant and deserves a break. Isn't it nice that the government is paying for his vacation?

Wouldn't you like the government to pay for your vacation? Or even better, wouldn't you like the government to subsidize your business by giving you big depreciation deductions?

Of course, you don't only get depreciation deductions for buildings. You also get them for equipment. In many countries, this includes your car so long as you use it primarily for business. It could even include the portion of your house that you use for an office. There are tons of possibilities.

Depreciation really is free money from the government, because if you're a smart investor or businessperson, you're going to make money from the buildings and equipment you purchase. And even though you're profiting from your purchases, you still get a tax deduction for them. How cool is that? This is why I call depreciation the *king of all deductions*. In essence, the government pays you for making money and being productive.

> *This is why I call depreciation the king of all deductions. In essence, the government pays you for making money and being productive.*

Real Estate Investing and Depreciation

Depreciation doesn't apply to only regular businesses. It also applies to real estate investing. Let's say that you don't want to be a business owner. Instead, you want to invest in real estate. Obviously, there are great financial benefits to being a real estate investor. You buy a property mostly with the bank's money and get a tenant to pay enough in rent to not only make your payments to the bank but also pad your pockets a little. And if you buy your real estate right, chances are it will increase in value over time.

The tax benefits of long-term real estate investing can be equal to or even greater than the cash flow and increase in value (appreciation) from your properties. Let's say that Pierre, in addition to buying a building for his restaurant, decides he wants to invest in real estate. He would like to buy a small apartment building. After a diligent search, he finds a good fit for his investment strategy, paying $800,000 for a great apartment building and its land. His cash flow from the apartments totals $12,000 a year after paying the bank and all other expenses.

The land is worth $200,000. So the building and its contents are worth $600,000. Let's suppose that $100,000 of the $600,000 is for the contents and $500,000 is for the building. Depreciation in the United States on residential property is about 3.6 percent per year. That means Pierre will get a depreciation deduction for the building of about $18,000 and another $20,000 of depreciation on the contents (20 percent, remember?) each year. That's a total of $38,000.

Example: Pierre's Depreciation on Investment Property	
Cost of Apartment Building	$800,000
Minus the Value of Land -	$200,000
Equals the Value of the Building and Contents =	$600,000
Depreciation of Building	
Value of the Building and Contents =	$600,000
Minus Contents of Building -	$100,000
Equals Value of Building =	$500,000
Multiply Value of Building by the Depreciation rate in the U.S. on Residential Property X	3.6%
Equals Building Depreciation Deduction =	$18,000
Depreciation of Contents	
Contents of Building =	$100,000
Multiplied by 20% X	20%
Equals Contents Depreciation Deduction =	$20,000
Total Depreciation for Building and Contents	

Building Depreciation Deduction =	$18,000
Plus Contents Depreciation Deduction +	$20,000
Equals total depreciation deduction =	$38,000

Since his cash flow from the apartment is only $12,000, when he subtracts the depreciation expense, Pierre ends up with a loss for tax purposes of $26,000. So Pierre's $12,000 of cash flow is entirely tax-free. In addition, Pierre has $26,000 of loss to use against other income. If Pierre is in a 40 percent tax bracket, this $26,000 of loss will create a tax refund for him of over $10,000. Again, Pierre can use that money to reinvest in his business or in real estate. Or he can take a vacation, improve his house, or do anything else he wants to do. After all, it's his money.

Tax Consequences	
Cash Flow from Real Estate =	$12,000
Minus total depreciation deduction (expense) -	$38,000
Equals a loss of =	($26,000)
Pierre's cash flow of $12,000 is Entirely Tax-Free.	
Potential Tax Refund	
Amount of loss that can be used against other income =	$26,000
Multiplied by 40% (tax bracket) X	40%
Equals a potential tax refund of =	$10,400

In Pierre's case, the government essentially paid him to invest in real estate. And they'll do the same for you. You can get the government to subsidize your business and your real estate, or pay for your vacation or home improvements, simply through the magic of depreciation.

Just a small note here: In some countries depreciation is called *capital cost allowance*. It's a different name for the same thing. Don't be fooled by the language. The same principles are at work.

You can get the government to subsidize your business and your real estate, or pay for your vacation or home improvements simply through the magic of depreciation.

The Magic of Amortization

Now let's say that you buy something that isn't a physical item. It's what we call an *intangible*. This means that you can't touch it. It could be a customer list, computer software, or a trademark or patent. Your government wants to subsidize your purchase and does so through a rule very similar to depreciation called *amortization*. Amortization is magical too. In fact, the only practical difference between amortization and depreciation is in the name. The principles are the same. You get to take a deduction for a portion of the cost of the asset over a period of years.

CAUTION!

Remember Your Tax Return Elections	
1.	You must elect to deduct amortization.
2.	Some amortization elections have to be clearly stated on your tax return in the year you first start using your intangible property.

In the United States that period of time ranges from 3 to 15 years. Other countries have different terms for amortizing nonphysical, or intangible, assets. But the rule works just the same as depreciation. Let's say, for example, that Pierre buys a bunch of recipes from another chef. This chef created some secret recipes that people love, and Pierre would like to utilize them to improve his business. Pierre pays $75,000 for the recipes.

Example: Pierre's Amortization on Cost of Recipes	
Cost of Recipes =	$75,000
Divided by 15 Years (based on U.S. period of time) ÷	15
Equals deduction taken for 15 years =	$5,000

Pierre gets to take a deduction for the cost of those recipes over fifteen years. That amounts to a deduction of $5,000 every year. And all the while Pierre is making oodles of money using the recipes to create wonderful food that he sells at his restaurant. He may even license his recipes and let other people use them, and he might make even more money from licensing than he does from his restaurant. And still, the government gives him a tax deduction each year for a portion of the cost of the recipes. Isn't amortization great?

Don't Cheat Yourself

Every so often I see a tax return from a new, real-estate-owning client that doesn't show depreciation. And it's not because the client has owned the real estate for 40 years. No, it's because for some reason the client or his or her accountant didn't take the depreciation deduction. This is not only wrong—it's also stupid. Why not take the deduction? If you don't, you're in essence cheating yourself. It makes no sense to me, but I see it at least once a month.

What's more, I rarely see a breakdown of the different components of a building on a new client's tax return. When you purchase a building, you really purchase the land, the building, the land improvements and the contents of the building. Just like Pierre did when he purchased the building to house his restaurant or when he purchased his apartment building, every investor should break out the land improvements and the contents of the building from the portion of the cost that related to the land and the building. What's inside of the building should be separated from the physical structure on the tax return.

Usually, I just see land, building, and whatever equipment the client purchased after he or she bought the building. This means that the taxpayer's tax preparer was too lazy or uneducated to break out the component parts of the purchase. (Breaking out the component parts of a building is called a cost segregation or chattel appraisal.) How dumb is this? The client's tax-return preparer has postponed the deduction to a much later year and penalized the client because of laziness. Instead of getting his money back from the government now, the client has to wait for several years. Remember, it's your money. Don't let the government have it any longer than needed.

Can you now see why I devoted an entire chapter to this magical deduction called depreciation? Nothing is better than a deduction you don't have to pay for. And nowhere do I see more mistakes made on tax returns than when it comes to this critical deduction. Take advantage of what the government has offered to you. Get your depreciation deduction done right. Find a reputable accountant who really knows what he or she is doing, and make sure to double-check your return before filing.

> *Nothing is better than a deduction you don't have to pay for.*

Ultimately, if you miss out on your fair return, it's nobody's fault but yours. Increase your financial intelligence and find good advisors to help you along the way.

In our next chapter, we're going to talk about what types of income are the best, what types are the worst, and everything in between.

<table>
<tr><td colspan="2" align="center">**CHAPTER 7: KEY POINTS**</td></tr>
<tr><td>1.</td><td>Depreciation is like magic. It creates money out of thin air.</td></tr>
<tr><td>2.</td><td>Deductions over a set number of years on hard assets such as buildings are called *depreciation*. Deductions over a set number of years for intangible assets such as recipes are called *amortization*.</td></tr>
<tr><td>3.</td><td>Many people don't take full advantage of their depreciation and amortization deductions either because of ignorance or laziness— or both—on their part or their accountant's part.</td></tr>
<tr><td>4.</td><td>Ultimately, you're the one responsible to make sure you're not cheating yourself. Always double-check your return.</td></tr>
</table>

Tax Strategy #7 – Cost Segregations of Business and Rental Properties

A few years ago, I was looking at the forum of a CPA website and noticed some chatter about cost segregations (pulling personal property out of real property classification to allow for quicker depreciation). What surprised me most was the amount of debate about whether cost segregations were legal. About 50 percent of the CPAs in the discussion felt they were illegal or admitted that they didn't know if they were legal. Another 30 percent thought they were very aggressive tax planning. So, here is the real scoop about cost segregations. Not only are cost segregations legal but they are specifically sanctioned by the IRS and technically required by law. Now, the IRS doesn't enforce the requirement because it means less revenue for them, and the IRS knows that the lazier the taxpayer and/or accountant, the more revenue the United States Treasury makes. Here is how you can tell they are legal. First, the IRS has an audit guide to tell their agents how to handle cost segregations. This guide is also useful for taxpayers. Anyone can see this guide on the IRS website at IRS.gov. Second, and more important, is how the law treats cost segregations. When you do a cost segregation on a building you have owned for several years, you must file a form 3115, "Change in Accounting Method." There are two types of changes on this form. One is a change from one correct method of accounting to another correct method of accounting. This is like when you change your basic accounting method from the cash method of accounting to the accrual method of accounting. (See Chapter 18 for an explanation of the cash and accrual methods of accounting.) The other change is a change from an incorrect method of accounting to a *correct* method of accounting. Guess where a cost segregation falls? That's right, it's a change from an incorrect method of accounting to a correct method of accounting. When you don't do a cost segregation, you are doing your depreciation incorrectly. Here are a couple of hints for doing a cost segregation. First, according to the IRS audit guide, you must employ professionals to do the study. You can either use engineers or CPAs. In my network of CPA firms, Tax-Free Wealth Network™, we use both an engineer and a CPA to do the cost segregation study. Next, remember that you can do a cost segregation at any time. You don't have to do it when you first buy the property. This allows for some great tax planning, as you want to do the cost segregation in a year when you are in the highest tax bracket so that you get the most tax benefits. Remember that depreciation is a deduction, not a credit, so your benefit is based on your tax bracket. We discuss credits in Chapter 10. A deduction in a high tax bracket is always better than a deduction in a low tax bracket. And here is a piece of information very few people understand. When you do a cost segregation, no matter how many years later, you get to catch up on all the depreciation you would have taken if you had done your cost segregation in the year you purchased the property. So, if you have owned the property for several years, you will have a lot of extra deductions in the year you do the cost segregation. Be sure you meet with your tax advisor and ask about cost segregations for all of your business and investment real estate. You could be missing out on a lot of tax savings otherwise.

Chapter Eight

Earn Better Income

"The only difference between death and taxes is that death doesn't get worse every time Congress meets."   *– Will Rogers*

When I was a kid looking for ways to make money, I didn't really care much about how or where I got it. I was just as happy (perhaps even happier) getting an allowance from my parents as I was earning money for shoveling snow in the winter or mowing lawns in the summer. I never distinguished between types of income because the end result to me was always the same—cash in my pocket.

Of course, back then I never earned enough money to worry about paying taxes. It didn't really matter how I got it, just so long as I had enough to buy candy or a baseball glove, or, later on, go on a date with a pretty girl (my favorite use for money in high school).

These days I care a lot about how I earn my money. And my favorite income is naturally the nontaxable variety. My least favorite income is the type that requires not only income tax but also other taxes such as employment taxes.

In every country, there are different types of income, and they all have different associated tax rates, costs, and benefits. For example, in most countries, long-term capital gains (income made from the sale of property and other assets) are taxed at a lower rate than ordinary

> *In every country, there are different types of income, and they all have different associated tax rates, costs, and benefits.*

income (retirement plans, bonds, etc.). In Australia, for instance, long-term capital gains are only taxed at half the rate of ordinary income, and some capital gains are not taxed at all, such as gains from the sale of a personal residence.

Earned income is taxed at the highest rate possible. This includes income you earn as an employee, self-employed individual, or partner. And in some countries, including the United States, earned income is subject to additional taxes called employment or self-employment taxes. The simplest way to determine if income is going to be taxed at a high rate or a low rate is to go back to the CASHFLOW Quadrant.

> *The simplest way to determine if income is going to be taxed at a high rate or a low rate is to go back to the CASHFLOW Quadrant.*

Income received on the left side of the quadrant will normally be taxed at a higher rate than income received on the right side of the quadrant. Remember what I told you about the government subsidizing businesses and investors? We already discussed one way they do that. They allow tax deductions for those people and organizations. Another way they benefit businesses and investors is by reducing the tax rate on their income.

Think about the super taxpayer. The super taxpayer is a business owner or investor. How does he earn his income? He probably gets some of his income from a salary, which is taxed at the highest rate. But most of his income is from either his business or his investments. Let's take a look at how this income (from the right side of the CASHFLOW Quadrant) is taxed.

First, there is the income the super taxpayer earns in his business that he puts back into the business to make it grow. This income isn't taxed at all. Why? Because when he spends the money to grow his business, he gets a deduction for every dollar he spends, either directly or through depreciation or amortization, as we discussed in the last chapter.

Let's use the example of my friend Pierre again. Remember, he's the one who owns the restaurant, Chez Pierre. Suppose he earns $200,000 after his normal expenses through his restaurant this year. If he took all of that money out of the business, it would be taxed at regular rates. He doesn't want to do that. So instead, let's say he puts $80,000 back into the business in the form of additional supplies and equipment that will make even more income for him in the future and then puts another $20,000 into marketing.

All of the money Pierre puts back into his business is deductible against his $200,000 of income. That would leave him with $100,000. Now let's say that he has a home office and that his van is used primarily for business; that when he spent money on a vacation, he took his wife and children, who are all owners of the business with him and that they spent more than half of each weekday on business; and that whenever Pierre and his wife went to dinner during the year, they had a business discussion.

In total, Pierre could easily have another $40,000 in expenses that he could use to offset his income. That leaves only $60,000 to be taxed. And after his deductions for his mortgage, taxes, and charitable donations, he's down to $30,000 of taxable income. If he's in the United States, this $30,000 will be taxed at about an 11 percent rate. So he only has to pay $3,300 in taxes on $200,000 of income. If he were an employee on the left side of the CASHFLOW Quadrant making a salary of $200,000, even after he took his deductions for mortgage interest, taxes, and charitable donations, he would've paid a tax rate of about 22 percent on the remaining $170,000—that's over $37,000.

Example of Possible Deductions	
Left Side of Cash Flow Quadrant	Right Side of Cash Flow Quadrant
1. Mortgage Interest	1. Business Supplies
2. Property Taxes	2. Business Equipment
3. Charitable Donations	3. Marketing Expenses for Business
	4. Home Office Expenses for Business
	5. Vehicle Use for Business
	6. Meals (discussing Business)
	7. Travel
	8. Mortgage Interest
	9. Property Taxes
	10. Charitable Donations

Of course, instead of putting the $100,000 back into his business, Pierre could've used his $100,000 to make other investments. With good tax planning, the money wouldn't be taxed in that case either. If the money is invested in energy or real estate, for instance, he's likely to get enough tax benefits from those investments to offset the tax he would otherwise have to pay on his business income.

Suppose, for example, Pierre invests the $100,000 in oil and gas drilling and development. In the United States, he'd receive a deduction equal to the entire $100,000 the year he made his investment. So he still doesn't have to pay more than $3,300 on his total income of $200,000. He could get almost as good of a result from investing in real estate, depending on the type of real estate he invests in and his meeting certain other technical requirements. And all the while, he'd be making even more money from the $100,000 investment while still getting these tax breaks.

TAX TIP: Modify your investment strategy. Some real estate investments have "built in" tax savings that don't require you to do anything extra to write off the losses against any other income you have. Oil and gas are examples of these investments, where as much as 100 percent of the investment can be written off in the first year.

Buckets of Money

Think about your income as if you had to put it into one of five buckets.

Earned Income

The first bucket is your *earned income.* This bucket has some serious holes in it. Your income runs out of those holes in the form of high income taxes and high employment taxes. Even if you're in a country where your employer pays the employment taxes, think about how much higher your income could be if your employer didn't have to pay those taxes.

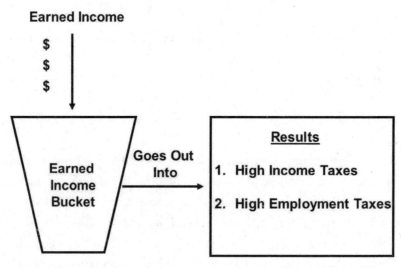

Ordinary Income

The second bucket is your *ordinary income*. This is income from your pension plan, your 401(k) plan, your registered retirement savings plan (RRSP), or Pension and certain other income that don't fit into one of the other buckets. While this bucket is better than the earned income bucket, it's still taxed at the highest income tax rates, but at least it doesn't get hit with employment taxes.

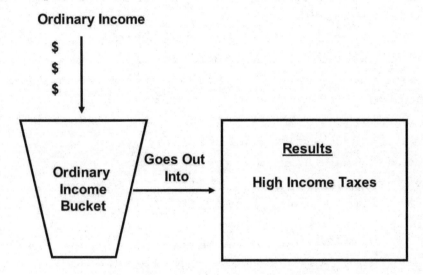

Investment Income

The third bucket is your *investment income*. This includes income from capital gains, interest, and dividends. In most countries, this also includes passive income from investments in businesses and real estate. As a rule, this income is taxed at lower rates. We've already discussed the example of capital gains. Dividend income also may be taxed at lower rates. For instance, in the United States, dividends are taxed at the capital gains rate. In Australia, dividends aren't really taxed at all due to a technicality called the franking credit. Other types of investment income get better tax rates as well. In the United States, interest income from state and local bonds isn't taxable. Life insurance proceeds are also tax-free.

And then there are the proceeds from like-kind (tax-free) exchanges. These are also called 1031 exchanges in the United States, after Internal Revenue Code section 1031. In Australia and Great Britain, these are referred to as rollovers, and in Canada they are referred to as replacements. The effect is the same in all of these countries and many others. If you sell one property that was used in a business (including a rental business) and replace it with a similar property, then the gain on the old property is not taxed until you sell the replacement property and don't roll that money into another property.

The magic of like-kind exchanges is that if you replace a new property with yet another property and continue to do so until you die, you may never have to pay any taxes. You get all of the depreciation deductions allowed under the law without ever paying a tax when the property is sold. And the new property doesn't have to be exactly like the old property. You can move from single-family homes to apartment complexes to commercial property to land and back again without ever having to pay tax.

Like-kind exchanges are particularly well suited for good estate planning.

Some people might be concerned that with like-kind exchanges they won't be able to get any actual cash in their pockets from the sale of their property. This isn't true, however, because you can always refinance the property and pull out tax-free appreciated value. And even if you do that, you can still do another rollover or exchange later on and not pay taxes.

Through like-kind exchanges you can keep buying more and more expensive properties as your properties go up in value, all without ever paying tax. Pretty cool, huh? This is one of my favorite types of income because it allows me to continue reinvesting without ever having to pay taxes. Be sure you meet with a good tax advisor who understands the rules of these types of exchanges. The rollover rules are very specific, and they don't apply to every type of asset. For example, in the United States, you cannot do a like-kind exchange with stock unless you own most of the stock in a company.

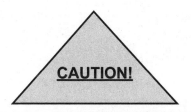

Dot Your 'I's and Cross Your 'T's in Your Like-Kind Exchange

1.	Tax-free exchanges have very detailed rules you must follow.
2.	If you don't follow EVERY rule precisely, your exchange will not be tax free. You will have to pay taxes.

My friend and client, Guy Zanti, can tell you all about the benefits of a like-kind exchange. One day as I sat in my office, Guy called me. He told me that he was about to finalize the sale on one of his rental properties, and he wanted to know if there was anything he could do to reduce his taxes on the sale since the gain was pretty big. I asked him what he was planning to do with the cash from the sale. He told me that he planned on buying more real estate.

Immediately, I thought of tax-free exchanges. I told Guy that if he made a few changes to his sales agreement he could completely avoid any tax from the sale. A few hours later he called me up to let me know that he'd made the changes. I was happy to inform him that by making these few changes he was going to save $20,000 in taxes. That was a good day for both Guy and for me. I love it when I can help a client convert income from taxable to nontaxable.

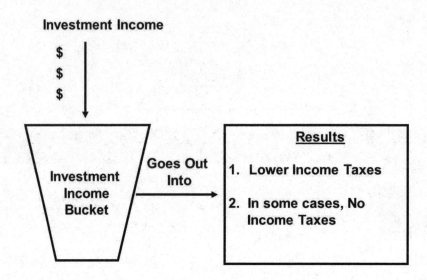

Gifts or Inheritance

The next bucket of income is the money you receive as a *gift or as an inheritance*. In most countries, the person who receives this money is not required to pay taxes on it. Instead, if it's taxed, the person who gives the money or the estate of the person who bequeaths the money is required to pay the tax. Later on, we'll spend an entire chapter on inheritance and gift taxes. There are many ways to avoid these special taxes. And in some countries, there's no inheritance tax at all.

Like-kind exchanges are particularly well suited for good estate planning. When you die, if you plan your estate well, you won't have to pay any estate tax and, at least in the United States, your heirs won't have to pay income tax on the gain when they sell the property because the gain goes away upon the death of the owner.

I had a client who has since passed away. She owned several rental properties. Let's take a look at how good estate planning helped her family on one particular property. She'd originally paid $200,000 for the property and took depreciation of $75,000 over the time she owned it. When she died, the property had grown in value to $300,000.

If she'd sold the property for cash the day before she died, she would've been taxed on her gain of $175,000 ($300,000 less $200,000 plus the $75,000 of depreciation she'd taken). But since she didn't sell the property, her son didn't have to pay any tax when he sold the property for $300,000 three months after she died. And since she had done her estate tax planning well, she (meaning her estate) didn't owe any estate tax either. In the end, she saved $35,000 in taxes during her lifetime and for her family by simply holding onto the property until she died. Now that's my kind of income—completely nontaxable.

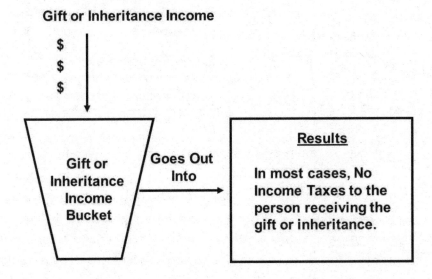

Passive Income

In the United States, there is one more bucket of income—*passive income*. This includes income from any business or real estate investment that you don't personally manage. This income is taxed at regular tax rates, but there are many ways to reduce the amount of income that is taxed.

Losses from passive investments in business and real estate can only offset income from those same or similar investments. While this may seem like a challenge for passive investment activities, it's really a great benefit. The key is to manage your investments so that you have both passive income and passive losses. Remember that the magical deduction of depreciation can really help here. For instance, depreciation from your real estate investments can offset the income from your business investments.

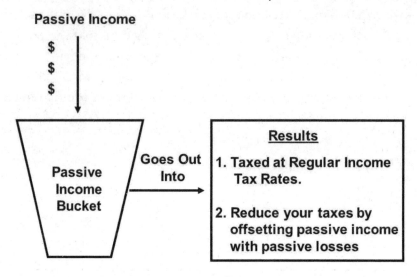

The buckets are important not only because of the different tax rates but also because of the deductions that may be available only to a certain bucket of income. For example, capital losses can only offset capital gains.

So it's just a matter of making sure that your losses and income in each bucket match up. This is where a good accountant and tax advisor can really help. There's no need for you to keep track of this all by yourself when help is only a phone call away. Having a specialist take care of this work will free you up to focus on making more money through your business or investments.

Now you see why it's important to understand how the different types of income are taxed so that you can have a real discussion with your accountant and so that you can keep a lookout for the good, better, and best types of income (i.e., those with the lowest taxes). Even if you aren't good at math or at keeping track of things like this, you can still have all of the advantages of low-taxed income just by having the right people on your team and finding a great accountant to assist you.

Next, we're going to talk about tax brackets. Most countries have a progressive income tax system, which means that the more income you make, the higher the tax rate on your income. So we want to get the benefit of as many low tax brackets as possible. There are a number of strategies available to accomplish this.

CHAPTER 8: KEY POINTS

1.	The more money you make, the more concerned you should be where it's coming from.
2.	Certain types of income, such as earned income, are taxed at higher rates than other types of income, such as passive income.
3.	One particularly good estate and tax planning strategy is like-kind exchanges whereby you can exchange one similar asset for another one tax-free.
4.	The rules on many of these tax strategies are detailed and the work involved in properly balancing your income and expenses is intensive. Hiring a good accountant will be very helpful to you and will allow you to focus on your business and investments.

Tax Strategy #8 – PIGS are your PALS

Most accountants seem scared to death of investments that create passive activity losses (PALs). I, however, love them. While other accountants are worried that the passive losses will not be used for many years, I like to find ways to use PALs. One of my favorite ways to use them is to modify your investment strategy to include passive income generators (PIGs).

The passive loss rules work like this. Suppose you invest in a business. If you spend a significant amount of your time in the business, generally 500 hours per year, you are considered to be "materially participating" in the business. This makes you an active business owner and the income and loss from the business is treated as ordinary income and loss. If you don't spend much time in the business, you are considered to be a passive investor, and income and loss from the business that is reported on your return (through a partnership or S corporation) is treated as passive income and loss.

Rental real estate is *per se* passive, meaning that regardless of any other facts, the income and loss from the real estate is passive. As we discussed in Chapter 7, it's fairly easy to create tax losses from your rental real estate. The challenge is that these losses will normally be considered passive losses, so they won't be available to offset ordinary income.

However, they can offset other passive income. The key is to develop a wealth strategy that takes into account your passive losses and also generates passive income. Let's look at an example.

Suppose you have $10,000 in passive losses from your real estate. Your friend, Paul, has a business that needs more capital. You research his business carefully and decide that it has great potential to grow. It's already earning income and doing fairly well. So you invest $100,000 in Paul's business in exchange for 5 percent ownership.

Paul's company is formed as an S corporation, so you will report 5 percent of the earnings from Paul's business on your tax return. Let's say that in the first year of your investment, Paul's company earns $100,000. You report $5,000 (5%) on your tax return. Your real estate losses of $10,000 will offset your income from Paul's company so you don't have to pay any tax on the $5,000 of income. And since you don't use all of the $10,000 of losses, the rest of those losses ($5,000) carry over to the next year.

Next year, you have another $10,000 of real estate losses. This time, Paul's company earns $300,000. Your share of the income from Paul's company is now $15,000 (5% x $300,000). Your real estate losses can totally offset this income. You have $10,000 from this year plus you carried over $5,000 from last year. So, you have totally sheltered the income from your investment in Paul's company. This makes your investment in Paul's company a lot more valuable. Imagine tax-free money. That's what happens when you combine PIGs with your PALs.

Chapter Nine

Take Advantage of Your Tax Brackets

"I take a very practical view of raising children. I put a sign in each of their rooms: 'Checkout Time is 18 years'."   *– Erma Bombeck*

My younger son turned 20 a while back. What a relief. No more teenagers. And yet, even at 20, he was still living at home. What's worse, so was his older brother. It's not that I don't love my boys. I do. In fact, I even *like* them. It's just that I left home at 19 and always figured that was also a good age for my children to leave home, get out on their own, experience life, get a job, or go into business—to be *independent*.

I understand that getting out on one's own isn't easy to do these days. At least they aren't teenagers anymore. Those teenage years can be rough. There were days I was sure that my 14-year-old son wasn't going to live to his 15th birthday and that I was going to be in prison for the rest of my life for killing him. I'm kidding, of course, but if you have teenagers, I'm sure you understand where I'm coming from.

A saving grace is that both of my boys have been and continue to be great for my taxes. And I'm not just talking about child tax credits. Those are very small tax benefits compared to the enormous tax benefit of using their tax brackets to reduce the taxes on income from my investments and businesses.

Believe it or not, children can be one of the best tax shelters around. And if you do it right, you can also reduce or get rid of your estate tax through good income tax planning with your children.

Believe it or not, children can be one of the best tax shelters around. And if you do it right, you can also reduce or get rid of your estate tax through good income tax planning with your children. Here's how it works.

No Kidding

My client and good friend George has six children. About 10 years ago George asked me to help him reduce his income taxes. He'd just started a business that hadn't made a profit yet. Because of this, the timing proved to be spectacular for tax planning purposes. Why? The business didn't have any value, which meant that giving a substantial portion of the business to his children was free of any gift tax.

George's goal was to have his income taxed at the lowest rate possible, preferably not more than 15 to 20 percent. He was serious about his tax planning, which made him a man after my own heart. He'd even looked into using offshore tax havens in the Caribbean to reduce his taxes. But when I looked at the proposal for his offshore tax planning, I saw that just the administration fees to the banking and tax professionals in the tax haven country for carrying out the plan were about 15 to 20 percent per year. Not to mention that the offshore tax strategy was pretty risky, since George would have lost control of his assets and the IRS would have likely challenged the plan and assessed additional taxes and penalties. I asked George if instead of this risky strategy, he'd rather keep his money on shore (in the United States), have less risk, and still only pay 15 to 20 percent per year with minimal administration costs. Of course, he said yes.

We looked at the tax brackets for both single and married individuals. Tax brackets are portions of your income that are taxed at a specific rate. For example, in 2018 the first $9,525 of taxable income for a single taxpayer is taxed at 10 percent in the United States. The next $29,175 of income is taxed at 12 percent, and so on up to the highest rate of 37 percent on income over $500,000. Using 2018 tax rates to reach

George's goal, we would have wanted each owner of the business who was married to receive no more than $77,400 of income and each owner who wasn't married to receive no more than $38,700 of income every year.

	2018 U.S. Projected Federal Income Tax Brackets	
Tax Rate	**Most Single Filers**	**Married Couples Filing Jointly**
10%	$0 – $9,525	$0 – $19,050
12%	$9,526 – $38,700	$19,051 – $77,400
22%	$38,701 – $82,500	$77,401 – $165,000
24%	$82,501 – $157,500	$165,001 – $315,000
32%	$157,501 – $200,000	$315,001 – $400,000
35%	$200,001 – $500,000	$400,001 – $600,000
37%	$500,001+	$600,001+

George had two married children and four unmarried children. Plus, of course, there was George and his wife, Martha. By dividing ownership of the business between himself and his family, George stood to save a lot of money. In total, because his children were all still in school at some stage and didn't have much taxable income of their own, the business could earn $387,000 and still have every dollar taxed at only 12 percent or less—provided it was structured correctly. Let's compare this to what would have happened with no tax planning.

If George and Martha were the sole owners of the business and had to pay tax on the entire $387,000, they would've paid over $87,000 of federal income tax on the business income (not taking into account the special 20% deduction in the U.S.) in addition to any employment taxes they owed. Instead, they paid less than $45,000 in taxes—a tax savings of more than $42,000. What's more, they received this benefit and more each year as the income grew. Even when the children started earning their own income, George and Martha were still saving thousands of dollars of tax every year because they were using their children's lower tax brackets.

George and Martha's Tax Planning Example		
Business Earnings	Federal Income Taxes Paid without Tax Planning	Federal Income Taxes Paid with Tax Planning
$387,000	> $87,000	< $45,000
Tax **SAVINGS** of **$42,000** Each Year...		

What makes this planning even better is that George was able to maintain control over the cash flow from his business by using trusts and other entities. His business was owned in a limited liability company (LLC), of which he was the manager. He controlled how the money was used and distributed. The children owned their interests in the company through trusts of which George and Martha were the trustees. So George had two levels of control, one as the manager of the company and another as the trustee of the children's trusts. (Of course, he also had parental control, which often is the best control of all.) This leads us to Rule #7.

RULE #7: It's not how much you own that matters, it's how much you control.

Every country is a little different when it comes to using children's tax brackets. Adult children get their own tax brackets in every country. When it comes to minors, some countries impose a flat tax on certain passive income. Others, such as the United States, tax minor children at higher rates (the United States taxes minor children at trust rates). Even so, there can be many other benefits to spreading income to your minor children, simply because it gets the income off of your tax return.

TAX TIP: Partner with your Parents' lower after-tax dollars. Form an LLC and have your elderly parents become members. You can give a portion of your LLC to your parents and the income will be taxed at their lower tax rates.

The Big Bad Corporation

Of course, children aren't the only way to take advantage of different tax brackets. Corporations are also good for this. Corporations are legal entities that own a business. They have their own tax rules and tax benefits, including their own tax bracket. So if you own your business in a corporation, the corporation pays tax on the income. You only pay tax on the portion of the income you take out of the corporation. Tax brackets for corporations work much as they do for individuals. In most countries, they start low and gradually increase as the corporation earns more income. In the United States, beginning in 2018 there is only one tax rate—21%. So all of the income you want to stay in a corporation can now be taxed at a flat rate of 21%.

So how do you split up a business between a pass-through company that is taxed to you individually and a corporation with its own tax rate? It's actually very simple in this day and age of specialization and outsourcing. Rule #8 is so important when you do corporate tax planning.

RULE #8:	**Treat your business just as you would if it were a big public company.**

Rule #8 means that you should look at your business just as a big company would look at its business. You've probably noticed that many big companies outsource much of their work to other companies. A marketing company may help with marketing. Accounting firms will handle their books. In fact, major corporations likely use hundreds of different companies to do special projects for them.

You can do the same thing with your small company. You can have your corporation do the marketing, the bookkeeping, or administrative work. If you are in the health care industry, you can have a separate company do the billings. My favorite service to place in a separate company is human resources. I love it when businesses use a separate corporation to handle all of the payroll and employee benefits.

There are also many good, non-tax reasons to use different companies for different services, which leads us to Rule #9.

RULE #9:	**All tax planning must have a business purpose other than reducing taxes.**

Outsourcing human resources is one example. Suppose you have multiple companies. You would normally have to do payroll and payroll tax reports for each of these companies. Instead of that, however, you can have a single company whose sole purpose is to handle payroll and other human resources for a variety of companies. This single company pays all of the employees of the other companies and handles all human resources. It charges the other companies for this service and their payroll costs, plus a profit. The formal term for a company such as this is a professional employment organization (PEO). There are many large PEOs in the United States and Canada. By utilizing a PEO, you have a company that has a business purpose outside of tax savings—you only have to do payroll and human resource reporting in one company. Can you see how a PEO might make life easier for you?

So let's put this all together. Start with your primary business (you have to have a business in the first place for this to work). If you are solely in the E quadrant, then this (and most of the other strategies in this book) won't work for you. This strategy also doesn't make a lot of sense in the I quadrant. But there's good news for you in the S quadrant. This strategy can work for you, though it works best in the B quadrant. You should be seeing a pattern here. Tax planning is always easiest from the B quadrant because governments favor business owners.

Let's take my friend, Sanjay, who is a dentist in the United States. Sanjay is definitely in the S quadrant, because he has only a single practice and is the primary dentist in that practice. Sanjay earns about $400,000 each year from his dental practice. This puts him in the 32 percent tax bracket. If he pays taxes on this income as a sole proprietor, his income tax will be about $92,000 using 2018 tax rates for married individuals. This doesn't even count the self-employment tax he has to pay. We'll talk about that in a later chapter.

Instead of being taxed personally as a sole proprietor, Sanjay could own his business through a corporation. In the United States, however, it may not be a good idea for him to own his dental practice through a regular, or C corporation if he plans on taking out all of the money from the practice. The reason is that in addition to the 21% corporate tax rate, he would also pay tax on the distributions from the company at the capital gains rate. If he placed his practice in a corporation, and assuming he took a $100,000 salary, his tax burden would actually increase from $92,000 to $112,000. Not a good idea.

Instead, he can own his practice through an LLC or an S corporation. This way, any income that is left in the company is taxed directly to Sanjay as the shareholder. But wait. Since we want to use the tax brackets available to regular corporations to reduce his overall income tax, we will need to form one more corporation.

Now we need to think of what services the other company can provide. It could provide human resources, marketing, bookkeeping, and/or administrative services. Whatever services it provides, they have to be services that justify being paid well.

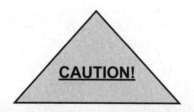

CAUTION!

All Transactions Must Have "Economic Substance"	
1.	There must be a business purpose for setting up your separate corporation.
2.	Your corporation must have a purpose other than just tax savings. It must otherwise help your business to be more profitable.

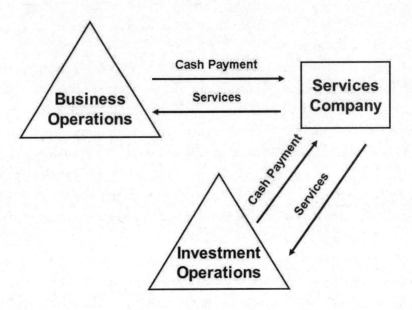

Ideally, we'd like the primary business to end up with no more than $315,000 of income, so we don't get above the 24% tax bracket. The rest of the income can go to the regular corporation. That way we shift the high-bracket income from Sanjay's personal 32 percent tax bracket to the corporations' lower 21 percent tax bracket. In addition, in the United States there is a 20% deduction if personal income is no more than $315,000. To accomplish this, we'll pay the company $85,000 from the dental practice.

Now, Sanjay's personal income is only $315,000. On that income, he will pay about $49,000 in taxes using 2018 tax rates. Then he will pay $18,000 on the income in the regular corporation, for a total tax burden of about $67,000. That's a tax reduction every year of $25,000. Even with the added cost of bookkeeping for the C corporation and for preparing the additional tax return, that's still a substantial savings.

Just think what Sanjay can do with an additional $25,000. He can take a very nice vacation, make those home improvements his wife has been wanting, or, better yet, invest the $25,000 either back into his business (he gets another tax deduction for that) or invest it into real estate or some other I-quadrant investment. The best part of all is that the $25,000 he saves in taxes is tax-free. So he gets the entire $25,000.

Remember to Document Your Intercompany Transactions	
1.	Payments from one of your companies to another must be well documented.
2.	Many good tax strategies have been lost because details and documents like notes for loans and management fee agreements have not been properly maintained.

This example, of course, uses U.S. income tax rates. Most other countries have even higher individual income tax rates than the United States. So this strategy works even better outside of the United States. In Canada, for instance, small business corporations have an especially low tax rate when compared with the individual tax rates. In Australia, the corporate tax rate is a flat 30 percent, while the individual tax rate goes as high as 45 percent. Anyone who makes more than $80,000 of income from their business in Australia can really benefit from using a corporation to take advantage of lower tax rates.

Plan Well

Of course, we always want to make sure that we are taking full advantage of our own personal tax brackets. Wouldn't it be a shame to lose our 10 percent or 15 percent tax brackets by not planning? You might think that could never happen, but it happens pretty often. I see it happen especially in down economies.

Let's say that you have a bad year in your business or investing and you lose money. You or your spouse may have a job, but overall, your income is a lot less than normal. You could end up losing the benefit of low tax brackets and even lose deductions that you can never get back. That's because if you don't have enough income during the year to use your itemized deductions, then you simply lose most of those tax benefits. You don't get to carry them over to a later year as you do with a loss from a business.

Of course, we always want to make sure we are taking full advantage of our own personal tax brackets. Wouldn't it be a shame to lose our 10% or 15% tax brackets by not planning?

For example, my friend Joe had a down year a couple of years ago. After taking all of his deductions, he had a loss for the year. The result was that he was about to lose a bunch of deductions and the benefit of his low tax brackets. So we did something that you may not normally think of. We created income. Actually, we just postponed some deductions and caused some income to be recognized that year that would normally have been recognized in a later year.

How we did this is a little too complicated for the scope of this book. If you find yourself in this situation, sit down with your tax advisor and figure out how you can have income taxed in your low-income year instead of a later, high-income year. And be sure you don't lose any of those precious deductions. It's not difficult. It just takes a little attention and realizing where you are financially during the year.

I hope you liked the great tax benefits I explained in this chapter. There are many great ways to save on taxes.

CHAPTER 9: KEY POINTS

1	A great way to reduce your taxable income is to take advantage of the tax brackets.
2.	By giving a portion of your business to your children and family, you can reduce the overall tax burden for you personally and take advantage of lower tax brackets.
3.	You can divide your business among family and partners without losing control by making sure your agreements are clear and by utilizing legal tools such as trusts. It's not how much you own that's important—it's how much you control.
4.	By creating a service company to handle things such as human resources and marketing, you can significantly lower your taxes.

Tax Strategy #9 – Make Your Parents Your Business Partners and Reap the Tax Benefits

We've discussed several tax strategies for your children. But what if you don't have children, or your children are grown, successful, and in a high tax bracket? You can use C corporations like we discussed earlier in this chapter, but another way to make the most of the tax brackets is to involve your parents. Many people have elderly parents who are in a very low tax bracket. Did you know that you can give a part of your business or real estate to your parents and reap major income tax savings? Here's how it works. You give a portion of your limited partnership, S corporation, or LLC to your parents. Any income from their share of the business then flows through to their income tax return and is taxed at their rates. Since you are still the manager of the LLC, majority stockholder of the S corporation, or general partner of the limited partnership, you remain in control. As long as you are careful about how much you give, you won't have any gift tax. And with the current estate and gift tax exemption, chances are they won't have any estate tax on the business when they pass away. There are other possible benefits as well. Be sure to go over this plan carefully with your tax advisor. When you do meet with your advisor, ask about the possibility of a "basis step-up" in the business when your parents pass away. This is an added benefit that requires some one-on-one discussion time with your advisor. And also check out the possibility of giving a lot more through the use of discounts, which we will discuss more in Chapter 13.

20% Pass-Through Deduction for U.S. Businesses

Beginning in 2018, there is a new deduction for businesses that operate as "pass-through" entities. Pass-through entities include sole proprietorships, partnerships and S corporations. The general rule for the new deduction is that pass-through entities receive a deduction equal to 20% of their net revenue for the year. There are several limitations to this rule.

Limitation #1 – 50% of Wages

The 20% deduction generally cannot exceed 50% of W-2 wages paid by the business. So, if there is $500,000 of net income and $120,000 of wages, the normal 20% of net income limitation ($100,000) would be limited to $60,000 (50% of wages).

Limitation #2 – 25% of Wages plus 2.5% of Depreciable Assets

If wages are low in a business and assets are significant, then this limitation might be better for the business than the 50% of wages limitation. The business gets to choose. For example, suppose in the example above that there was $2 million of depreciable assets, such as real estate and equipment. 25% of wages would be $30,000 and 2.5% of assets would be $50,000, so the limitation would be $80,000 instead of $60,000.

Limitation #3 - $315,000 of Taxable Income

If the taxable income of the owner is less than $315,000 ($157,500 for single individuals) (before the 20% deduction), then there is no wage or asset limitation. So if the net income from the business is $300,000 and total taxable income is less than $315,000, then the deduction would be $60,000 (20% x $300,000).

Limitation #4 – Specified Service Businesses

Businesses that are in the accounting, legal, health, performing arts, actuarial, athletic, consulting, financial services and brokerage services do not qualify for the 20% pass-through business deduction unless the taxable income of the owner is less than $315,000 ($157,500 for single individuals). This limitation also applies to any business whose principal asset is the skill or reputation of one of the employees or owners, such as an independent contractor.

Phase-Out

The pass-through (also referred to as QBI) deduction phases out for businesses with income between $315,000 and $415,000 ($157,500 and $207,500 for single individuals). Specified Services Businesses with income in excess of these amounts do not receive any of the benefit. Other businesses with income in excess of these amounts are subject to additional deduction restrictions. Be sure to sit down with your tax advisor to figure out your actual deduction.

Chapter Ten

Credits: The Cream of the Tax-Saving Crop

"There may be liberty and justice for all, but there are tax breaks only for some." – Martin A. Sullivan

A few years ago, I looked at myself in the mirror and didn't like what I saw. And I liked it even less when I got on my bathroom scale. I was 40 pounds overweight, and it showed. I was wearing size 40 pants and had no muscle tone. Right then I decided I was going to lose the weight and get into shape.

My son Max was also working on his weight at the time. He'd signed up for a program where he received training on what foods to eat, and weighed in every week. He also received some books listing the calories and fat content for a large variety of foods, including most of the chain restaurants. I decided to join him. What was most attractive to me about the program was that I could choose what food I ate as long as I kept within a certain number of "points."

The program was tough. I was hungry much of the time in the early stages and had to be disciplined. I wouldn't be lying if I said it was one of the most difficult things I've ever done. Within three months, I'd lost 20 pounds. Over the next 12 months, I lost the rest of the weight. When I was finally finished, I promised myself I'd never gain the weight back because I never wanted to go through such a difficult process again.

Many times during the program, I'd wished I had a magic pill to lose weight instead of going through all the pain and hard work to lose those 40 pounds. Isn't this what everyone wants, a magic pill to lose weight and be healthy? But it doesn't work that way, does it? We all know that exercise and dieting are hard work and take great discipline.

Though there's no such thing as a magic weight-loss pill, if you're looking to lose those excess pounds (or dollars or euros) of tax weight, there's good news. There's a magic pill for some major tax reductions without doing a lot of work. That magic pill is the *tax credit*.

Cream of the Crop

Here's how tax credits work. You do certain things that Congress or Parliament wants you to do and you get an immediate reduction in your taxes. What could be easier than that? All you have to do is learn which things that the government wants you to do and know that there is a tax credit available for doing them. You may already do some of these things without even knowing that the credit is there for you.

A tax credit is the cream of the tax savings crop because it offsets your taxes dollar for dollar. It's not like a deduction that only reduces your taxable income. It goes directly against your taxes. So if you have a tax credit of $1,000, it reduces your taxes by $1,000, no matter what your tax bracket is.

> *A tax credit is the cream of the tax savings crop because it offsets your taxes dollar for dollar.*

TAX CREDITS		TAX DEDUCTIONS
Go directly against your taxes – dollar for dollar	-VS-	Reduce your taxable income

Tax credits are really a direct subsidy. The reason that the government doesn't just send you a check is that it's much simpler for them if you instead claim the credit on your income tax return. And, of course, subsidies are never as politically correct as tax credits. In addition, not everyone has the knowledge required to claim tax credits. So the government isn't out as much money as they would be if they sent you a check directly. Of course, sometimes they do send out checks—but only when they need votes.

There are two primary versions of tax credits. The first is a *refundable credit.* You can receive this credit even if you don't have any taxes due in the first place. So you could completely eliminate your taxable income through some of the techniques I'm teaching you in this book and you would still get a refund from the government for the amount of the credit.

The other version of tax credits is the *nonrefundable credit.* You only get this credit if you actually have tax due. Most credits are like this. For some of these credits, if you don't use them, you can carry them over to another year. For others, if you don't use them, you lose them. It's critical that you know what your taxes are going to be during the year so that you can make sure you have enough income to use up the credits. If you don't have sufficient income, you could lose some of the credits just as you could lose your deductions. And we certainly don't want to lose any tax benefits, do we?

Types of Tax Credits

So what are activities that governments typically reward with credits? They fall into several categories.

Family Credits

First, there are the *family credits.* Many countries, including Australia and the United States, give tax credits for children. The amount of the credit depends on the ages of the children and how many you have in your home. When you think about it, this is a reward and encouragement for raising children. Countries with child tax credits want to help those who increase the population of the country.

Education Credits

Many countries also have *education credits*. Typically, these credits help you offset the cost of tuition and related costs at universities. These credits may be a portion of your tuition and book costs, or they may be a flat amount per student. They also tend to vary based on how long the individual has been in school.

TAX TIP:	Watch out for traps. Many education savings vehicles permit earnings to grow tax-free and distributions to be taken tax-free. While this sounds like a great idea, be sure to take a closer look. Often, these education savings vehicles severely limit your investment options and how the funds can be used. This can in turn limit the overall earning potential and work against the goal of making your child's education more affordable. Understanding how education savings vehicles work can help you maximize your overall earning potential.

Working-Poor Credits

There are also *working-poor credits*. These credits include the earned income credit in the United States and credits for helping the working poor. Credits for earning poverty-level income are usually refundable. Credits like this are primarily intended to provide assistance to those who are at the poverty level or just above.

Still, don't fall into the trap of thinking that just because you make a good income that you aren't eligible for working-poor credits. Remember, if you are in business or if you're an investor, your deductions may be high enough to reduce your income to a very low level. We have several clients who do this and are then able to qualify for earned income and child credits even though their cash flow may be $200,000 or more per year.

Some of you are thinking this isn't fair. People who make a substantial income should not receive benefits presumably designed for those who can't afford many of the basic necessities of life. You would be right in thinking the tax law isn't fair. And it's not meant to be fair. *It's meant to encourage certain activities.* The primary activities that the tax code encourages are business and investing. Business owners and investors get certain privileges. These privileges include receiving credits that

> *You would be right in thinking that the tax law isn't fair. And it's not meant to be fair. It's meant to encourage certain activities.*

help the working poor as long as the taxpayer can so arrange his affairs to qualify for the credit.

So don't send me letters complaining that the tax law should or shouldn't benefit a certain group of people. Instead, become one of those it benefits. The reason you're reading this book is to learn how to reduce your taxes and have more cash flow to create a better lifestyle for yourself, your family, and those around you, right? Focus on that. If you want to give back some of that money, you can. And you'll get a deduction for it. That's what the deduction for charitable donations is for, to encourage you to give back.

Charity Credits

And speaking of credits for giving back, that's what we're discussing next—*charity credits.* Many countries and states or provinces give tax credits to incentivize people to give to schools, to the poor, and to other charities. Often, these credits are in addition to the deduction allowed for charitable donations. There may even be times when you end up with more money in your pocket by giving through the combination of a tax credit and a tax deduction than if you hadn't donated the money in the first place. Now that's an incentive to give.

Investment Tax Credits

As you've probably already guessed, the biggest tax credits are reserved for business owners and investors. These are called *investment tax credits.* They range from credits for building low-income housing and buying equipment to credits for doing research and development of new products and processes. There are literally hundreds of investment-type credits.

If you want to know what the government really values the most, look at what credits it offers to business owners and investors. Think of tax credits as super deductions, because they directly offset your taxes.

Sample of Tax Credits	
1. Family Credits	These credits are for having children, and the amount depends on the ages and how many there are in the home.
2. Education Credits	These credits help offset the cost of tuition and related costs at universities.
3. Working-Poor Credits	These credits are primarily intended to provide assistance to those who are at the poverty level or just above.
4. Charity Credits	These credits incentivize people to give to schools, to the poor, and to other charities.
5. Investment Tax Credits	These credits are reserved for business owners and investors, and include credits for building low-income housing, buying equipment and doing research, and development for new products and processes.

Let's take a look at one of my clients and see how she's used credits to reduce her taxes. Debbie is in the construction business. She spends most of her time building apartment complexes for real estate developers. It's definitely a specialty. As a result, she really knows the apartment business. She's good at what she does, and she makes a lot of money. In a good year, her income can be as high as $10 million or more.

As you can imagine, Debbie has a serious tax challenge—a $4 million tax challenge to be exact. She asked me how she could reduce her taxes to a more reasonable level, and we discussed her situation. I suggested that she invest some of her excess cash into low-income housing projects and that she could even invest in projects that her company builds. The credits are very high for this type of investment in the United States.

By doing this, Debbie has an additional benefit of investing in something that she understands, and she knows which low-income housing projects are likely to be profitable. So not only is she getting an excellent tax benefit through the credits but she'll also receive good cash flow from this passive investment.

Let's look at another type of investment tax credit. My friend and long-time client Melissa decided that she wanted to learn how to renovate old houses. She has a knack for design and loves bringing older homes back to their original condition. She and I sat down to discuss her situation. I recommended that she choose homes that qualify for the historic building tax credit, a 20 percent tax credit. Of course, there are certain requirements she'd have to meet, but that didn't stop her. She actually found that the requirements fit right into her plans.

The result was that the government contributed 20 percent of the construction costs of the renovations through tax credits. That more than doubles her profit from each project.

Debbie and Melissa are typical examples of people who take advantage of tax credits to not only reduce their taxes but to also increase their profits. By following the government's rules, they focus on projects that will increase their cash flow now and for years into the future.

CAUTION!

Your Credits Must Have "Economic Substance"	
1.	Beware of promoters who want to "sell" you tax credits.
2.	If you don't have a profit motive for your investment other than tax credits, you probably won't get to use the credits.

Notice that in both cases these clients chose investments that not only had good tax benefits but also made good sense from a profit and cash flow standpoint. This is essential. *Don't ever invest in a project solely for the tax benefits.* Always look at the profit opportunities first. And, as Debbie and Melissa did, choose investments that you know something about. You'll make a lot more money (and lose a lot less) if you're knowledgeable about the industry and projects in which you invest.

> *Don't ever invest in a project solely for the tax benefits. Always look at the profit opportunities first.*

That's it for our discussion on the super tax benefits called tax credits. Start looking for these incentive packages right away. Chances are that you already qualify for some tax credits and you may not even know it.

We're going to talk next about payroll taxes, such as Social Security and health insurance taxes such as Medicare.

CHAPTER 10: KEY POINTS

1.	Tax credits are the cream of the tax-savings crop because they reduce your taxes dollar for dollar rather than just reducing your taxable income.
2.	There are two types of tax credits: refundable and nonrefundable. Refundable tax credits are receivable even if you make no income. Nonrefundable tax credits require taxable income. Most credits are nonrefundable.
3.	Many tax credits meant for low-income families are available to investors and business owners—if they plan right. This isn't fair, but taxes aren't fair. Incentives are meant to encourage certain behaviors.
4.	Never invest in a project because it has good tax benefits. First find solid projects of which you have knowledge and then take advantage of tax credits.

Tax Strategy #10 – Saving for Your Child's Education with Maximum Tax Benefits

The challenge I have with government-sponsored educational savings plans is that the government is in control of your money, how you use it, when you use it, and how it's taxed. For example, in a 529 plan (also called a Coverdell IRA), the earnings of the plan are tax free when you use it for your child's education. Sounds almost too good to be true, doesn't it? What sort of limitations do you think the government places on these funds in order to control your money? First, they control how much you can contribute. Then, they control what you can do with the money in the plan, even controlling how you invest the money. Next, they control what expenses you can pay for with the fund. Only certain educational expenses qualify. Finally, if you don't use the funds for education, you have only two choices. One choice is to transfer the money to a relative who can use it for their education. The other is to distribute it to yourself and pay taxes and penalties. So, if you make too much money from your investments in the plan, you pay a penalty for not using all of the money for education. What if you could have all of the tax benefits of a 529 plan without giving the government any control over your money? Wouldn't that be a lot better? In tax strategy #5 we talked about paying your children to work in your business. When I teach this principle in my Tax and Asset Protection class, the question always comes up about what to do with the money you pay them. This is the perfect opportunity to have your children pay for their own education without having to rely on Section 529 plans or other tax-deferred, government controlled educational savings plans. Your children can contribute their money to an LLC, limited partnership, or S corporation that owns a business or investments. Like a 529 plan, you get a deduction when you pay your child a salary. Like a 529 plan, there is no tax to the child when received. Like the 529 plan, with good planning, especially in real estate, there is no tax on the cash flow from the investment. But unlike a 529 plan, you have full control over the investment. Unlike a 529 plan, you can take it out and use it for any expense for your child (except for support, like food and clothing), and you can take it out any time you like. Unlike a 529 plan, there are no penalties for distributing the money or accumulating a huge amount over a lifetime. Now isn't that a much better plan than a government-controlled savings plan? Stop using government plans and make your own plan. You will have much more control and get better tax benefits than the government plans.

Chapter Eleven

Conquer Your Employment Tax Troll

"There is no worse tyranny than to force a man to pay for what he does not want merely because you think it would be good for him."
– Robert A. Heinlein

I'm the youngest of six children. So growing up, I always had five people, plus my parents, telling me what to do. That doesn't even count schoolteachers and church leaders. When I was young, this wasn't really a challenge. It was nice to have someone else directing my life.

But by the time I was eight or nine years old I was getting pretty tired of being told what to do all the time. If you have older siblings, then you understand that they have a way of telling you what to do in a not-so-nice way. One of my brothers liked telling me what to do at dinner by kicking my leg under the table. So if I put my elbows on the table, chewed with my mouth open, or said something he didn't like, I'd get a sharp one to the shins. Pretty annoying.

My sister and brothers also liked to play tricks on me. I remember they once tricked me into eating a turnip. As a child, I hated vegetables (I still don't like most of them). I would never have eaten a turnip if I knew it was a vegetable. They convinced me it was a new kind of potato that we were trying out. Since my mother was always signing up to try out new products, this was totally believable. I liked potatoes. In fact, meat and potatoes were two of my four primary food groups (the other two were peanut butter and milk). But yuck. This new kind of potato was awful. My siblings started laughing hysterically. This was just one of many ways they got me to do something I didn't really want to do.

With all of these tricky and domineering family members, I started rebelling anytime someone told me what to do. You can imagine what kind of employee I turned out to be. My first job out of college was with Ernst Young (then Ernst & Whinney) in Salt Lake City. I'd only been there about a year the first time I told my boss, the partner in charge of tax accounting for the office, to take a hike. I wasn't very calm about it either. He had made a mistake and then loudly confronted me in the hallway suggesting that the mistake was mine, not his. I turned right into him and, in full voice so the entire office could hear, told him to go to hell. Fortunately, I didn't lose my job, and later he even came into my office and apologized.

I remember two other times while I was working at Ernst that I did something similar. When I was in the company's national tax department in Washington, DC, I had a rather frank conversation with my immediate supervisor. And that happened again with one of the tax partners when I moved to Phoenix as a senior tax manager.

Do you see the pattern? I didn't at the time. I didn't recognize how much I hated being told what to do. So I stayed on as an employee for a long time—13 years, in fact. When I finally left the big-company employment world and started my own firm, the first thing my friends said to me was, "It's about time."

Perhaps this is the reason I feel so strongly about the government not telling me what to do. I don't mind them offering me incentives to be in business and to invest in real estate, oil, and gas. I love that. But what I hate is the government telling me that I *have* to contribute to Social Security and Medicare—especially since I'll probably never use them.

For those of you who are employers, I suspect you feel the same way. I've done some research on Social Security, national insurance, and other government-sponsored "savings plans" around the world. It's pretty amazing how much all of the government programs are alike. A small saving grace is that the United States has lower employment taxes than many other governments. Germany and Great Britain, for example, are both higher than the United States.

Still, would you pay employment taxes if you didn't have to? As an employee, even, would you pay into Social Security if you had a choice? For those in France, wouldn't you rather have your employer give you the money they pay into the CSG (general social contribution). My guess is that most of you would rather have control over your money instead of entrusting that control to a government program. And that's probably true even if you aren't the youngest of six children.

If you don't feel this way, that's fine. You can skip this chapter and pay the maximum national insurance rates, Social Security, or CSG payments. But if you do want to reduce your payments to the government for employment-related taxes, read on.

If you happen to be in a country with low employer contribution rates, consider this: If your employees didn't have to contribute so much into the state-sponsored pension plans, you could probably pay them less.

If your employees didn't have to contribute so much into the state-sponsored pension plans, you could probably pay them less.

The reality is that you can always get higher returns on your investments than the government will give you through the state-sponsored pension plan. In the United States, most people under the age of 50 (and many older than that) expect that they will never get payments out of Social Security. By the time they get to retirement age, Social Security will be bankrupt. Heck, by the time most people in the United States get to retirement, the entire U.S. government may be bankrupt. But I'll leave that discussion to my friend Robert Kiyosaki and his book *Conspiracy of the Rich: The 8 New Rules of Money*.

Let's move on with assuming that you'd like to reduce how much you pay into your country's government-sponsored medical insurance and pension plans. There are many compelling reasons for wanting to pay less. You'd have a lot more money to invest for yourself, and with the proper education you'd receive much higher returns on those investments and have control over when you receive the income from those investments—and how that income is taxed.

Remember, pension benefits, even when they come from the government, are normally taxed. Many of these benefits are not deductible to you when you pay them into the plan either. How is that fair? You don't get a deduction for the payment and you still get taxed if and when you receive the payment back to you. That's just what happens in the United States with Social Security. Not all countries work this way, but many do.

As an employee, there is very little, if anything, you can do to reduce your employment taxes. This includes your Social Security, Medicare, or other national insurance contributions. But you can reduce these payments in many cases if you are self-employed and plan correctly, or if you are in business. And in many countries, investment income is not subject to these taxes at all.

Think about that. As an employee or even as a self-employed individual, you will have to pay high government insurance (e.g., Medicare) and/or Social Security taxes on most or all of your income. If, on the other hand, you earn all of your income through investments, such as stock dividends and capital gains, real estate rentals, oil and gas investments, or business distributions, you can avoid most if not all of these additional taxes. And yes, they are additional taxes because they are taxes in addition to your income tax.

E and S *Left Side of the Cash Flow* *Quadrant*		B and I *Right Side of the Cash Flow* *Quadrant*
☐ Pay high government insurance taxes	VS	☐ Can avoid most if not all of these taxes.
☐ Pay high Social Security taxes		

Understanding Your Base

In figuring out how to reduce your payroll-related taxes if you are running a business, start by looking at the "tax base" for these taxes. How are the taxes measured? Are they a flat rate per employee? Are they based on a percentage of total wages? Are they a percentage of net income from the business? And are there limits? In Canada and the United States, at least for now, some of the payroll taxes only apply to a certain amount of wages. After that, the taxes don't apply at all.

In the United States, for example, wages and salaries in excess of about $129,000 are not subject to Social Security taxes. They are only subject to income and Medicare taxes. In Canada, the amount subject to employment insurance premiums is a lot less.

Once you understand the base or measure of the tax, you can find ways to reduce that base in order to reduce the tax. Let's take a simple example in the United States.

Once you understand the base or measure of the tax, you can find ways to reduce that base in order to reduce the tax.

My client Michael is a chiropractor. Like many chiropractors, he is self-employed. He also has a couple of other chiropractors working for him on a contract basis. He used to report all of his income on Schedule C of his personal income tax return. In other words, he didn't use a separate entity for his business. Not only was this a bad idea from the standpoint of legal liability (he was personally liable for everything that could go wrong in his practice, whether or not he was the one who caused the problem), this also caused him to pay the maximum amount of Social Security and Medicare taxes. Like many countries, the United States treats self-employment income in the same way it treats salaries and wages. So the key to reducing his employment taxes was to reduce his amount of "self-employment" income (see Rule #10).

RULE #10:	When you want to reduce a tax, reduce the base on which it's measured.

In the United States, dividends from corporations are not subject to all employment taxes. This is true in many other countries as well, since they are not "earned income." We reduced the amount of Michael's self-employment income by converting some of his income to dividend distributions. We did that by setting up a company to own Michael's medical practice.

Now, instead of being self-employed, Michael is an employee of his company, as well as an owner. As an owner, his share of the income is paid to him as a distribution of the company's earnings. This amount is not subject to employment taxes. As an employee, his earnings for serving his patients are paid to him as salary.

We want the salary portion of the money Michael makes from his company to be as low as possible and his distributions or dividends to be as high as possible so that he can pay the least amount of employment taxes. The government tax collectors understand this as well. So they want the salary to be, at the least, reasonable for the services Michael renders to the company.

Unreasonably Low Salaries Can Cost You in an Audit	
1.	Tax collectors are always on the lookout for salaries that are much higher or much lower than normal for your industry.
2.	If you take too low of a salary, the government may treat ALL of the income from your company as self-employment income subject to employment taxes.

What's reasonable? Reasonable is what Michael would pay someone else to do the work that he does for the company. Well, Michael knows what he would pay someone else because he is already doing so—he pays contracted chiropractors. Michael just has to pay himself the same rate he pays the other chiropractors.

If you don't know what a reasonable rate is to pay for your position at your company, there are many resources, such as www.salary.com, that will provide you with a good estimate. And if you still can't find the information you're looking for, just estimate. So long as you make a reasonable effort to pay a fair salary to yourself, you should be okay. And don't forget, you can always ask your tax advisor for help with this. They have lots of other clients and probably some in your industry. They can give you some ideas.

TAX TIP:	Don't pay yourself too much or too little. Too much salary may mean overpaying payroll taxes. But too little salary and your company could be a target for an audit. Reduce your chances of audit by paying a reasonable salary. It can save you over $4,500 in annual employment taxes and reduce your chances of audit.

EXAMPLE Converting Michael from an S to a B (Moving from the Left to the Right Side of the CASHFLOW Quadrant)	
Before Conversion *Left Side of CASHFLOW* *Quadrant*	After Conversion *Right Side of CASHFLOW* *Quadrant*
• Michael is self-employed.	• Set up a new entity that owns Michael's practice.
• Michael reports all income on Schedule C of his personal tax return.	• Michael files a separate tax return for his company.
• Michael is personally liable for all risks.	• Michael is only liable for his own mistakes and not those of his employees or partners.
• Michael pays the maximum amount of Social Security tax.	• As an owner, parts of Michael's earnings are now paid to him as distributions, which are not subject to employment taxes.
• Michael pays the maximum amount of Medicare tax.	• Only the portion Michael receives as salary is subject to employment taxes.

Choose Your Entity Wisely

Now in the United States, in particular, the type of company you form is going to be important for income tax purposes. You probably want to be taxed as an S corporation for your primary business. An S corporation is pretty simple to operate and avoids any potential double taxation that comes from operating your main business as a C corporation.

In other countries, you may want to be a limited partner in a partnership or a small business corporation. Again, you'll want to sit down with your tax advisor to determine the exact type of entity that makes the most sense for your business. Just remember that one of the goals of forming an entity is to reduce the employment-related taxes you pay on your income from your business.

As long as you focus on the tax base, that is, the amount the national insurance or pension or other "contribution" (don't you love that word—contribution—as though it were voluntary?) is based on, you can reduce your employment-related taxes fairly easily. And isn't it a lot better for you to have that money to control and invest for yourself than to give it to the government to control, invest, and maybe pay back to you sometime in the distant future? You don't have to be the youngest child to enjoy the benefits of controlling your own money and your financial future, and controlling your employment taxes is one of the best ways to do this.

You thought this was going to be a book that only talks about how to reduce your income tax didn't you? Not so. In fact, it's not only employment taxes that we can and ought to control and reduce; it's also property tax, value-added tax, and other sales and excise taxes. We'll talk about those next.

CHAPTER 11: KEY POINTS

1.	Some of your biggest tax costs will come from employment taxes into government-sponsored programs such as Social Security and Medicare.
2.	In order to lower your employment taxes, you must understand your tax base and lower your tax-base liability.
3.	Income derived from investments such as dividends and distributions are not taxed as "earned income" and significantly reduce your employment-tax burden.
4.	It's important to consult with your tax advisor to discuss what type of entity can best help reduce your tax-base liability and lower your employment taxes.

Tax Strategy #11 – Reduce the Wages You Take from Your Business

When you own your own corporation, you are required to pay yourself a reasonable salary. By definition, you are an employee of your company. You want to pay yourself the lowest salary possible, however, because you want to keep your employment taxes down. So how do you determine the amount of salary you should pay yourself? The basic answer is pretty simple. You have to pay yourself what you would pay someone else if you hired someone to do your job. So, if you own a C corporation that does billings for your medical office, and you do the billing work, you have to pay yourself what you would pay someone else to do that billing work. There are several websites to go to, such as salary.com, for an idea of what someone would make in your position. The same is true if you own an S corporation. You must pay yourself a "reasonable" salary. Otherwise, the IRS can (and likely will) challenge the amount of pay and will reclassify some or all (probably all) of your distributions as salary. This will result in a much higher salary than if you had just been reasonable in the first place. Remember, though, that pay includes all forms of compensation. So if you have a medical expense reimbursement plan in your C corporation, your pay includes your medical benefits even though the medical benefits aren't taxed to you. The same is true of any other benefits that you provide your employee(s). So, you may end up with a smaller salary than what you find on the Internet. You also need to pay your salary at least monthly, since that's what you would do with someone working for you. Don't put this off until the end of the year. If you do, the IRS has additional ammunition for saying that your salary is not reasonable.

Chapter Twelve

Lower Your Property, Sales, and Value-Added Taxes

"The art of taxation consists in so plucking the goose as to obtain the largest possible amount of feathers with the smallest possible amount of hissing."
– Jean-Baptist Colbert

Most tax professionals spend their entire career dealing only with their country's income tax system. They never think about the other taxes their clients have to pay. For the first seven years of my career, I was no different. That is, until my first day on the job at Pinnacle West.

Pinnacle West is one of the largest companies in Arizona. It owns the largest public utility in Arizona, and at one time also owned one of the largest real estate developers in the state. I didn't have any experience in public utilities when I started at the company, but I had a tremendous amount of experience in real estate. So I was hired to handle the income tax work for the real estate company and contribute to the income tax matters for the public utility company as well as other Pinnacle West companies.

Soon after I started my new job, my boss told me that we'd be heading to Washington, DC, to speak to some tax attorneys about a ruling we were seeking from the IRS. A few years earlier, Pinnacle West had purchased a savings and loan right before the collapse of the entire U.S. savings and loan industry. By the time I arrived in 1990, the savings and loan company was worthless.

We were asking the IRS whether Pinnacle West could deduct in full the losses from the purchase and subsequent demise of the savings and loan company against the incomes taxes of our other companies. Within a couple of months we had the answer, and it was yes. This was a huge win for Pinnacle West and its shareholders.

Of course, it also meant that Pinnacle West wouldn't have to pay income taxes for years to come. My job as tax advisor seemed a lot less important. So I looked for other ways I could help the company. I discovered that there were many other taxes that the company was required to pay that weren't offset by the loss from the savings and loan. These consisted mostly of sales taxes and property taxes. At the time, public utilities in Arizona paid huge property taxes, much more than many other taxpayers. And since Pinnacle West operated several coal-fired electric generating plants and one of the largest nuclear energy plants in the world, the company paid a lot of sales taxes on its purchases.

From that experience, I learned that property tax and sales tax could be reduced almost as easily as income tax. Just as income tax, all it took was learning the rules and then applying them to reduce the taxes. This was great for me. It was a free education. I discovered two new taxes that I'd known nothing about before joining Pinnacle West, and the company gave me all the resources I needed to learn about them and then reduce them.

There are as many exemptions and tax benefits in the sales and property tax rules as there are in the income tax law. These are taxes that many times are simply ignored by business owners and their tax advisors. We just come to accept them as normal. We have a tendency to complain a lot less about sales tax in particular than we do about income tax. Yet the dollars involved are enormous. Let me show you just how important these taxes can be.

> *There are as many exemptions and tax benefits in the sales and property tax rules as there are in the income tax law.*

Sales Taxes

Let's say your business earns $100 in income. Most businesses have expenses equal to at least 80 percent of their income. So in this case, you have $80 of expenses to offset your $100 of income. That leaves you with net income of $20. Suppose you have a tax rate of 30 percent on your net income. That means that on the $100 of gross income, you end up paying income tax of $6.

Compare that to your sales tax, goods and services tax, or value-added tax. Even in the United States, where there is no national sales tax, the sales tax on your $100 of income could be around $8, depending on what state you live in. That's two more dollars than your income tax. And in most countries where there is a national sales tax it can be as high as 15 to 20 percent or more. You could have three times as much sales tax as income tax on the same revenue.

So potentially, the sales tax is a lot more than the income tax on the same amount of income. Of course, the standard answer to this is that, as the seller, you get to pass on this tax to the buyer. So you really don't have to pay the tax at all, right? This is true for the taxes on your sales. But what about the sales taxes on your purchases? How much are you paying in taxes each time you purchase supplies or equipment?

While at Pinnacle West, I found that there are many deductions and other benefits related to sales taxes. In Arizona, as in most states, purchases of manufacturing equipment are not subject to sales tax. The same is true for purchases of equipment used in research and development, and purchases of inventory and raw materials that you eventually sell to your customers. In fact, there are hundreds of different items that are not subject to tax.

You may think that your accountant knows all of this. As an accountant, I didn't, and your accountant probably doesn't either. I'd been in the national tax department of one of the largest accounting firms in the world and didn't know all of this. So

You may think that your accountant knows all of this. I didn't, and your accountant probably doesn't either.

what makes you so sure that your accountant knows about these sales tax benefits?

Purchases Not Subject to Sales Tax (In Many U.S. States)
• Purchases of Manufacturing Equipment
• Purchases of Inventory
• Purchases of Equipment used in Research and Development
• Purchases of other Supplies
Be sure to check with your accountant to ensure you are getting all the sales tax benefits available to you.

If you don't live in the United States, it can be even worse. Canada, Australia, and Europe all have higher sales tax rates than the United States. The value added tax (VAT) in France, for example, is 22 percent. You pay a tax of over 20 percent on every purchase. What if you could reduce that to only paying tax on 80 percent of your purchases? Or even less? All the money saved would go straight to your bottom line, which, if you're the owner of the company, actually goes straight into your pocket. It's like getting a 20 percent discount on everything you buy.

And then there is the question of charging these taxes to your customers. Who do you charge? Do you charge everyone? What about people who don't live in your province or your state? Or even your country? In this age of Internet sales, which customers have to pay tax?

Many people think they don't have to charge sales tax to anyone who lives outside of the province or state where their company's home office is based. This may not be true. Your company could be required to collect sales tax or value added tax on Internet sales or catalog sales to people in several different states or provinces. And what happens if you don't? It isn't pretty.

TAX TIP:	When in doubt, collect it. Not sure if your business needs to collect sales tax? When in doubt, collect it, remit it, and file a tax return. The cost is minimal but the result is substantial, because it significantly reduces your exposure.

Not too long ago I was talking to my friend Tim, who puts on seminars. Tim often has several different speakers teaching at his seminars. After they're done speaking, these presenters will often sell books, tapes, or other educational tools to the audience. These presenters travel from all over the United States to Tim's seminar. And many of the students are also from different states. So Tim doesn't have to worry about collecting sales tax at the seminar, right? Wrong.

Only a few months ago, the state tax examiners came to Tim and asked him if he'd been charging sales tax on all of the sales at his seminars. He hadn't. They told him that he'd have to pay tax on all of the sales for the past four years at every one of his seminars. The cost? In excess of $1 million. Ouch.

Ask Yourself This:
If the state tax examiners came to visit you today, can you confidently say you are charging sales tax on all taxable sales?

Could Tim go back to the students, or even the speakers, and charge them for the sales tax? No way. Think of the bad feelings people would have towards him if he tried to do that. Fortunately, Tim was able to pay the tax and stay in business. But this isn't always the case. Sales tax has put a lot of companies out of business. And the worst part is that if an owner of a company simply understands to whom he has to charge sales tax, the customers will gladly pay the tax. Instead, it becomes a problem that potentially puts him out of business.

Think of all the things my friend could've done with that $1 million that he ended up paying the state. I'm sure all of the things you can come up with are better than paying off the government. So get with your accountant or tax advisor and find out which customers will owe sales taxes when they buy from you. You may even have to charge tax to some customers who live outside of your state, province, or country. As the old adage goes, it's better to be safe than sorry.

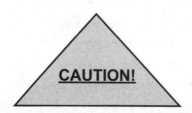

Unreported Sales Tax Could Put You Out of Business	
1.	Sales tax should always be collected unless you have clear proof that no tax is due.
2.	Unpaid sales taxes can grow without your knowledge for many years. All companies should have a sales tax professional do a review of their collection requirements every few years.

Property Taxes

Sales tax isn't the only local tax that can be challenging. Property tax is another. Every country I've looked at charges some level of tax on the value of property that you own. And this can be true for individuals who are not in business as well as those who are in business.

Property tax is especially hard to swallow in difficult economic times, because property tax isn't charged only if you make a profit. And it doesn't necessarily go down when the value of your property decreases. That's because sometimes the government will raise the tax rate to make up for the decrease in value.

The good news is that just as with income and sales taxes there are many ways to reduce your property tax. Let's spend a few minutes talking about two different types of property taxes: the real estate property tax and the personal property tax.

Real Estate Property Tax

One type of property tax is on the value of your real estate. This is the tax people most often associate with property taxes because in many countries you have to pay property tax on your home. In most countries, these taxes are also levied against your rental and business properties.

> *The good news is that just as with income and sales taxes there are many ways to reduce your property tax.*

The property tax is usually calculated as a percentage of the value of your real estate. So the obvious way to reduce your property tax is to challenge the value placed on your property. This is especially true when property values are going down. The assessor (the person at the tax office who determines what the value of your property is for tax purposes) doesn't always keep up with what's happening in the market. So you could end up paying tax on last year's value. In some cases, such as in the U.S. housing downturn, this could be devastating.

Be sure to pay attention when you get your property tax bill, even if your mortgage company or bank pays your property tax. Only you can protest the value they put on your property. Keep in mind that there are time limits for protesting the value as well.

There are two ways to argue that your property should be valued at a lower figure than what the tax assessor says. One is to show that the value of your property is a lot less than what they say. You could get an appraisal, or, if the property is a rental property or used in your business, you may be able to use your reduced rental income and the reduced rents of similar properties as evidence that your property should be valued at a lower dollar value than it was valued at originally.

Another way to pay less property tax is to show that your property is being valued at a higher dollar value than a similar property. In many cases, properties of similar use, size, and location are required to be valued the same.

I had an interesting experience several years ago when I built my house. My house was one of the few houses at the time with a basement. The basement was a little less than half the size of the main floor. I loved my basement. It stayed warm in the winter and cool in the summer. As a result, my utility bill for the basement was a lot lower than for the main floor.

When I received my first property tax valuation notice, I was shocked. It showed a value much higher than I'd expected. I went to the county and checked the value of my next-door neighbor's home. That house is two stories without a basement. It's a little bigger than mine in total. When I checked the value, though, the county showed it to be a much lower value than my house.

I decided to appeal my valuation. I had a friend who was an expert in property tax. He agreed to go with me to the assessor's office to help me with my appeal. I sat down with the assessor, and he explained that my house was valued more than my neighbor's even though it was smaller because mine was all one level.

It seems that one-level houses in Arizona are worth more per square foot than two-story houses, and because of this they are taxed higher than two-level houses. That was all fine and dandy. Only my house wasn't one level. It was two. What I learned that day about the rules was more than a little surprising.

It turns out that the county only counts a house as having two floors if the smaller of the two floors is at least half the size of the larger floor. My neighbor's house was about the same size on both floors. Since my basement was less than half the size of the upstairs, it was treated as a single-story home. I've been paying higher taxes for fifteen years on my home simply because I didn't build it big enough. It's a tax accountant's worst nightmare.

Had I known the rules when I designed the house, I probably would've made it larger. It would've cost a little more to build, but I would've had the extra space and my taxes actually would've gone down.

	Reducing Your Real Estate Property Tax	
1.	To reduce your property tax, challenge the value placed on your property.	
2.	Pay attention to the fact that your property tax bill states the time period within which you must protest or appeal the value placed on your property.	
	Challenge or protest your property taxes by:	
a. Getting an appraisal that will prove your value is less than what is stated		b. Showing that your property is being valued higher than a similar property

Personal Property Tax

The other property taxes you need to know about aren't levied on real estate. They're called personal property taxes, and they usually only apply to business property. And they can be huge.

The good news is that there are many benefits to businesses that can seriously reduce the taxes on business personal property. Just like income tax, these benefits go to those businesses that the government wants to encourage. Your business could be one of them.

The good news is that there are many special benefits to businesses that can seriously reduce the taxes on business personal property.

There are many tax reductions for property used in research and development and in high-tech manufacturing. These benefits come through the methodology used to set a value on the equipment and other property. Instead of looking at comparisons of value to other similar equipment, these types of property are usually taxed based on their cost less a reduction for depreciation.

Two Types of Tax-Favored Personal Property	
1.	Personal property used in research and development.
2.	Personal property used in high-tech manufacturing.
Be sure to check with your accountant to ensure you are getting all the tax benefits you deserve.	

Don't be fooled into thinking that the depreciation for property tax purposes is the same as for income tax. They don't have anything in common. The depreciation for property tax is often a lot more than what you would get for income tax. And the depreciation often depends not only on the type of equipment but on the industry.

Take a serious look at your business property taxes, both for real property, such as land and buildings and personal property, such as machinery and equipment, and look for ways to reduce the property tax on your home if you live in a country that taxes personal homes.

Most of all, remember that there are many taxes you can reduce besides your income tax. I've just scratched the surface here. Besides sales and property taxes, there are also many excise taxes on everything from tires to oil and gas. These taxes combined can be much more than your income taxes, and they have just as many deductions and other benefits available. Just be sure that your tax advisor is experienced in these taxes and that you know what you need to do to reduce them.

We are going to talk next about another tax—the estate tax. This is the tax that attempts to confiscate at your death what the income tax wasn't able to get during your life.

<table>
<tr><td colspan="2" align="center">**CHAPTER 12: KEY POINTS**</td></tr>
<tr><td>1.</td><td>Most people and tax professionals only focus on reducing income taxes, ignoring potentially bigger taxes such as sales, property, and excise taxes.</td></tr>
<tr><td>2.</td><td>There are as many exemptions and tax benefits in the sales and property tax rules as there are in the income tax law.</td></tr>
<tr><td>3.</td><td>Not understanding when to charge sales taxes and how to reduce your sales tax liability can add up to major losses for you and your company.</td></tr>
<tr><td>4.</td><td>There are two types of property taxes, real estate property and personal property. Each has its own set of deductions and ways of being reduced, along with their potential for major savings.</td></tr>
</table>

Tax Strategy #12 – Reduce Your Sales Tax Burden

As a business owner, you pay sales tax on two basic types of transactions: items you buy for your business and products your company sells. Do you know which of these two transactions has the biggest effect on your bottom line? Most people would say that the items you purchase for your business are a bigger expense since you can't pass on those taxes to your customers. The reality is that for most companies the bigger challenge is the tax on products you sell.

The reason is that if you don't collect tax on products that you sell, and the state later audits you and assesses tax, the tax burden shifts from your customers to your business. For this reason, you should always collect sales tax unless you are sure that no sales tax is due. Let me give you an example.

A number of years ago a big bank moved into Arizona and purchased another bank's assets. Among these assets was an automobile leasing company. The new bank didn't realize that in Arizona you must charge sales tax on automobile lease payments. When the state came in and audited them, they were presented with an enormous—and unexpected—tax bill. The bank went back to its customers and asked them to pay the sales tax. For most of the customers, this amounted to $1,000 or more in back taxes. The customers rebelled, called the newspaper, and the bank made front-page headlines—and not in a good way. The bank had to back off and pay the taxes. This story, while unfortunate, is not uncommon. I have seen more businesses put out of business for uncollected sales tax than for any other tax reason. It's rare for the IRS to put a company out of business. It's not nearly as rare for the state sales tax auditors to put a company out of business.

Customers are used to paying sales tax. So, they don't mind seeing it on the bottom of an invoice. Unless your customer can prove that they shouldn't pay sales tax, be sure to collect it. If you are unsure about whether you are collecting tax in the right states, hire a qualified CPA to do a sales tax study for your business. You might find that there are more states in which you should be collecting tax. It's always cheaper to collect a tax and file a sales tax report than to find out too late that you should have been collecting tax in that state.

Chapter Thirteen

Estate Planning is Good Tax Planning

"The purpose of a tax cut is to leave more money where it belongs: in the hands of the working men and working women who earned it in the first place." – *Senator Robert Dole*

My mother was brilliant. By the time she was four years old she was an avid reader. By the time she was 12 years old she was in high school, and by the time she was 15 years old she'd graduated. She had some very distinct thoughts on how to live her life—and she never wavered from her principles.

One of my mother's philosophies was that her children should work from a young age. I think every one of us six children had a job by the time we were 12. We all did some kind of work at "The Plant." The Plant was my father's printing business. It was a pretty sizable company, at one time having 40 employees. We all worked in different parts of the business. For example, my sister worked in the art department, one of my brothers worked in the photography department and pressroom and, of course, I worked in the accounting department.

My mother felt that work was a good thing, something that should be started as early as possible and continued throughout life. It was her belief that her children should be able to have a good work ethic to provide for their own families when they were older. So when she and my dad prepared for retirement, she made a decision that was consistent with her philosophy. She decided that they should break even when they died. She didn't want to leave any debts outstanding that we would have to pay—and she didn't want to leave us any assets either.

And that's pretty much what happened. My mother died at the age of eighty, a few years before my father passed away. When she died, they had a little bit of stock and two houses, their primary home and their summer home in Bear Lake, Idaho. The stock shares carried my dad for the rest of his life. When he passed away, the summer home went to my sister, Peggy, who, along with her husband, took care of my parents in their later years. The only thing left to the rest of the kids was the primary house.

I've always been happy about this. My parents took good care of us when we were children. We always had plenty of food on the table and shelter over our heads, and we took a vacation every year. And they passed on their values and their wisdom to us kids—that's far more important than their money.

That being said, I do like the idea of building some assets for my children and grandchildren. While I was fine with my parents' decision to spend most of their wealth while they were alive, there are a few things I want to provide my children and grandchildren. For example, I'd like to have plenty of money for my grandchildren to attend the best schools throughout their lives and for me to be able to travel with them. And, of course, I want to own my dream homes free and clear of any mortgages so that my family can enjoy them even after I'm gone.

I'd also like to leave money to charity when I die. There is a lot of good that can be done in this world when money is used for the right purpose. I suspect a lot of you feel the same. I know my clients do. Most people, I find, want to provide for their families and for some charitable causes when they die.

The challenge comes with getting your estate set up just right so that you get to choose who gets your wealth. That includes choosing how much of your wealth the government gets when you die. Like my mother, I don't want to leave anyone with my debts. Nor do I want the government to have my assets. You know by now how I feel about the government getting anything more than I have to pay them. This includes when I die.

More than anything, I don't want my family to have any hassles when I die. I want everything to go smoothly for them. It's enough that they'll have to deal with my death. I don't want them worrying about how my assets will be distributed, dealing with courts over a contested will, or anything else, for that matter.

That's why I feel so strongly about doing good estate planning. Estate planning comes down to two things: making the financial aspects of your death as easy as possible for your family to handle and making sure all, or at least most, of your assets go to your family, your charities, and others you choose— and not to the government.

> *Estate planning comes down to two things: making the financial aspect of your death as easy as possible for your family to handle and making sure all, or at least most, of your assets go to your family, your charities, and others you choose — and not to the government.*

Estate Planning			
1.	Think about who will inherit or acquire your assets upon your death.		
Spouse	Children	Grandchildren	Great-Grandchildren
Step-Children	Siblings	Other Relatives	Charities
Care Givers	Friends	Schools/ Universities	Foundations
2.	Estate Planning allows you to:		
a. Ensure your heirs have a painless financial experience.		b. Leave your assets with your loved ones instead of the government.	

Three Steps to Successful Estate Planning

In the remainder of this chapter, we'll look at steps you should take that will simplify the process your heirs will need to follow after your death and increase the amount of your wealth that they have available to them.

Three Steps to Successful Estate Planning	
1.	Placing assets in trusts
2.	Creating a will
3.	Avoiding the estate tax

Placing Assets in Trusts

Let's start with making the financial aspects as easy as possible. While not all countries have an inheritance tax (Australia and Canada got rid of it years ago), everyone has to deal with the other financial aspects of death. I'm not just talking about having insurance so that there's enough money for your coffin and funeral expenses. I'm also talking about having the title of your assets taken care of before you die so that your family doesn't have to go through probate.

Probate is the process of changing an asset's title (i.e., who owns it) from the person who died to that person's heirs. Heirs are simply the people or organizations that get your assets when you die, such as your family or your favorite charity. Probate is bad for a few reasons. It's bad because it's a painful process that includes the court, a judge, and lawyers. It's bad because it can be expensive. And it's bad because it's public. That means that all the financial pirates out there can (and will) pounce on your spouse and your children trying to convince them to invest or spend their inheritance on scams.

	Probate is to be AVOIDED because:
1.	It includes courts, judges, and lawyers
2.	It's expensive
3.	It's public (everyone knows)

There is an easy way out of probate in most countries. Make sure all of your assets are titled to a trust. You can be the trustee (owner) of the trust, and you can even be the beneficiary (the recipient) of the trust assets while you're alive. The trust document says what will happen to the assets when you die. It's basically your ticket to control your assets after death. Wouldn't it be great for your loved ones to not have any arguments over who gets what? And to not have to go through probate, keeping your family matters private? You get all this and more simply by setting up a trust that owns all of your major assets.

> *There is an easy way out of probate in most countries. Make sure all of your assets are titled to a trust.*

TAX TIP:	Give and take with your charitable giving. If you have charitable intentions with your estate, then consider a charitable trust. With a charitable trust, you can give your assets to the charity now but still take the income stream from the assets for the rest of your life. You still get the income, but the value of the assets in the trust will avoid estate tax.

Where There's a Will

One other document you need in order to make life easier for those who survive you is a will. Just because you have a trust doesn't mean you can skip putting together a rock-solid will. This is particularly true if you have small children. A will allows you to appoint the person who is going to be the guardian of your children. In a will you can also be very specific about who gets which of your assets, and you can share your funeral requests and any other special requests. Between a will and a trust, you should have most bases covered.

> Between a will and a trust, you should have most bases covered.

Set Up a Trust and a Will	
1.	A Trust will:
a.	Control your assets after your death.
b.	Avoid probate.
c.	Maintain privacy.
2.	A Will can:
a.	Appoint a guardian for your children.
b.	Specify the distribution of your assets.
c.	Specify any other special requests.

Avoiding the Estate Tax

Determining where your assets go is only one part of the equation. You still have to figure out how to keep the government out of your affairs and out of your pocket when you're gone. This is especially true for those of you who live in a country with an estate tax, a tax levied on your assets when you die.

France, Great Britain and the United States, among other countries, all have an inheritance tax or estate tax that's based on the value of your assets when you die. And the tax can be high—as much as 60 percent in France. In other places, such as Canada, there isn't a tax on the value of your assets. But in Canada you still get taxed when you die. That's right. Just because there isn't an estate tax in Canada doesn't mean that there isn't a tax when someone dies. It just goes by a different name. It's basically an income tax levied on a person's assets, which are considered sold at the fair market value on the day the person dies. The effect is the same as an estate tax, though you do get favorable capital gains rates on many of the assets. So if you live in Canada, estate planning is still very important.

Lower Is Better

The key to getting around an estate tax is to learn the rules. The first rule is that the lower your assets' value, the lower your estate tax. That means that the fewer assets you own when you die, the lower your taxes will be. The key is to get as many assets as you can out of your estate (i.e., your ownership) during your lifetime while still maintaining control of those assets.

The key to getting around an estate tax is to learn the rules.

ESTATE TAX RULE #1:	The lower your assets' value, the lower your estate tax.

The obvious thing to do would seem to be to give your assets away, right? Well, that's fine except for two things. One, you want to still control the assets while you're alive in case you need them. And two, every country with an estate tax also has a gift tax that is at least as much as the estate tax. The gift tax is specifically created to nip this kind of behavior in the bud.

To lower the value of your estate, then, you need to learn some more of the estate tax rules. The second rule in every country is that portions of your assets aren't taxable. This is called an exemption. Some countries, such as the United States, have a very high exemption. Others, such as Great Britain, have a lower exemption. Still others, such as France, have a different exemption depending on who is inheriting the assets. So you will need to find out the exemption amount in your country. On the plus side, most countries' exemptions work not only when you die but also for the gifts you make during your lifetime.

ESTATE TAX RULE #2:	There is a portion of your assets that are not taxable (this is called an exemption).

Since you want to reduce the value of your estate, one of the tricks to lowering your estate tax is to give away assets such as real estate and businesses that you think will go up in value. There are two reasons these assets are good ones to give away during your lifetime. First, you can give away the value without giving away the control by using a limited partnership or similar entity. Second, you can utilize discounts.

In your estate planning, give away assets where:	
1.	You give away value without giving away control
2.	You can minimize the gift tax by giving away portions of each asset

Giving Away Value without Giving Away Control – Limited Partnerships

A limited partnership is an entity that has two types of owners. One owner is a general partner and one is a limited partner. A general partner is in charge of the partnership even if he only owns a small portion of the partnership. A limited partner has no say in the day-to-day operations of the partnership. This means that you can be the general partner, owning as little as one percent of the partnership and still be in control.

So when you give away a limited share of the partnership, the person you give it to won't have any say in what happens in the partnership. I love this. I can control something that I don't even own. And during my lifetime, all I care about is controlling the business or real estate—not whether I technically own it. As the general partner, I can even pay myself a salary from the partnership.

During my lifetime, all I care about is controlling the business or real estate—not whether I technically own it.

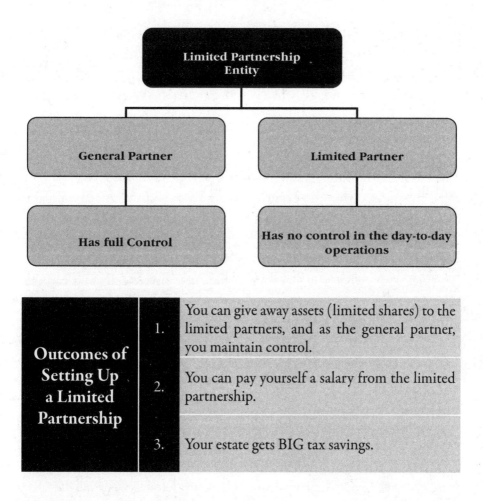

Outcomes of Setting Up a Limited Partnership	1.	You can give away assets (limited shares) to the limited partners, and as the general partner, you maintain control.
	2.	You can pay yourself a salary from the limited partnership.
	3.	Your estate gets BIG tax savings.

Reducing Your Gift Tax by Only Giving away a Portion of Each Asset

The second reason I like to give away business and real estate shares is that I can give more of them away than I can with some other assets, all the while not using up all of my exemption. I do this by giving away only a portion of each asset at a time, using a tool called a *discount*. Gift tax is a tax on the value of a gift. In some cases, the value is obvious. For example, if you make a gift of cash, the value of the cash is the amount of money you gave away. The same would be true of gold or silver or shares of stock in a publicly traded company, such as IBM or Microsoft. That's because the person who receives the gold, silver or shares could turn around and convert them to cash simply by selling them to the public.

What happens, though, when you give away a small portion of a private company? The person you give these shares to may not have any vote or other control of the company. This would make the shares less valuable. A small share of a company where the owner has little control or vote is called a "minority interest." Nobody will pay the same amount for shares of a company that they can't control as they would for shares of a company that gives them a right to vote on how the company is run. So a minority interest has less value then an interest that controls the management and sale of a company.

Then again, when you give away a share of a private company, can the person you give it to easily go out and sell it for cash? It could be very difficult to sell the shares, as there may be restrictions on who can buy the shares or there may simply be no market for the shares. So you may have to sell them at a discount, or a reduced price from what they would be worth if the shares were of a public company and could be sold in the stock market.

These two reductions in value are called "discounts."

The first discount is called a "minority share" discount. It works like this. Suppose your business is worth $500,000 in total. That means that there is someone out there who would be willing to buy your business for that amount. Let's say you decide to give away 20 percent of your business to your children. You might think that 20 percent of a $500,000 business is worth $100,000, right? Wrong. Because 20 percent won't let someone have any say in what happens in the business, it's worth a lot less than $100,000. It could be worth as little as $60,000. This is called a *minority discount*. This means that you could give away 20 percent of your business and you might only use up $60,000 of your exemption. That's like getting an extra $40,000 exemption.

Outcomes of a Minority Discount	1.	You can give away assets (minority shares) and still maintain control.
	2.	The portion or percentage you give away could be worth less than the actual figure, which means you only use a portion of your lifetime exemption.
	3.	Your estate gets BIG tax savings.

The other discount that could be available is for a partial ownership that is difficult to sell. This is called a marketability discount. Let's use the business example again. If the shares of the business were listed on the stock exchange, you would be able to sell your shares any time you want at the price listed on the exchange. Private company shares don't work this way. People don't like buying into a family business when they are not part of the family. There is a lot of risk that they may not know about. Or, the shares might have restrictions on who can buy them or at what price. So the courts allow a discount on the value of the shares.

In summary, the marketability discount is allowed because it's difficult to market and sell a partial interest in a closely held business. The minority discount is simply because you don't control the business (you may not have any say at all). You could even own a majority of a business without controlling it.

Outcomes of Partial Ownership Discount	1.	You can give away assets (partial ownership) and still maintain control.
	2.	The partial ownership you give away is discounted.
	3.	Your estate gets BIG tax savings.

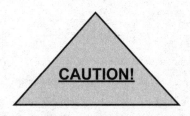

Be Sure to Use a Qualified Appraiser When Gifting Assets

| 1. | Determining the value of the assets and discounts allowed requires the services of a valuation expert. |
| 2. | Make sure your valuation expert is experienced in gift and estate tax valuations and discounts. |

In the end, all that really matters is that the value of your gift is discounted if the asset is a small (less than controlling) share of a business that isn't publicly traded. Real estate works the same way as a business when it comes to value. So you can give a small or minority share of real estate away and still get a discount. In doing so, you end up with a smaller estate tax because you've given away some of your assets. And since you expect those assets to go up in value, it's a really good deal to give them away early.

As a quick example of how valuable good estate planning is, let's take a look at my friend from Chapter 9, George, who gave most of his business to his children because he wanted to use their income tax brackets. By planning his estate well, not only does he get the income tax benefit he was seeking, he also gets an estate tax benefit. That's right, since his children now own 80 percent of his business only 20 percent is taxed when he dies. That will add up to some big savings for his loved ones.

There are many other, more complex, ways to reduce your estate tax. A good estate-planning attorney and accountant can help you with those. In most cases, you can completely eliminate the estate tax. The key is to control your assets, not own them. And with good estate

In most cases, you can completely eliminate the estate tax. The key is to control your assets, not own them.

planning, you can even control them after you die. That's especially good news for all of you control freaks out there.

Even for those of you who aren't control freaks. Wouldn't you still love to keep the government from getting at your hard-earned wealth when you die? It just takes a good gifting program like the one we described here and good knowledge to plan well. And the more you know, the less tax you and your family will have to pay when you die.

We're going to go over taxes in multiple locations next. We'll look at taxes you might have to pay in foreign countries and taxes you might have to pay in different states and provinces. You'll be amazed at how easy it is to reduce your taxes in these different places and how it's just as easy to end up paying much more than needed. .

CHAPTER 13: KEY POINTS

1.	Estate planning is important because it saves your family the stress of managing your affairs and it allows you to keep control over your assets.
2.	An essential part of your estate planning should be a trust and a will. Many of your bases will be covered with just these two items.
3.	Many countries have an estate tax that is levied against the value of your assets after your death. Good planning can eliminate much if not all of your estate tax.
4.	Two valuable ways to lower your estate tax are limited partnerships and discounts.

Tax Strategy #13 – Reducing Your Estate Taxes through Charitable Trusts

Lots of people these days are very charitably minded. People want to give as much as they can to their favorite charity. Charitable trusts are an amazing tool for doing this, especially since they allow you to reduce your income and/or your estate taxes even though the charity may not get the assets until you die. There are two primary types of charitable trusts that you can use. Here is a little primer on them.

The first question to ask yourself is what you want to do with the assets during your lifetime and where you want them to go when you die. If you want the income from the assets for your lifetime and then want a charity to have the assets when you die, you should use a charitable remainder trust (CRT). In a CRT, you get all of the income during your lifetime. Once you die, the assets go directly to the charity. They don't go through your will, since you don't own them any more—the trust owns them.

If you want the charity to get the income while you are alive and then you want the assets to go to your family when you die, you want a charitable lead trust (CLT). In a CLT, the charity gets the income while you are alive or for a specific number of years. When you die, your assets go to your family or anyone else you choose.

The great thing about both of these trusts is that you get an income tax deduction for the donation in the year you set up the trust. In addition, with a CRT, you get an estate tax deduction for the full value of the assets when you die. Even in a CLT, you may get an estate tax deduction.

These valuable tools require detailed set up and assistance from your tax advisor. Do not set them up by yourself. And be sure you talk to your family about what you are doing so that they aren't surprised to find out that some of your assets are in a charitable trust.

Chapter Fourteen

Reducing Your Taxes in Other Locations

"I am proud to be paying taxes in the United States. The only thing is I could be just as proud for half of the money." – *Arthur Godfrey*

I love to travel. Ever since I was little, I've loved seeing new places, meeting new people, and experiencing different cultures. As a child, we took family road trips. Sometimes we went to California to see my Grandma Marco and visit Disneyland. Other times we'd go to the Four Corners area to see the Native American ruins at Mesa Verde. Or we went to the Grand Canyon, Bryce Canyon, or Yellowstone.

When I got a little older, I started taking trips on my own. As a teenager, I twice visited Washington, DC, once when I was a Boy Scout and again with my high school choir. It was fascinating to see all of the different people and sites.

As I stated at the beginning of the book, when I was 19 I went to France to serve a mission for the Mormon Church. I loved being a missionary and going out to talk to people about the Church. Every day I met someone new and interesting. I remember often having long conversations with people on a street corner or at a bus stop. The French love to argue, and I learned to enjoy the French argument—never personal, always intense and educational. It wasn't long before I fell in love with the French people. I've loved them ever since.

These days, I do most of my traveling for business. I speak at seminars or visit clients. I've been to Australia, Europe, Asia, South America, Africa, Mexico and Canada and around the United States on business.

Sometimes I'm in a location for just a day or two and other times for an entire week.

I'm not alone in doing business in a lot of different places. These days, most businesses have customers throughout the country and around the world. The Internet can bring us customers from even the remotest corners of the planet.

You're probably wondering what all this has to do with taxes, right? A lot, actually. Ever wonder if a business has to pay taxes in all the places it has customers? Wouldn't that be a nightmare? But wouldn't it be worse if you were supposed to pay taxes in those places and didn't until the tax collector came knocking at your door, wanting back-taxes, penalties, and interest? If a business waits for the tax collector to come knocking, chances are it will pay much higher taxes than if it did a little planning early on.

Doing business or investing in multiple locations can be a little tricky. Understanding the basic principles involved can make things much easier. And you'll be able to sleep better at night not worrying about tax collectors from other states, provinces, and countries coming after you for unpaid taxes. Not only that, chances are you can reduce your taxes overall just with a bit of simple planning.

> *Doing business or investing in multiple locations can be a little tricky. Understanding the basic principles involved can make things much easier.*

Know Your Geography

Let's start with some of the most basic principles of doing business in multiple locations. The first thing you have to know is where you're going to be taxed. Of course, you're going to be taxed wherever you own property or have an office. You'll probably also be taxed wherever you have employees and sometimes even where you just have contractors.

	Basic Principles **When Doing Business in Multiple Locations**
1.	You'll be taxed where you have property.
2.	You'll be taxed where you have an office.
3.	You'll be taxed where you have employees.
4.	You may be taxed where you have contractors.

For example, take my network of accounting firms, Tax-Free Wealth Network™. Because we service clients all over the world, we do everything by phone, fax, and email. Clients can be anywhere, and we can still take excellent care of their tax and wealth strategy needs. The same is true for our employees. They don't really have to live, where we have an office. Everything we do is done electronically, over the Internet, fax, and phone lines; we don't even have to use the Post Office most of the time.

At any one time, we may have employees in Arizona, Utah, North Carolina, Iowa, or any of several other states. We could even have employees in different countries. And we have to file income tax returns in any state (or country) in which we have employees.

You may also be taxed where you have customers, even if you have no office and no employees in that location. Many of the states in the United States are very aggressive in forcing businesses to pay taxes wherever they have a lot of customers. And they're winning in court. The rule in the United States is that if you get financial, legal or other benefits from a state, such as fire protection for a rental property or just the legal protection of the state court system, the state can tax you. More and more courts are saying that if you get sales from a state, then you are financially benefiting from the state enough to allow the state to tax you. There may come a time in the near future when businesses have to pay income tax in every state or country where they have a customer.

U.S. GENERAL **STATE RULE:**	If you get benefits from a state, the state can tax you.

This may not be all bad. When you are taxed in multiple locations, you can end up paying a lot less tax. That's because different states have different rules about how much of your income is taxable in their state (see Rule #11).

RULE #11:	**Every location has different tax rules, and paying tax in several locations can result in paying less total tax than you would if you did business in only one location.**

Work the Rules

In many cases, you can pay tax on as little as half of your income just by working the rules of the different tax locations against each other. Have you ever wondered what it would be like to pay half the taxes you do now? Sounds too good to be true, doesn't it? Well, I have good news for you. Not everything that sounds too good to be true really is untrue. Sometimes, it's just true. And that's how it is

In many cases, you can pay tax on as little as half of your income just by working the rules of the different tax locations against each other.

with your local (state, city, and provincial) taxes. With the right planning, you can cut your local income taxes by as much as 50 percent.

There are some basic principles you can use to seriously reduce these taxes. The most important principle to remember is that it is better to be taxed in two states than in just one. If you are only taxed in one state, all of your income will be taxed by that state. If you are taxed in two or more states, then sales to states in which you don't have any connection (employees, property or contractors), could escape tax altogether. This is because of the formula the states use to determine how much income goes to each state, called the apportionment formula. The same can happen when you are taxed in multiple countries. Sales to countries in which you have no connection could escape tax altogether, and at the very least they could escape state or provincial taxes.

TAX TIP:	Operating in multiple states can work to your benefit. Doing business in states that have low or no income tax rates can help reduce your overall state taxes. When structured properly, some of your business income can become "nowhere" income and escape state tax altogether.

This is no small matter. Planning your local tax strategy well can save you tons of cash. Many locales have taxes as high as 10 percent or even higher. In the United States, some states have rates as high as 11-13 percent. In Canada, provincial rates can exceed 17 percent.

If you know the rules, you can end up paying taxes on less than 100 percent of your income. Conversely, if you don't know the rules, you can end up paying tax on more than 100 percent of your income. It's actually possible for your sales to be taxed in both your home state and the state you sell into. This is also true when you are doing business in more than one country. If you aren't careful, you can easily pay tax twice on the same income, once in your home country (or state) and once in the other countries (or states) where you have offices, employees, or customers. So be sure to formulate a complete multi-state and multi-country tax strategy with your tax advisor so that you can be sure to pay the least amount of tax possible.

CAUTION!

If You Don't Understand the Rules in Different Locations:	
1.	You could end up paying tax in two locations.
2.	You could pay tax twice on the same income.

The Foreign Tax Credit

Let's talk about the mechanics of paying taxes in another country. In most countries, you must have an office in that country before you'll be required to pay taxes there. Of course, that might be as trivial as the office your foreign employee uses out of his house. Each country has different rules for this. So you'll want to work with your tax advisor to find out which countries require you to file a tax return.

Suppose you do have to pay taxes in another country besides your own. How do you make sure you don't end up paying taxes twice? The key is the *foreign tax credit*. Most countries allow a credit for taxes paid to a foreign country on income that's earned in that country. The credit is usually the smaller of the amount of taxes you actually paid in that country or the taxes you paid in your home country on that income. Let's look at an example.

Ted has a business with a location in New York and another location in Frankfurt. Because his business is headquartered in New York, he has to pay tax on 100% of the income of his business, no matter where it is earned. Of course, Germany also wants to tax the income his business earns in Frankfurt. So the potential is double taxation on the German income; once in the United States and again in Germany. The way this double taxation is avoided is through the foreign tax credit.

Let's say Ted's business earns $1 million of net income overall. In the United States, he pays tax of $210,000 on that net income. Suppose his business earns $100,000 in Frankfurt and that the German income tax on that $100,000 is $45,000. Ted receives a foreign tax credit of $21,000 to offset his U.S. tax liability of $210,000. This is computed as the lesser of the tax he paid in Germany on his German income ($45,000) or the income earned in Germany multiplied by his U.S. tax rate ($100,000 x 21% = $21,000). Because his U.S. tax rate is lower than his German tax rate, he receives a credit for the amount he paid in the United States that was also taxed in Germany, but at the U.S. tax rates. While he still pays more than if he had earned the entire amount in the United States, Ted still only pays taxes once on the income he earns, just at the higher of the two tax rates.

Foreign tax credits usually depend on your country having a tax treaty with the other country. The treaty will say that the other country's citizens and businesses will get a credit for taxes paid to your country and that your country's citizens and businesses will receive the same treatment. A little tit for tat, you might say. The challenge is making sure that you are using the right entities in both countries so that you're able to take full advantage of the foreign tax credit for that country. Here's the key.

> *How do you make sure you don't end up paying taxes twice? The key is the foreign tax credit.*

RULE #12:	To receive the foreign tax credit, the same taxpayer (entity) who pays the tax in the foreign country has to report the income in the home country.

This seems obvious, doesn't it? But what happens when the entity you use for your business in the foreign country is taxed differently than it is in your home country? I find this a lot. Let's take a look at Canada and the United States as an example.

Suppose you live and work in the United States and your business is owned through a limited liability company (LLC). In the United States, your business is taxed to you as a sole proprietor. You decide to open an office in Canada, and wanting things to be easy, you open the office in the name of your U.S.-based LLC.

What you don't realize is that LLCs in Canada are treated as corporations—not as sole proprietorships. So the LLC will be subject to corporate income tax in Canada. In the United States, though, you'll be taxed personally on the income earned in Canada. The result is that a different taxpayer (your corporation) is paying the Canadian tax than the taxpayer (you, individually) paying the U.S. tax. The problem here is that you'll only get the foreign tax credit if the same taxpayer paying the U.S. tax is also paying the foreign tax. A very easy mistake like this can end up making you liable to pay corporate tax in Canada and individual income tax in the United States *on the same income*. That's double taxation.

How do you fix this? It's simply a matter of choosing the right entity in both countries. One option would be for you to use a corporation for your business in the United States and use that same corporation or a corporation owned by your corporation for the office in Canada. That way, it's the corporation paying the tax in both countries. In the United States, your corporation will receive a tax credit for the corporate taxes paid in Canada. You only pay tax once.

Going Offshore

Now let's talk about how to reduce your taxes even further. Start by looking at where you're taxed. Chances are you'll be taxed in your home country on all of the income you earn around the world. So you may want to change your home country. That doesn't mean you personally have to move. You simply form and operate your business out of another country.

Other countries may have lower tax rates than yours. Or they may have tax benefits for your industry that are a lot better than the country where you live. Some countries don't have any tax at all. There are many businesses that can easily operate out of one of these non-tax countries, many of which are in the Caribbean. And you just might enjoy visiting your operations and spending a little time on the beach while you're there.

Setting up business operations offshore (i.e., not in your home country) can be a bit challenging. I can't stress enough how easy it is to mess up structuring a foreign business. You'll want to have great advisors, including an attorney, a tax advisor, and a banker who understand the laws of both your home country and the country where you want to set up business.

That it's a challenge doesn't mean you shouldn't do it. Every business owner and investor who has done great things has had a great team. Don't be afraid. Just get the right team in place.

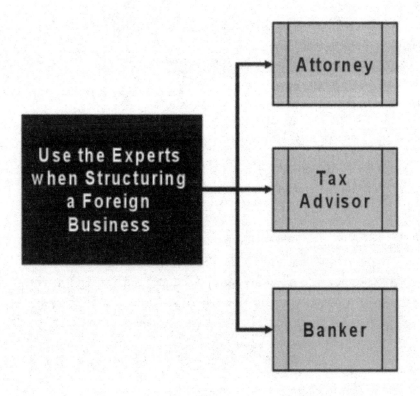

If your business isn't one that you can easily set up in a country without taxes, then look at how you can operate in countries and still pay the lowest taxes. Let's say your home country is Germany and you want to set up a business or investment operation in the United States. Unless you have to be in a specific state, choose a state that has good tax laws. For instance, there are four states in the United States that don't have a corporate income tax: Nevada, Washington, South Dakota, and Wyoming. These states, plus Florida, don't have individual income taxes either.

In Canada, the provincial tax rates vary widely. Alberta has made a conscious effort to keep its tax rate as low as possible. For small businesses, Canada has an especially low federal tax rate, and some of the provinces have low tax rates as well. France has great tax credits for research and development. So if your company is looking to do research and development offshore, you may want to consider France.

Every country has tax benefits for business. All you have to do is work with your tax advisor to determine which countries offer the best ones for *your* business. If you don't want to choose your location based on where they have the lowest taxes, then be sure to learn all of the tax benefits that are available where you locate your business or investing.

> *Every country has tax benefits for business. All you have to do is work with your tax advisor to determine which countries offer the best ones for your business.*

You may even be able to avoid your business being taxable in your new location. If you don't have to have an office or employees in that location, and if you aren't buying or leasing real estate, you may be able to avoid being taxed at all. It will depend on the local laws and how much other presence you have there.

In the end, there are many ways to reduce your tax liability for doing business in other locations. Make sure to consult your tax advisor on putting together a winning strategy for you and your assets.

So far in this book we've discussed a lot of ways to reduce your taxes. Now we need to talk about how to put all of these rules together to create a life-long tax-savings plan.

CHAPTER 14: KEY POINTS

1. Every location has different tax rules, and you can use those rules to pay lower taxes than if you only did business in one location. Many states and countries have low taxes—or even no taxes at all.

2. You can avoid double taxation if you take advantage of the foreign tax credit. To receive the foreign tax credit, the same taxpayer (entity) who pays the tax in the foreign country has to report the income in the home country.

3. You can set up your business so that you don't have to pay taxes anywhere besides your home country.

4. All states, provinces, and countries have specially designed tax benefits for certain investors and industries. You just have to find the location that has the best tax benefits for your business or investing.

Tax Strategy #14 – Being Taxed in Multiple States or Countries Can Seriously Reduce Your Taxes

One of the biggest mistakes I see with taxpayers who have businesses or investments in multiple states is a tendency to ignore the impact of state taxes. Because state taxes are so much smaller than federal taxes, all of the emphasis goes on reducing federal income tax. Consider, though, that state income taxes can be as high as 10 percent or more. Wouldn't it be worthwhile to spend time reducing these taxes as well?

One of the best ways to reduce your state taxes in a business is to make sure that you are taxed in more than one state. Most people understand that they will be taxed in the state where they have their business. You may not know that you are also taxed in any state where you have employees, or where you have an office or inventory. While some business owners are trying to avoid being taxed in more than one state, members of our Tax-Free Wealth Network™ want all of our business clients to be taxed in at least two states.

If you are only taxed in one state, you will pay tax on 100 percent of your income to that state. However, if you are taxed in multiple states, you can actually pay tax on less than 100 percent of your income. Sometimes you can reduce your state tax by 40 to 50 percent. Wouldn't that be worth a little time and effort? Here is how it works.

When you are taxed in multiple states, the states divide up your income by a formula to decide how much income is taxed in which state. While each state has its own formula, all of the states' formulas include what is called a sales factor. How many sales you have in the state helps determine how much of your income is taxed in the state. Whether a sale belongs in a state depends on where the product is shipped. If the product is shipped to New Mexico, that sale belongs to New Mexico. If it's shipped to Nebraska, the sale belongs to Nebraska.

So, let's say you have your main office in Arizona and you have a warehouse operation in Nevada. You don't have any offices or employees anywhere other than in these two states. That means that when you do your Arizona tax return, you will only report sales shipped to Arizona.

Since Nevada doesn't have an income tax, all other sales will be "nowhere" sales. So you end up being taxed on only a small portion of your income in Arizona and you aren't subject to tax in any other state. Pretty great, isn't it? If you were only subject to taxes in Arizona, all of your income would be taxed in Arizona no matter where the sales were shipped.

So make sure you are subject to tax in more than one state where you have sales. Sit down with your tax advisor and figure out how you can be sure you are taxed in at least one additional state so that you don't have to pay state taxes on all of your business income.

Part Two

Your Tax Strategy for Tax-Free Wealth

Chapter Fifteen

Plan to Take Control of Your Taxes: Entities

"You got to be careful if you don't know where you're going, because you might not get there." – *Yogi Berra*

Being the youngest of six children, I've never liked being told what to do. I've always wanted to do things my way, to be in control of my life. That's why early on I learned to plan ahead. Any time I didn't plan, I found that I was left to the whims of others. By planning, I was able to take control, like when I went to graduate school at the University of Texas at Austin (UT).

I looked at a lot of graduate schools before settling on UT. I'd looked at New York University's law school, Brigham Young University's master's program, as well as the master's programs at the University of Southern California and Arizona State University. What I liked best about UT's program was the flexibility it gave me to plan my own schedule and what courses I could take. I wanted to take some business law classes (I ended up taking three of them at UT), and I wanted some other diverse classes such as a class on investing and another on insurance. University of Texas gave me the flexibility to do this while still taking all of my tax classes. I was in control of my education.

It's only natural that my career specialty is tax planning. Creative tax planning is the ultimate in flexibility and control over your life. Instead of the government controlling your life, you control it. Any time you plan for something long-range, you increase the flexibility in your life.

At our Tax-Free Wealth Network™ CPA firms we've taken tax planning to an entirely new level. We start with every new client by creating a long-term, comprehensive tax strategy specifically suited to their specific needs. A strategy is simply a plan of action intended to

> *A strategy is simply a plan of action intended to accomplish a specific purpose.*

accomplish a specific purpose. In the case of our tax clients, the specific purpose is to permanently lower their taxes for the rest of their life—and for generations to come.

RULE #13:	Taxpayers with long-term, flexible tax strategies will always pay less tax than those without strategies.

Tax strategies are a pretty simple concept. Start by deciding what you want to accomplish. Do you want to decrease your income taxes? Are there state and local or provincial taxes you want to reduce? What about property taxes? Do you own equipment in your business or real estate that's taxed on its value? If you own a business, you also want to reduce your sales tax, value-added tax, excise taxes, and payroll taxes. And you probably want to reduce your estate taxes if you plan on leaving anything to your children or grandchildren.

Permanent Tax Savings

Each of these taxes requires its own specific strategy to keep them as low as possible. Let's focus right now on income tax, since that's the one that keeps people up at night. Say you're in a 30 percent tax bracket. It's pretty easy to be in this bracket when you count both the federal income tax and the local income taxes. And let's say you want to permanently reduce your taxes.

What do I mean by permanent tax reduction? As you would expect, permanent is the opposite of temporary. Most tax planning throughout the world is temporary. Like many people, you probably have an IRA or

401(k) if you are in the United States, an RRSP if you are in Canada, a pension contribution if you are in the UK, or some other plan that you put your money in now, get a tax deduction when you do, and pay tax on the money when you take it out for retirement (i.e., the taxes are deferred or postponed).

The primary argument for this type of tax planning is that you will be in a lower tax bracket when you take the money out than when you put the money in. Really? This suggests that you are planning to retire on less money than you earn now. *So in other words, you are expecting to retire poor.* My clients and I have a tough time with this way of thinking. We want to retire rich. In fact, there are several reasons not to put your money into a 401(k), IRA, RRSP or Pension.

Planning on Retiring Poor?
☑ Higher Tax Bracket with Same Income
☑ Shift 15% Capital Gains to 35% or Higher Ordinary Income Tax Rates
☑ Lose all Tax Benefits of Real Estate and Business
☑ Inflation Creates even Higher Tax Brackets

The reality is that if you're going to have as much money when you retire as you do now, then you probably will be in a *higher* tax bracket than you are today. Why? Because you likely won't have the deductions, exemptions, or credits you currently enjoy for your children, for your house, or even for your business. After all, you want to be retired.

> *The reality is that if you're going to have as much money when you retire as you do now, then you probably will be in a higher tax bracket than you are today.*

The real reason that most tax planning around the world is temporary is that this type of planning is easy. It's particularly easy for the tax planners. The challenge is that besides being in a higher tax bracket when you retire, you lose control over your money while it's in the tax-deferred savings plan. The types of investing you can do and the type of income you can earn is limited. Also, most countries restrict when you can take out your own money.

Tax Planning	
Deferral	**Permanent**
• Temporary Tax Savings	• Permanent Tax Savings
• Retire Poor	• Retire Rich
• Limited Earnings	• Unlimited Earnings
• Restricted Withdrawals	• Unrestricted Withdrawals
• Limited Control	• Unlimited Control

As I've said, I like to be in control of my money and my taxes. So when I create a tax strategy for a client, I also want them to be in control of their money and their taxes. In my firm, we focus almost entirely on permanent tax savings. By permanent, I mean tax savings that we never have to give back to the government. All of the tax savings we have discussed over the previous chapters are permanent tax-saving opportunities. Using the permanent tax-savings techniques available to entrepreneurs and investors avoids all of the pitfalls of temporary or deferral techniques. Instead of raising your tax rates, you permanently lower your tax rates; instead of losing control over your wealth, you increase your control over your wealth; rather than increasing your risk in the market, you reduce your risk; and by maintaining control over your wealth, you are able to increase your returns.

When you build your tax strategy, remember two things: You want it to be flexible and you want to look at the big picture.

Tax Deferral Plans

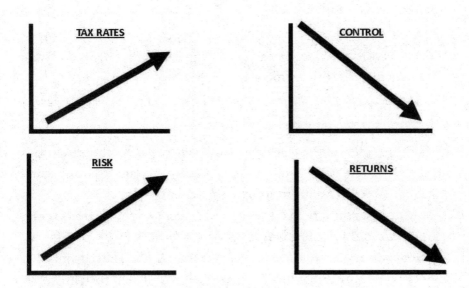

Thinking Through Your Tax Strategy

Let's move on with your tax strategy. You're now focusing on a goal of permanent income tax savings. Of course, we want your income tax to be as low as possible under the law. The next step is to determine where you are today and where you want to be in the future. Just as if you were going on a trip, knowing where you are starting from and where you want to go will have a major impact on the direction you take. A few questions you should ask are:

- What investments do I have now?
- What business entities (e.g., corporations and partnerships) do I own now?
- What are my plans for my businesses and investments?
- How sure am I that my tax returns are being prepared in the best way possible?

- How often do I hear from my tax advisor? (You should hear a minimum of four times a year from your tax advisor.)
- How old are my children?
- Do I plan to have more children?
- Are my children interested in working in my business (or do I want them to be, if they are too young right now)?
- Do I need to set aside money to help my parents in their old age?
- How secure is my job?

These are a few of the questions to ask yourself as you begin your tax strategy. Once you have a good picture of where you want to go and where you are today, you can start forming your strategy.

When you build your tax strategy, remember two things: *You want it to be flexible and you want to look at the big picture.* By flexible, I mean you want your strategy to allow for changes in your life. The only thing we really know for sure is that life tomorrow will be different than life today. You may have more children tomorrow, your business might change, and even your marital status can change. Be sure your tax strategy is built with these possible changes in mind.

And be sure to look at the big picture. Don't do something that gives you big tax savings only to cause problems for you in your business or your family. I had a client years ago who did some very good tax planning. He'd put the ownership of his company into the name of his four children. This was both good estate planning (he transferred the ownership when the business was not worth much) and good income tax planning (the children had lower tax rates than my client).

The challenge was that this created personal issues for at least one of his daughters when she was grown. She married a man who'd never had much money. He was a good guy, but didn't have much financial education. Each year, he would look at their tax return and wonder why he was working so hard when his wife was a trust-fund baby. He put pressure on her to get money from her dad since she was an owner of the business. Her dad (my client) said no, that this was just a tax-planning strategy, and that there wasn't money to give to them. This caused hard feelings with the daughter's husband. Eventually, it contributed to the breakup of their marriage.

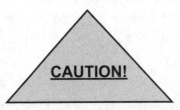

Don't Let the Tax Tail Wag the Dog	
1.	Taxes are important but not nearly as important as personal and business goals.
2.	Make sure your tax planning doesn't interfere with personal, wealth and/or business goals.

The reality is that good tax planning isn't always good family planning. In the case of this client, a simple change to the planning early on in the process would have allowed my client some flexibility, and the income for his business would not have shown up on his daughter's tax return. You may wonder if this was simply a case of bad advice. I don't think so. I know the tax attorney who helped with the planning. I think they just didn't anticipate the daughter marrying someone for whom this could be an issue.

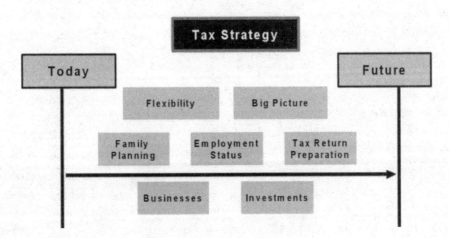

Pick an Entity

When working with a client to create their tax strategy, I always like to begin with the business entities. The right entity can reduce your taxes almost immediately. Remember, an entity is just a form of ownership, such as a corporation or a limited liability company. Each country has its own best entities for different purposes. Let's look at the different types of entities and some general rules for when you will want to use them. There are four primary entity types. Most countries have some form of each of these entities, though they may be called different names in different countries. These entities are trusts, partnerships, corporations, and limited liability companies.

Trusts

Trusts are pretty universal throughout the world. Three primary people are involved in a trust. First is the *settlor* or *grantor*. This is the person who forms the trust and puts the assets into the trust. The second is the *trustee*. This is the person or company in charge of taking care of the trust. Technically, the trustee is the owner of the trust. The third person is the *beneficiary*. This is the person who will reap the rewards of the trust assets. Any trust can have one or multiple grantors, trustees, and beneficiaries.

Trusts are used for a variety of purposes, but they're primarily used to transfer assets from one person to another. They're particularly useful in family planning where parents or grandparents want to transfer assets to their children or grandchildren. They can also be used in transferring assets to charities and other people or organizations. They're essential for doing good estate planning.

Partnerships

Partnerships are perhaps the most flexible of the different entities. A partnership exists whenever two or more individuals or entities own and operate a business or investment together and haven't decided to use another type of entity, such as a corporation. The income and loss from partnerships is reported on the partners' tax returns instead of paying tax in the partnership. Partnerships come in two common varieties; *general partnerships* and *limited partnerships*.

General partnerships allow every partner to make decisions for the partnership. And all partners are typically responsible for the debts of the partnership. So you can imagine that general partnerships can be a little dangerous if there is a chance the partnership might get sued at some time in the future.

Limited partnerships include at least one *general partner* and one *limited partner*. A limited partner is limited to investing and has no say in the daily operation of the partnership. And they don't have any personal responsibility for partnership debts beyond the amount they invested. Additionally, in the United States, the income received by limited partners usually is classified as passive income.

Limited partnerships are good to use when one person is in charge of the business and the others are passive investors. They also work well as part of an estate plan in which children or grandchildren are the limited partners and the parents or grandparents are the general partners. This is one way to transfer partial ownership of some assets to the younger generation while keeping control of the assets in the hands of the older generation.

Every country has tax benefits for business. All you have to do is work with your tax advisor to determine which countries offer the best ones for your business.

Corporations

Corporations are the entities most recognized around the world for owning and operating businesses. Most countries have special tax rules for small businesses that give special incentives to these businesses. In Canada, there are special, lower tax rates for small businesses. In the United States, there are lower capital gains rates for small businesses, special benefits when a small business loses money or goes out of business, and there is even a special class of small businesses called an S corporation that allows the owners to report the business income on their personal tax returns instead of paying taxes in the corporation.

> **TAX TIP:** Have a business partner? Form your own entity taxed as an S Corporation and have that entity be the partner in your business rather than you personally. This structure will reduce your self-employment taxes and provide maximum flexibility to you and your partner.

Corporations are particularly useful if you plan to become a public company, that is, a company that is owned by lots of people. They're also good for protecting your personal assets from lawsuits, as we will see in the next chapter.

Limited Liability Companies

Finally, we have limited liability companies (LLC). These entities are known by other names in other countries. In Germany, they are called a GMBH. The United States was one of the last countries to start using these entities. LLCs have different tax rules in each country. In Canada, for example, LLCs are taxed as corporations. In the United States, they're taxed as partnerships unless you choose to have them taxed as corporations.

Limited liability companies exist so that you can have the asset protection that you would normally get as a limited partner while still having a say in the company. Remember, limited partners cannot control the company. Members of an LLC, though, can have full management control without being fully liable. For this reason, many businesses in the United States are now formed using the LLC instead of as a partnership.

Each of these entities has a place in your tax strategy. For example, you may want to use an LLC to own your real estate investment properties, a corporation (or LLC taxed as a corporation) to own your business, and a limited partnership to own assets you want to transfer to your children. And you likely will want to use trusts to protect assets you set aside for your children from creditors and others, particularly while they're young.

You'll definitely want your attorney involved in this process along with your tax advisor, especially in the United States where there are so many lawsuits and protecting your assets from those lawsuits is so important.

Entities are the foundation for your tax strategy. Once you have your entities in place, you can begin to use all of the other tax benefits we've already discussed to permanently reduce your income, estate, and other taxes now and for generations to come. In summary, there are four parts to a good tax strategy:

Four parts of a good Tax Strategy	
Part 1	Know where you're starting.
Part 2	Know where you're going.
Part 3	Build flexibility into your strategy
Part 4	Look at the big picture.

Once you have your strategy in place, you need to implement it. This means living it every day of your life. The more you use your strategy, the more comfortable you will become with it. Remember that you can lower your taxes every day just by putting your tax strategy into action.

In the next chapter we'll turn to an aspect of your tax strategy that doesn't involve taxes. I'm talking about asset protection. Particularly in the United States, you must protect your assets from lawsuits at the same time you are protecting them from the government tax collectors. The best time to create your asset protection strategy is while you're forming your tax strategy.

CHAPTER 15: KEY POINTS	
1.	The best way to protect your assets and reduce your taxes permanently and in the long term is to develop a comprehensive tax strategy.
2.	It's essential for a tax strategy to be both flexible and deal with the big picture.
3.	When developing your strategy, it's important to know where you are starting from and where you want to end up.
4.	The first step to developing a solid tax strategy is to decide which type of entity is most appropriate for your goals.

Tax Strategy #15 – Use a Combination of Entity Types to Reduce your Taxes

One of the questions I get the most when I'm out speaking is which entity someone should use for business or investing. This is a little like asking what car you should buy. The answer is always going to be, "It depends." Like a car, which entity to use depends on what you use it for and how you use it.

Business entity advice isn't as easy as suggesting that you use an S corporation for a business or a partnership for real estate. Some businesses are better off taxed as partnerships, and sometimes real estate should be held in an S corporation (such as when you are planning to quickly sell the real estate).

One of my favorite tax strategies is to combine different entities into a single strategy. Let me give you one good combination—a partnership and two S corporations. Let's suppose you and your friend decide to open a business selling widgets. You would like to have the self-employment tax benefits of an S corporation. (Remember Chapter 11?) You are a little worried, though, about some of the corporate tax rules and are thinking that maybe you would like a partnership. Which one do you choose?

Why not choose both? Why not own the business in an LLC taxed as a partnership and then own your interest in the partnership through an LLC taxed as an S corporation. It would look something like this:

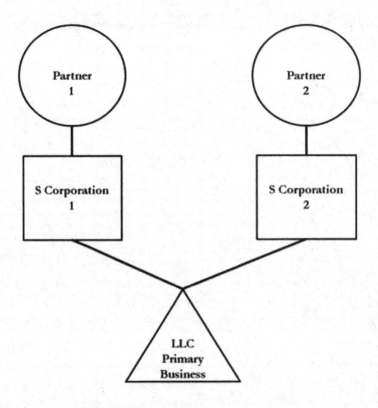

The benefits of this combined entity structure are huge. Because you own the business as a partnership, you can distribute income differently than you allocate income. Or suppose you both need company cars. You want to drive a Ferrari and your friend wants to drive a Honda. Chances are that your friend doesn't want to pay for half of your Ferrari. If you formed your business as an S corporation, you wouldn't have a choice. Since your friend owned half of the S corporation stock, her share of the income from the company would go in part to pay for your Ferrari. In a partnership, you can specially allocate deductions. You could allocate the cost of the Ferrari to you and the cost of the Honda to her. You might want to do the same with home office deductions, travel, meals, or education expenses.

This is just one simple example of a combined entity structure. At Tax-Free Wealth Network™ CPA firms, we have clients that use several different types of entities within their tax strategy and who receive thousands and thousands of dollars in tax benefits for doing so. It's one of the few ways you can have your cake and eat it too. So, don't get caught in the trap of thinking that one type of entity fits all or that you should even only have one entity as part of your tax strategy. There is a lot of flexibility when you have a clear understanding of the different entity types and your tax advisor has a clear understanding of your goals and circumstances.

Maximizing the 20% Pass-through Deduction

Remember in Chapter 9 that the United States now has a special deduction equal to the lesser of 20% of business net income or 50% of wages from a business. Payments to a partner don't qualify as wages for this purpose. So if the two business owners in the strategy above formed as a partnership and they had no employees, they would receive no 20% deduction if their income is over a certain level. And they would pay high social security taxes on all of their partnership income.

However, if they own their partnerships through their S corporations, not only would they severely reduce their social security taxes, they would also create W-2 income that would allow them to take the 20% deduction.

For example, suppose the net income of the business was $1,000,000. Assuming this is split equally between the two partners, social security taxes on this income would be over $65,000. Plus there would be no 20% deduction to either of the partners.

If, instead, they own the partnership through their S corporations and are each paid a reasonable salary out of their S corporation of $100,000, they reduce their social security taxes and get the 20% deduction. Their social security taxes reduce from $65,000 to just over $30,000. Their 20% deduction will be $100,000 (the lesser of 20% of $800,000 or 50% of their $200,000 salary). Since they will be in the 35% income tax bracket, the $100,000 deduction lowers their income tax by $35,000. In total, simply by owning their business through S corporations instead of directly through a partnership, they lower their taxes by about $70,000 between the two of them. This is the magic of a good tax strategy.

Chapter Sixteen

Protect Your Wealth from Pirates, Predators, and Other Plaintiffs

"A government which robs Peter to pay Paul can always depend on the support of Paul." – George Bernard Shaw.

True Freedom

My passion is building wealth for others and for myself. I love the freedom that comes with having enough money to not worry about the price of the groceries I'm buying, whether I can afford a personal trainer, if I'm going to make my mortgage payment this month, or whether I can afford to take my family on our annual trip to Hawaii. That's true freedom.

I haven't always had that kind of freedom. Like many of you, I had a job and a mortgage, and I knew that if I didn't have that job, I wasn't going to be able to pay that mortgage—let alone put food on the table. It's only been in the last several years that I've had enough assets to pay my expenses without working every day.

I love Robert Kiyosaki's definition of an asset. He says that an asset is something that puts money in your pocket. Anything else is a liability because it takes money out of your pocket. So by this definition, your home is not an asset because it takes money out of your pocket and doesn't put money into it. On the other hand, your business or investments (including investment homes) can be assets if they produce cash flow.

In recent years, I've been fortunate to build my assets, especially my business, to the point where I don't have to go into the office very often and have the luxury of living off the income they provide. Much of my current wealth is tied up in my business. The rest is in my real estate. This wealth is the foundation of my freedom. It's why I have the time to write this book and teach seminars all over the world. There's nothing more important to me than protecting my family's freedom. So I have to protect my wealth just as I expect our government to protect our personal freedoms.

Asset Protection

Part of protecting this freedom is setting up adequate asset protection. I haven't always done a great job of protecting my assets. A number of years ago, we had an office in another state. We found a CPA to put in charge of that office and worked with an attorney to develop a partnership agreement. We had high hopes for that practice office because we had many clients living in that area even before we opened it.

For several years the office struggled to make money. It never seemed to make as much as our other offices, even though we seemed to spend at least as much time working with its staff and clients as we did with the staff and clients in our local office. My partner Ann and I decided that we were spending too much time and effort on this office for the small amount of money it made and that we needed to sell it.

We told our partner about our plans and that we wanted to include him in the discussions so that he'd be comfortable with whoever purchased the practice and so that he could continue to manage the clients. We thought this would be a great win for us and for him, and we put the practice on the market in late November. The listing broker who was marketing our practice didn't find a buyer prior to January. We decided to get through tax season (January through April) and then put it back on the market in the spring.

This decision turned out to be catastrophic. At the end of January, we received an email from our partner. He decided that rather than sell the practice, he'd just take it over, keep all of the clients and employees, and leave us with nothing. Of course, this was completely contrary to our partnership agreement. Our partnership agreement, written by some excellent lawyers, spelled out exactly what was supposed to happen if a partner decided to leave. Instead of following our agreement, however, our partner decided to take a completely different path than we'd anticipated. We spent the next nine months in court dealing with this challenge while doing our best to keep our clients happy.

The result was thousands of dollars in attorneys' fees, hundreds of hours of lost time, uncertainty for many of our clients, and the eventual loss of many of our clients in that state, not to mention an incredible amount of stress and lost sleep. That translated to a loss of about 75 percent of the total value of that entire practice. How did this happen? We'd worked so hard to build this business, and now most of it was gone. The simple reason was that we'd ignored the most important rule for protecting your assets.

RULE #14:	You must maintain control of your assets at all times and in all circumstances.

We thought we were in control. We had a great partnership agreement. We spoke to our partner at least twice every week. But we weren't *really* in control. We didn't have control of our files, our office, or our clients. So we were vulnerable, and lost enormous amounts of time and money as a result.

Why are we talking about this in a book about taxes? Because saving on taxes is simply one way of protecting your assets. You're protecting them from the government. When you take the time and energy to create a strategy for protecting your assets from the government, it's also the best time to create a strategy for protecting your assets from financial pirates and other potential predators, including your partners,

When you take the time and energy to create a strategy for protecting your assets from the government, it's also a good time to create a strategy for protecting your assets from financial pirates and other potential predators, including your partners, your employees, and your tenants.

your employees, and your tenants. When you create a tax strategy, you are looking at which entities to use and how to control your business and investments. These all impact your asset protection strategy as well.

The rules for protecting your assets are fairly simple. You have three goals.

Asset Protection Goals	
Goal #1	Prevent a lawsuit.
Goal #2	Stay under the radar so that you are less likely to be sued.
Goal #3	Win any lawsuit.

In this chapter, I'm only going to discuss Goal #1. Goal #3 is good, but even if you win a lawsuit, you still have to spend time, money, and energy on it. While my partner Ann and I hired great lawyers to write our partnership agreement, and while we won our lawsuit, in the end we still lost hundreds of thousands of dollars and enormous amounts of time and energy. This is why having good insurance, while important, is not enough. And as for Goal #2, it's certainly nice to stay under the radar, but my experience is that a smart attorney will find you eventually. So let's focus on Goal #1.

Preventing Lawsuits

If you're ever wondering how someone will act in a financial situation, it's a good practice to simply follow the money. For instance, if you're investing, follow the money to find out who is going to benefit from your investment—you or your financial advisor? If you want to protect your assets, you also want to follow the money. Who is going to benefit from a lawsuit against you?

The obvious people who could make money from suing you are the plaintiffs (those suing you). Who might want to sue you? The answer is anyone who thinks they can get at your assets. If people believe that they can get money from you, they'll do everything in their power to use the court system to dip into your pocket.

And it's not just the plaintiffs that make money in a lawsuit. It's the lawyers. Sometimes the lawyers make even more money than the plaintiffs. It's often the lawyers who convince their clients to file the lawsuit in the first place. That's why attorneys in the United States pay millions of dollars to run television ads throughout the day telling you to talk to them first if you're in an accident or otherwise feel damaged.

CAUTION!

Don't Rely Solely on Insurance to Protect Your Assets	
1.	Insurance, especially a personal umbrella policy, while critical to your asset protection is not enough.
2.	Be sure your asset protection strategy works to prevent lawsuits, not just protect you in case you lose a lawsuit.

The key to protecting your assets from both plaintiffs and their attorneys is to set up your business and investments so that if they do sue you, they likely won't get any money. In many countries, lawyers get paid even if they don't win the lawsuit since they charge their clients an hourly fee. In these countries, the client has to be confident they're going to win (or be so upset they lose reason) before they go ahead with a lawsuit.

This isn't the case in the United States. The United States allows lawyers to accept contingent fees. A contingent fee is a fee that is only paid if the plaintiff wins the case or convinces you or your insurance company to settle the case. If you can convince the lawyers they won't get any money even if they win, then they likely won't take the case. Lawyers hate not getting paid.

How do you set up your business and investments so that the chances are slim that a plaintiff will get money from you even if they win a lawsuit? Let's look at a few tips for protecting your assets from lawyers and their clients that can be done while you are creating your tax strategy. My disclaimer here is that I'm not an attorney. The tips I'm giving you are what I've learned through my own experience and from discussions I've had with attorneys. You must have any tax and asset protection strategy reviewed by a qualified attorney before setting it up. I would also suggest reading Garrett Sutton's book, *Start Your Own Corporation*, for a complete analysis of asset protection strategies.

TAX TIP:	Combine your tax strategy with an asset protection strategy. The two go hand in hand. In the end, you will have a strategy that protects you both from the government and from potential plaintiffs.

The Right Entity

Just as protecting your money from the government requires the right entity structure, the most important step in protecting assets from pirates, predators, and other plaintiffs is to use the proper entity to own your business and investments. Remember that the laws that protect your assets from plaintiffs are often different than the tax laws. So you want to form a tax strategy using entities that also protect you from future plaintiffs.

Make sure that your tax advisor has a good understanding of the asset protection rules in your state, province, and country as well as a thorough understanding of the tax law. You will also want your tax advisor and your asset protection attorney to speak to each other at least once or twice as you formulate your tax and asset protection strategy.

Fortunately, in many locations, you can get both maximum tax savings and asset protection through the use of the right entities. There are so many different asset protection entities and opportunities that I can't possibly cover them all in this one chapter. So I'm going to review some of the basic entities like I did in the previous tax strategies chapter and explain how these entities could help (or hinder) your asset protection. We'll look at asset protection entities in the same order we did when we talked about tax strategy.

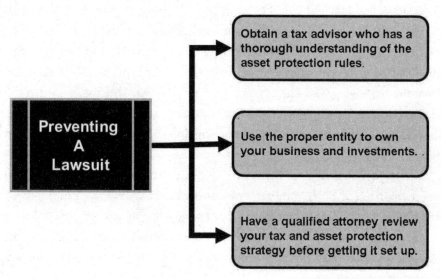

Preventing A Lawsuit

Obtain a tax advisor who has a thorough understanding of the asset protection rules.

Use the proper entity to own your business and investments.

Have a qualified attorney review your tax and asset protection strategy before getting it set up.

Trusts

Let's start with trusts. I mentioned in the previous chapter that trusts are particularly good for moving assets from one generation to another. They are also particularly good for asset protection.

Trusts have been available for thousands of years, so there are many cases telling us how trusts will be handled in a lawsuit. The general rule is that if the beneficiary of the trust (the person who eventually gets the income or the assets) is different than the grantor (the person putting the money or assets into the trust), then creditors (people to whom you owe money, including plaintiffs) cannot get at the assets of the trust.

Let's say you want to leave your money to your children and that you want them to be taxed on

Trusts have been available for thousands of years, so there are many cases telling us how trusts will be handled in a lawsuit.

the assets now but to not get the assets until after you die. You can do this by putting the assets into a trust. Another great aspect of trusts is that the trust document says who can get the income or assets of the trust and when. The trust document, which you need to write with the help of an attorney, can say when your children get the assets or income of the trust. In this way, you can even control your assets after you die.

You can also use trusts for giving assets to a charity. In fact, you can give the asset to the charity (the "corpus" in legal terms) and keep the income. This way, the charity gets the asset when you die, you get the income while you live, and the asset is protected from potential lawsuits. In addition, you can get a tax deduction for the charitable contribution now even though the asset isn't actually used by the charity until you die.

There are lots of uses for trusts in asset protection strategies. You'll need the help of both your attorney and your tax advisor to make these strategies work. Don't be afraid of them just because there are a lot of legal documents and lots of options. Ask questions and be sure your tax advisor and attorney can speak plainly and explain simply what they are suggesting to you.

Partnerships

When it comes to asset protection, partnerships can be either very good or very bad. General partnerships are awful. Think of a general partnership as though you and your partner are standing naked in the middle of a field with people throwing rocks at you both. You just might get hit with a rock aimed at your partner.

When it comes to asset protection, partnerships can be either very good or very bad. General partnerships are awful.

General partnerships offer no protection from plaintiffs. You are responsible (liable) for everything you do, everything your partner does, and everything your employees do. When someone sues a general partnership, they also sue all of the partners. The scary part is that you may be in a general partnership and not even know it. You may be investing with someone or doing a little side business together. That makes you a general partnership. You don't have to have a written agreement to be considered a general partnership. So be careful. I run into new clients all the time who have general partnerships without realizing it.

Limited partnerships are good for asset protection because the limited partners don't have any responsibility (liability) for what goes on in the partnership. They can only lose their investment—no more. Limited partnerships can be good for estate planning and for businesses where only one or two of the partners are running the business and the rest are passive investors. In some countries, such as Canada, the general partner can be a corporation without many assets. That way, even the general partner doesn't have a lot of liability because there aren't any assets to go after if the general partner is sued.

Corporations

Corporations are good entities for protecting you from any lawsuits that are directed at the company. As a shareholder, you cannot personally be sued unless you personally did something wrong. You're a bit like a limited partner, because all you can lose is the amount you have invested into the business. In countries other than the United States, where there aren't a lot of personal injury lawsuits, corporations can be great, so long as they also meet your tax goals.

LLCs

Limited liability companies (LLCs) can be the absolute best way to protect your business and investment assets from lawsuits. They give you the protection of a corporation. You can only lose what you put into the company. But they actually give you more protection than a corporation if you're personally sued.

> *Limited liability companies (LLCs) can be the absolute best way to protect your business and investment assets from lawsuits.*

Limited liability companies generally have the protection of a *charging order*. Here's an example of how a charging order works.

A few years ago, not long after my son turned 16 years old, I bought him a car. It was a sporty little Mazda. He had his driver's license, and I'd worked with him on his driving skills and was pretty comfortable with him out on the road. About six months later, my wife Rosie and I took a vacation in Hawaii. We'd left my 16-year-old and his 22-year-old brother at home to fend for themselves.

It was a great trip. That is, it was great until we got frantic calls one night from both sons. We'd been attending the LDS temple in Kona that night, and cell phones aren't allowed in the temple. When we got out, we had 10 missed calls from each of the boys. I called the older one, Max, first. He said Sam, our younger son, had been in a car accident. No one was badly hurt, but the car was badly damaged.

We called Sam, and he confirmed that he was okay. He told us the driver of the other car was fine, too. Sam's car, however, really was a mess. It took more than a month to get it fixed and working again. Thankfully, the other driver wasn't injured, but what if he had been? What if he'd been badly hurt? He might very well have sued us, the parents, for Sam's accident.

My CPA firm is owned through a limited liability company. What would have happened to my business if the driver of the other car had sued us and won a large judgment against us? Would my business have been protected? If I'd owned my business through a corporation, I'd have been in trouble. The plaintiff could've been awarded my shares of the company. He could've stepped into my shoes, voted my shares, and, if I owned a majority of my company, he could've sold it.

But since my company is a limited liability company, he couldn't have done any of those things. Were he to sue, he wouldn't have gotten my shares, and he wouldn't have gotten my vote. He couldn't have liquidated my company. All he could've done was get a charging order against my share of the LLCs distributions. A charging order against the income of an LLC is a bit like garnishing wages. Yes, he might have received any cash flow that came out of the company, but was I, as the manager of the LLC, going to allow any cash flow to be distributed to me when I knew he was going to get all of the money? No, of course not.

I would never have distributed any income to me. My partner could still get her income. We simply wouldn't distribute any to me. So the plaintiff, *and the plaintiff's lawyer*, would have received nothing. The charging order rule varies from state to state. Some states, such as Wyoming and Nevada, have strong charging order rules while others have been weakened as a result of the decisions in recent court cases. See Garrett Sutton's book, *Start Your Own Corporation*, for a more thorough discussion of the charging order rules.

Plaintiffs' lawyers know this about LLCs. So they tend not to sue people whose assets are owned in them. Lawyers like to get paid. Talk to your attorney and tax advisor about using LLCs to own your business. And don't forget all of the great tax benefits of using an LLC we talked about in the previous chapter.

I could go on forever about other ways to protect your assets, but I won't. I just want you to know the basics so that you can have an intelligent conversation when you talk to your attorney and your tax advisor. You don't have to learn all the details. But you do have to learn the basic rules. Then you can have a much better understanding of how asset protection can work for you. And when you do your tax strategy, you can keep these rules in mind to form an asset protection strategy at the same time.

Using Entities for Asset Protection			
	Not Good	Good	Best
Trusts	☐	☐	☑
Trusts can be used in a variety of asset protection strategies.			
General Partnership	☑	☐	☐
GP offers no protection from plaintiffs.			
Limited Partnership	☐	☑	☐
LP can also be used in a variety of asset protection strategies.			

Corporations	☐	☑	☐
Corporations are good for protection against lawsuits directed at your business.			
Limited Liability Company	☐	☐	☑
LLCs can be the absolute best to protect your business and investment assets.			

We're going to talk next about the single biggest fear of all taxpayers: the government audit. What can you do to win an audit, and how do you prevent one from happening? My goal is to eliminate your fear of government tax audits.

CHAPTER 16: KEY POINTS

1.	The best time to put together an asset protection strategy is at the same time you are putting together your tax strategy.
2.	Just as you are protecting your assets from the government with a tax strategy, you need to protect your assets from financial predators—plaintiffs.
3.	One of the surest ways to protect your assets is by choosing the right entity. Of all the entities, an LLC may be the best for you.
4.	Always seek the advice and help of a qualified lawyer and tax advisor when putting together an asset protection strategy.

Tax Strategy #16 – Include Asset Protection Planning When You Create Your Tax Strategy

My friend and fellow Rich Dad Advisor, Garrett Sutton, likes to say that CPA stands for "Cannot Protect Assets." Unfortunately, this is the case with many of my CPA colleagues. They never consider asset protection when they advise their clients on which entities to set up.

Recently, one of my students at our Tax and Asset Protection course came up to me and said that his accountant had recommended he set up his LLC in Florida. Unfortunately, there is some case law in Florida that weakens the LLC protection when the LLC has a single member. This student had read Garrett's book and was concerned that he should instead set up the LLC in a strong asset protection state such as Nevada or Wyoming. His CPA, though, insisted that that would just be a waste of money and that he should set up in Florida.

I have two issues with this advice, and they go hand in hand. First, the CPA is not understanding that in his client's situation, forming in Nevada or Wyoming and registering to do business in Florida would provide better asset protection than forming directly in Florida. Second, the CPA did not recommend that his client speak to an attorney. Instead, he took it on himself to give an answer to a question he was not fully qualified to answer.

At Tax-Free Wealth Network™ CPA firms, we *always* recommend that the client go over their entity structure with their asset protection attorney. In fact, we draw a diagram of how the entity structure should work for tax purposes and then, with the client's permission, we send this diagram to their attorney for review. Once the attorney has reviewed the entity structure, we schedule a call with the attorney to go over any changes the attorney may want to make in order to ensure the best asset protection while not interrupting the tax benefits from our recommended structure.

Of course, we also see the mistake of someone getting entities set up by an attorney without consulting a tax advisor. Then, when they come to us and we suggest different entities, they often have to make costly changes. Asset protection attorneys rarely have a thorough understanding of the tax law. Their expertise is asset protection, not tax.

Be sure to have both an attorney and a CPA help you with your entity structure. The best way to do this is to begin with a good tax advisor. You and your tax advisor can come up with a solid entity structure that will give you the best tax benefits. Then, go over this entity structure with your asset protection attorney. Doing your planning in this order will be the most efficient and effective.

Chapter Seventeen

Plan to Retire Rich, Not Poor

"Retirement: It's nice to get out of the rat race, but you have to learn to get along with less cheese."   – Gene Perret

My father never retired. He used to say that when you retire, you die. He owned and ran his business as long as he could. When he was 88 years old, and no longer able to handle it, he turned the business over to my sister. I feel the same way about retirement as my father. Why would I retire from my work when I love it so much? What could be better than a career developing new methods to learn about building wealth and reducing taxes, and then teaching those methods to millions of people? To me, retiring and giving up the work that I love would be a sort of death.

Most people don't think about retirement like my father and me. Instead, most people have jobs or situations that make them anxious to retire as soon as possible. I get it. Only a few years ago, I was working so many hours (Ann and I were both working over 3,500 hours a year at one point), that I was completely burned out. It got to the point that Ann and I decided that we would have to do something different—or quit altogether.

Fortunately, we figured out how to change the way we do our business. We did only that part of the business that we each love to do. Ann loves to create systems and processes and implement them into our business. I love to create new ways to build wealth and teach those innovations to clients and staff. Plus, we have the advantage of having a business that doesn't require our personal services. In reality, we have a passive investment that we can work at if and when we choose. And we could retire anytime we want.

The challenge of retirement

If you're aching to retire, I have some bad news for you. You have a challenge ahead of you—you may never be able to retire, at least not with the income you enjoy now while you're working. And this is especially true if you are using the same methods to retire that our parents used—relying on pension, profit sharing, RRSPs, and 401(k) plans. These government-qualified retirement plans provide temporary tax benefits, but they're also the reason most people will never be able to stop working for money.

Here is how the basic government-qualified retirement plan works. You and/or your employer (as allowed or directed by the government) decide how much you put into the plan each year. Under a typical plan, you're not taxed on the income you put into the plan. This has the same effect as if you received the income and then received a deduction for putting it into the plan. In fact, some plans work just this way, like a standard IRA in the United States or an RRSP in Canada.

The money in your plan is then invested in some type of government-approved asset. Most governments require you to decide between mutual funds or an account that earns interest, called a guaranteed contract. If you have a self-managed or self-directed account, you have more options for your investment and you have more control over where the money is invested.

Your money stays in the retirement account until you retire. At that point, you are allowed to take some or all of the money out. When you do take the money out, the government taxes you at ordinary income tax rates. The effect of this is to postpone or defer the tax on this income and the related earnings until you retire. The argument for this type of program is that this gives you a way to save for retirement without the added burden of paying taxes on the earnings of your retirement investments until you retire. When you retire, as the argument goes, you will be in a lower tax bracket because you won't need as much income, as your expenses will be lower.

There are some important exceptions to the general rule that government-qualified retirement plans postpone your tax. In the United States, if you put your money into a Roth IRA or Roth 401(k), you don't get a deduction when you put your money into the plan and you don't pay tax when you take it out. In Australia, you don't pay tax when you or your employer puts money into your Superannuation account. The account pays tax on the earnings, and you don't pay tax when you take the money out of the account.

Most tax planning in the United States and around the rest of the world is focused on maximizing the amount you can put into these types of accounts. The idea being that the more you put in the less you pay now and the more money you earn tax deferred. If you're like most people, you've been told your entire working life to maximize your 401(k) or RRSP. You may even work for an employer that adds some of the company's money to the money you choose to put into the plan. This is commonly referred to as a matching contribution from your employer.

The retirement plan lie

This all sounds pretty good, doesn't it? Don't pay tax until later and get a tax deduction today. You may even be expecting me to show you how to increase the amount you can put into your retirement account.

That's not going to happen—not in this book or in any other book I author or to which I contribute. I'm not going to tell you how to maximize the amount you put into these so-called retirement plans that are the creation of your country's government and are qualified by that government. In my mind, this would be unconscionable.

Instead, I'm going to tell you everything that's wrong with these plans and why you shouldn't use them. Then, in the next several chapters, I'm going to tell you how to permanently reduce your taxes by actively investing in any of the four asset classes—business, real estate, stocks, and commodities instead of investing in a government-qualified retirement plan.

Let's begin with the lie contained within their basic premise of these retirement plans. They presume that when you retire, you will be in a lower tax bracket than you are when you are working. The only way this could possibly be true is if your goal is to retire poor. If you plan on retiring with even the same amount of income you have while you are working, you will be in a higher tax bracket when you retire.

Retirement = *higher* tax bracket

The reason for this is that while you are working, you can take advantage of a whole host of tax benefits. Let's start with the tax benefits you get for your children. When you retire, your children are no longer dependent on you (if you're lucky), so you don't have that tax benefit. While you are working, you probably pay interest on a home mortgage. When you retire, you hopefully have paid off your mortgage, so you no longer have that deduction. While you are working, you likely have business deductions or employment-related deductions. These obviously go away when you retire.

There are people who say that the fact these deductions go away is precisely why you don't need as much income when you retire as you do while you are working—the point being that you don't have to pay for kids, a mortgage, and business expenses when retired. That may be true if you plan to just sit around the house and watch television when you retire. If you're like most people, however, you've put off a lot of life's pleasures while you were working in hopes to enjoy them in retirement when you have more time.

These pleasures may simply be more rounds of golf or more travel. Or, you may have always wanted a house in the mountains or on the beach. These are additional expenses that you didn't have when you were working. Plus, you'll probably have cute grandchildren who need to be spoiled. And these days, you may also have to contribute to the income of your children who are struggling to make ends meet. So, you really do need at least as much money when you retire as you do while you are working—if you're hoping to have any quality standard of living. You just don't get all of the tax deductions you had while you were working.

This doesn't even take into account the effects of inflation on your tax bracket. You may be earning $100,000 now as a couple and be in a fairly low tax bracket. But by the time you retire, you may need $200,000 of income to maintain your current lifestyle. Tax brackets rarely keep pace with real inflation, so you could find yourself in a much higher tax bracket just from inflation.

Effective Tax Rate Increase on Income of $100,000 Using a 15% Inflation Rate		
Year	Taxable Income	Effective Tax Rate
1	$100,000	14%
2	$115,000	15%
3	$132,250	16%
4	$152,088	17%
5	$174,901	17%
6	$201,136	18%
7	$231,305	19%
8	$266,002	20%
9	$305,902	20%
10	$351,788	22%

This isn't the only way you will end up paying more taxes by using government-qualified retirement plans. Think about what investments are allowed in an RRSP, 401(k), or pension plan. Typically, you will invest in the stock market. What types of income do you earn from stock market investing? You earn capital gains and dividends.

In most countries, capital gains are taxed at a lower rate than ordinary income. In New Zealand, for instance, they are totally exempt from tax. And dividend income is also taxed at a lower rate in many parts of the world. In the United States, dividends are taxed at the low capital gains rate. But when you invest in the stock market through your government-sponsored retirement plan, these lower tax rates go away.

When you invest in the stock market through a qualified retirement plan, like a 401(k), all of the income you earn is eventually taxed at the regular tax rates. So, instead of the preferred capital gains rate, that same income is taxed at ordinary income rates when you withdraw it from your retirement plan. This alone can more than double the tax rate on your investment earnings.

Tax penalties and self-directed retirement plans

Suppose you are in a country that allows some flexibility in your investments. Take, for example, the self-directed IRA in the United States or the self-managed Super in Australia. You decide that you want to invest your retirement savings into rental real estate. This could be a huge mistake. Remember from Chapter 7 that real estate is a great tax shelter because of depreciation. Let's look at Rule # 15

RULE #15:	**Never ever put a tax shelter investment inside another tax shelter.**

Isn't that exactly what you are doing when you invest in rental real estate through your IRA or Super? You take an investment that can save taxes not just on the income from the real estate but can actually reduce the rest of your taxes, and instead you convert it to an investment that can cost you a lot of additional taxes!

Remember when you were in grade school and you first learned that negative 1 (-1) multiplied by negative 1 equals positive 1 (-1 x -1=1)? That's exactly what happens when you put a tax shelter inside another tax shelter.

You take a tax shelter, multiply it by another tax shelter, and end up with a tax liability. Here is how this works.

Let's say you own rental real estate that earns $10,000 each year in cash flow. Depreciation on this property is $15,000, so you get to report a $5,000 loss on your tax return ($10,000 positive cash flow less $15,000 depreciation equals $5,000 tax loss). In a 40 percent tax bracket, this $5,000 loss is worth $2,000 in tax savings to you.

Tax Benefits Outside of an IRA	
Rental real estate annual earnings is positive cash flow of:	$10,000
Minus property depreciation of:	$15,000
Equals loss of:	$ 5,000
The loss of $5,000 in a 40% tax bracket = **$2,000** dollars in **TAX SAVINGS!**	

If you were to make this same investment in a government-regulated retirement plan like an IRA, you lose this $2,000 of tax savings because the depreciation deduction gets trapped inside the IRA. This is true even with Australian Super or a Roth IRA. I love self-managed Supers and Roth IRAs for certain types of investments, just not for an investment like rental real estate that can be a great tax shelter when it's owned outside of a retirement plan.

TAX TIP:	Roth IRAs can be very useful for certain types of investments. Develop your wealth strategy first and then decide whether a Roth IRA works within your wealth strategy.

Consider also that in many countries there are significant penalties for taking money out of your retirement account before you reach a certain age. These penalties are in addition to the tax you will pay when you take it out.

The reality is that if you're going to have as much money when you retire as you do now, then you probably will be in a *higher* tax bracket than you are today. Why? Because you likely won't have the deductions, exemptions, or credits that you currently enjoy for your children, for your house, or even for your business. After all, you want to be retired.

> *The reality is that if you're going to have as much money when you retire as you do now, then you probably will be in a higher tax bracket than you are today.*

	Planning on Retiring Poor?
☑	Higher tax bracket with same income
☑	Shift 15% capital gains to 35% or higher ordinary income tax rates
☑	Lose all tax benefits of real estate and business
☑	Inflation creates even higher tax brackets
☑	Pay penalties when you withdraw early

The power of leverage

I'll let my friend, Andy Tanner, Rich Dad Advisor for stocks and paper assets, explain all of the investment reasons not to use government-regulated retirement accounts in his book, *401(k)aos*—except for one investment aspect I want to talk about, *leverage*.

Leverage is the difference between building massive amounts of wealth and barely getting by in retirement. Leverage, in the form of mortgages, is what makes real estate such a good investment. Without debt, real estate is a mediocre way to make money. The returns on investment are no better than buying and holding stock. We will discuss how to use leverage to build massive amounts of wealth in Chapter 24.

The same is true for business. With leverage, business can be a great investment. You can borrow to improve your return on your equipment. You can borrow to purchase the business. And, of course, the best leverage in business comes from leveraging your time by hiring employees. Like real estate, without leverage, business is just a mediocre investment. Just ask any self-employed person who does all of the work in their business by themselves. They merely own their job. They don't get much more of a return on their investment than the time they put into their business.

In a 401(k), IRA, RRSP, or even in a Super, it can be difficult to get much leverage for your investments. Banks simply don't like to lend money to retirement accounts. They prefer to lend money to corporations and to individuals. Retirement accounts are trusts, and they can put a lot of restrictions on bank loans. In the United States, the person who owns the retirement account cannot guarantee a loan in their IRA, and banks like personal guarantees because they don't want to have to rely on just the real estate to pay for the mortgage. So you may find that when you go to buy that great piece of real estate inside your IRA that you can't get much of a bank loan to finance it.

CAUTION!

Leverage Inside a Retirement Plan Can Mean Big Taxes

1. Some countries, like the US, tax investment earnings in a retirement plan that come from borrowed funds.

2. Be sure to meet with your tax advisor before using debt to buy assets in your qualified retirement plan.

Government restrictions

The worst part of any government-qualified retirement plan is the amount of control you have to give up. The term "qualified" implies that you have to meet certain restrictions for the plan to be qualified for tax benefits from the government. Let's start with the investment restrictions. Only certain types of investments are allowed. In an IRA, you can't own collectibles, such as paintings, musical instruments, or collectible gold and silver coins. In a 401(k), you are severely restricted on the types of investments you can make.

We already talked about the restrictions on leverage, but we were only talking about the bank's restrictions. What about the government restrictions? The primary benefit of a government-qualified retirement plan is that normally the plan doesn't have to pay tax on its earnings. You don't pay tax on the earnings until you pull the money out of the plan. However, in the United States, when you leverage your investments inside your retirement plan, the income earned inside the plan is taxed when it's earned. You lose the tax-deferred benefit of the qualified plan. So even if the stock brokerage will give you leverage, your retirement plan ends up paying tax on the earnings because of the leverage.

Then there are the restrictions on how much you can put into the account and when you can take it out. In Canada and Australia, these restrictions are fairly liberal, and you can put in quite a bit and have some good flexibility for taking the money out. Not so in the United States.

In the United States, money you put into a 401(k) plan cannot be withdrawn until you leave your company. There is an exception that allows you to borrow out 50 percent of the money you have in your 401(k), but even this exception is only allowed on one loan at a time. And most employers only allow you to take out a loan once every few years.

There are also restrictions on when you can have full access to your money. As I mentioned before, in most countries you are restricted on when you can take the money out without a substantial penalty.

Control, or lack of it, is the worst part of government-qualified retirement plans. Even in Australia, where the self-managed Super is pretty amazing, the regulations about how to manage your Super are in excess of 3,000 pages. You even have to get your Super audited by a professional accountant every year. That's great for us accountants who get paid to do the audits and understand the regulations, but it's a huge additional cost for you.

So you end up with several challenges when you use a government-qualified plan for retirement. First, you increase your tax rates. Second, you increase your risk since you are leaving your money in the hands of someone else. Third, you reduce your overall returns because you are limited in using leverage. And fourth, you lose control over what you can do with your money and when you can use it.

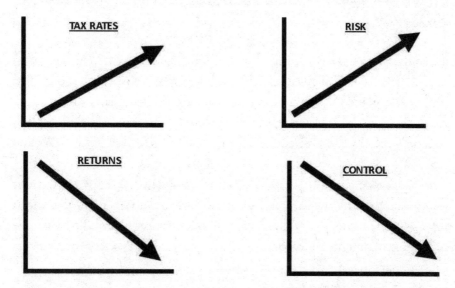

For the entire chapter, I've told you what *not* to do to prepare for retirement. In the next several chapters, I'm going to tell you what you can do without being subject to massive government control over your money. We're going to talk about how to use business, real estate, stocks and bonds, and commodities such as gold and silver to prepare for retirement and take advantage of the tax incentives provided for each of these asset classes.

CHAPTER 17: KEY POINTS	
1.	Using retirement methods your parents used only provide temporary tax benefits.
2.	Placing a tax shelter investment inside another tax shelter investment creates a tax liability.
3.	You lose control of your money when investing in government qualified plans for retirement.

Tax Strategy #17 – Use a Roth IRA for Certain Wealth Strategies

The only type of tax planning I like is planning that permanently reduces taxes. This is my biggest challenge with most government-qualified retirement plans. While most government-qualified plans are horrible for permanent tax savings, there are certain government-qualified plans that do work. In the United States, these plans are called Roth IRAs and Roth 401(k)s.

I don't love Roth 401(k)s because there are still too many restrictions on them regarding investment options and distributions from them. But Roth IRAs can be a very good part of a tax strategy, provided that the types of investments that work in a Roth are also the types of investments that are part of your wealth strategy.

Most people invest without any strategy at all. At Tax-Free Wealth Network™ CPA firms, we always suggest you begin your tax planning by forming your wealth strategy. And one of the first steps in a wealth strategy is determining which types of assets you are going to use to build your wealth.

We recommend that you focus on a single type of asset. Begin with the asset class you are going to use, whether business, real estate, paper, or commodities. Once you have the asset class figured out, choose which type of investment you want to use within that asset class. For example, if you choose paper assets, then decide which type of paper assets you are going to use to build your wealth. Are you going to use stocks, options, futures contracts, or maybe hard money loans?

Once you have decided on the asset you are going to use for building wealth, then you can decide how to get the best tax benefits from using that asset. As we discussed earlier in this chapter, if you choose multi-family housing as your asset, then you won't want to use a government-qualified retirement plan to hold your wealth. That would be putting a tax shelter inside another tax shelter.

There are several assets that work well in a government-qualified plan, particularly a Roth IRA that provides permanent tax savings. These assets all have certain things in common. First, they don't use debt for leverage. Second, their tax rate when invested outside of a government-qualified plan is fairly high. And third, they produce income that you will not need or want until you reach 59 ½ years old. Finally, all you have to do to manage these assets is to direct the purchase and sale of the assets. Here is a table showing some of these assets.

	Assets that work well in a Government Qualified Plan
1.	Tax Liens
2.	Hard Money Loans
3.	Stock Trading
4.	Gold and Silver Bullion
5.	Cryptocurrency

Notice that each of these assets meets our four qualifications of assets that make sense in a Roth IRA. (In Tax Strategy #20 at the end of Chapter 20, we will discuss in detail how to use stock options in a Roth IRA.) So be sure to build your wealth strategy *before* you decide on your tax strategy. For more on wealth strategies, visit us online at TaxFreeWealthBook.com.

Chapter Eighteen

Business Can Be Your Best Tax Shelter

"Business, that's easily defined - it's other people's money."
– Peter Drucker

At our Tax-Free Wealth Network™ CPA firms, much of our time is spent with our clients developing wealth strategies. One of the first things we work on is determining which asset class will be a client's primary focus. Nobody gets rich by investing in several asset classes at once. Rather, it's important to discover which asset class, whether business, real estate, paper, or commodities, should be the primary focus. We help our clients figure this out.

We begin by using the Kolbe™ personal assessment to determine their natural instincts. When you know your natural instincts, you can focus your attention on those activities that will be the most productive for you.

Next, we ask a series of questions to determine a client's personal preferences when working with investments. For example, how important is it to work with people? If someone doesn't want to work with people, then maybe focusing on stock investing and other paper assets would be a good fit. On the other hand, if working with people all the time is desired, business might be a better fit.

Personally, I love working with people. In fact, if I go too many hours without personal contact with another person, I start going into withdrawals. My partner, Ann, on the other hand, can work for hours on end without ever talking to anyone and is happy as can be. Ironically, of the two of us, she is much better in social situations than I am. Because of her willingness and desire to work on projects for hours at a time, however, Ann could do extremely well trading stocks and options. I would hate it.

I want as much people interaction as possible. So my focus is entirely on business. When people ask me about my investing, I explain to them that I'm a serial business owner. I own several businesses and continually develop new businesses and new ways to do business. Fortunately, business is also one of the best ways to reduce your taxes. Especially if you can turn your business into a passive investment like I've done with my accounting firm.

> **TAX TIP:** Turn your business into a passive investment. When you do, you can use your real estate losses to offset the income from your business.

Business and reducing taxes

The reason business gets so many tax breaks is because the government understands that the single most important task for the economy is to create jobs—and businesses create jobs. So there are literally thousands of tax breaks for businesses and business owners. This is as true in Japan as it is in Germany, France, or the US.

> *The reason business gets so many tax breaks is because the government understands that the single most important task for the economy is to create jobs.*

We have already discussed several of the benefits of a business in the earlier chapters in this book. To put things into context, let's look at the life of a business from start to finish and review the major tax benefits at each stage. You might think we would start with the formation of the business. The good news is that we can start even earlier than that. Let's start with the first time we begin thinking about starting a business.

Startup costs

You may have quite a few expenses when you begin investigating a new business. Likely you will have some educational expenses, and you may have some travel. You probably will pay some team members to help you get the new business going. And you may have some professional fees to accountants and lawyers. All of these costs together are called startup costs.

> *Since the first requirement for a business deduction is that you are in business, you don't get to deduct start up costs until you are "in business."*

Since the first requirement for a business deduction is that you are in business, you don't get to deduct startup costs until you are "in business." You aren't in business until you open your doors and are ready for your first customer. Once you open your doors, you can begin taking a portion of the startup costs as a deduction over several years. This is called amortization, which we discussed in Chapter 7 when we also discussed depreciation.

The reason you have to wait to begin deducting your startup costs is because those costs create an asset that will generate income for many years (we hope). Any time you have expenses that will benefit future years, you don't get to take an immediate deduction for them. Instead, you capitalize them, or, in other words, you treat them as an asset.

> *Startup costs are amortized over a period of time, just like real estate or equipment are depreciated over time.*

Startup costs are amortized over a period of time, just like real estate or equipment are depreciated over time. Some countries are specific about the period of time for certain assets. In the United States, for instance, the IRS tells you exactly how much depreciation or amortization you get each year for specific types of assets. For startup costs, that amount is 6.7 percent per year. In other countries, you look at how long you expect the asset to last. Some assets don't wear out over a specific time period, so you may not get a deduction until you go out of business. Be sure you check

---

with your personal tax advisor to find out how startup costs are treated in your country.

You can start deducting your amortization as soon as you open your doors for business. And while you're planning to open your business, you might want to look into where you open your business. Many countries, states, and cities offer tax breaks for companies that locate in areas that the government is trying to improve. These are called enterprise zones. You could receive a tax credit for leasing or buying a building in an enterprise zone. Or you could receive employment tax credits for hiring people to work in an enterprise zone.

CAUTION!

	Be Sure to Start Deducting Start Up Costs as Soon as Possible
1.	If you don't begin deducting start up costs in the year you begin business, you may never get to deduct them.
2.	Start deducting your start up costs in the first year you may have begun business. If the government says you started too early, then you can still deduct them in later years.

Business tax advantages

Business expenses

Of course, as soon as you open your doors for business, you can begin deducting all of your business expenses as you pay for them. Remember the basic premise we discussed in Chapter 6? You can deduct almost anything as long as it is ordinary and necessary in the course of operating your business. Once you can show that your expense is for your business and that it is ordinary (typical) and necessary, the expense becomes fully deductible against your business income. This is true even for many expenses that you would have even if you didn't have a business, such as travel, meals, education, and auto expense. Even medical expenses that you might not be able to deduct personally can become deductions with the right business structure.

Tax brackets

Once you have a business, you can also take advantage of different tax brackets. You can use multiple corporations to take advantage of their lower brackets, just as we discussed in Chapter 9.

Depreciation and tax credits

Remember the magic of depreciation we discussed in Chapter 7? In addition to the depreciation deduction for equipment, many countries give credits for investment in business equipment. In the US, there is a credit for research and development expenses, including equipment. In some countries, all new equipment purchases used in business create a tax credit for the business owner. This credit is commonly called an investment tax credit.

Employees

Besides equipment, every business needs employees. And since the goal of the government is to increase employment, it would be natural that there would be tax benefits specifically for hiring more employees, right? And there are.

Employment credits are a favorite tool of governments to encourage companies to hire more people or certain types of people. Many governments give credits for hiring people who have been unemployed for a long period of time. In France, there is an enormous credit for hiring engineers who do research and development work.

There are other tax incentives for adding employees. Of course, the obvious benefit is that you get to deduct salaries and wages paid to employees. You may also decide you want to give certain employees stock options (the option to buy stock at a lower price than if they bought it in the stock market). Typically, you can deduct the value of these options as soon as the employees have the right to exercise (use) them. Or, you may be able to give the employees a special benefit by using qualified stock options, sometimes called "incentive stock options," or ISOs. These allow the employees to receive the options without paying ordinary income tax. So long as they hold them for more than a year, the employees get to pay the lower long-term capital gains rates when they sell the stock.

Business Tax Strategies	
Tax Credits	
☐	Leasing or buying a building in an enterprise zone
☐	Hiring people to work in an enterprise zone
☐	Hiring specific types of people
☐	Increasing your employee work force
☐	Business equipment
☐	Research and development
Deductions	
☐	Travel
☐	Meals
☐	Auto expenses
☐	Medical expenses
☐	Depreciation
☐	Salaries and wages paid to employees

Tax Brackets	
☐	Using multiple types of entities

Note: Be sure to check with your tax advisor to determine how these business tax strategies apply to your personal business situation.

Choosing your accounting method

As you start your business, you will need to make certain decisions about how to account, or record, your income and expense. Most businesses have the option to either use the cash method of accounting or the accrual method of accounting. The cash method means that you record your income and deduct your expenses when you pay for them. This gives the best tax benefits for most businesses because often a business will have many customers who pay over time, and by using the cash method, you don't have to pay tax on these sales until you actually receive the money from the customer.

The accrual method means that you record income when it's earned, even if the customer doesn't pay you until several months later. It also means that you get a deduction when you purchase an item, even if you don't pay for it until months later. So, if you are postponing payment for a lot of purchases, the accrual method of accounting could save you a lot of taxes. So be sure to sit down with your tax advisor when you first start your business to make the best decision about which method of accounting to use.

Recording Your Income and Expenses	
Cash method of accounting	Record income and deduct expenses when you pay for them.
Accrual method of accounting	Record income when it's earned, and deduct expenses when you purchase them, even if you don't pay for them until months later.

You also need to choose your year-end for accounting purposes. Individuals are required to use the calendar year as their period for reporting income and expenses on their tax return. Businesses, however, have more options. Corporations typically can choose to end their business year in any month they desire. So you could have your business year-end on March 31 even though your personal tax year ends on December 31. This might give you some flexibility about when you pay taxes on your income. For example, you could pay yourself a bonus in March. Your company could deduct the bonus for their year that ends that March while you don't have to personally report the income until you file your tax return for the following year that ends on December 31.

> *Income from overseas customers often can be sheltered from taxes in your country as well as from taxes in the country where your customer lives.*

Offshore planning

Most businesses these days sell a lot of their products to customers who live in other countries. Income from overseas customers often can be sheltered from taxes in your country, as well as from taxes in the country where your customer lives. This type of tax planning is called "offshore" tax planning. There is an entire industry of tax planning dedicated to it.

At our Tax-Free Wealth Network™ CPA firms, we have so many business clients who do business around the world, that we have teams of tax advisors who specialize in offshore tax planning. Be careful with offshore planning, however, as your government doesn't like to see their tax revenues reduced this way. You need a tax advisor who specializes in this type of planning. I know a little bit about it, but not enough to do anything other than get me in trouble. That's why I hire tax advisors who specialize in this area.

Selling your business

What about when you decide to sell your business? There are lots of ways to reduce your taxes when you sell your business.

Let's suppose you find a buyer that is a public company whose stock trades on an exchange. You may be willing to "sell" your company in exchange for stock in the public company. After all, when you do, you have an asset that you could easily turn into cash later on. When you do this, you could end up paying zero taxes when you sell your company. Later, when you sell the stock of the new company, you only pay tax at the lower capital gains rates.

Or what if you're selling your company to a private buyer—perhaps a competitor in your industry? If you sell the stock of your company, you only have to pay tax at capital gains rates. And even if you sell the assets of your company, most of your gain should be capital gain, so long as your tax advisor has done a good job negotiating the agreement.

Yes, this does mean that you should have your tax advisor heavily involved in the negotiations when you sell your business. I can't tell you how many times I've had someone come to me after they had agreed on the way they would sell their business and ask if I could do something to lower their taxes. By then, it is usually too late. Instead, involve your tax advisor from the beginning, before you even start talking to the potential buyer.

In some cases, your business won't succeed. Even in failure, there are tax benefits. Many countries allow businesses to deduct their entire investment in the business as an ordinary deduction in the year they fail, if certain elections and planning are done ahead of time. Nobody wants to plan to fail. However, since nine out of ten businesses do fail, it's smart to plan ahead of time to get the maximum tax benefits if you do fail.

The tax benefits of owning a business are part of why I like business so much. That and all of the great people I get to meet, like Robert Kiyosaki and all of the Rich Dad Advisors.

Not all people want to be in business. In the next chapter, we will focus on another asset class that provides tremendous tax benefits to investors—real estate. First, let's look at a very creative tax tip that allows you to seriously reduce the taxes you pay on your business income

	CHAPTER 18: KEY POINTS
1.	Businesses get tax breaks because they create jobs that help the economy grow.
2.	"Start up" costs can be deducted over a period of time once a business opens its doors.
3.	There are a host of tax strategies to help a business reduce its tax liability – such as tax credits, various deductions and using tax brackets.

Tax Strategy #18 – Turn Your Business Into a Passive Investment

Many times over the years I have heard people talk about how it's possible to turn your business into an investment where you don't have to go to work. For years, I didn't understand how this was possible, and I certainly didn't think it would ever be possible for my CPA firm. After all, there is no more labor-intensive business than a CPA firm. With Ann's amazing skills in creating systems and procedures, however, we were able to turn our firm into a passive investment. We now have a business that runs without us.

Turning a business into a passive investment where you don't have to go to work takes some serious effort. It took Ann and me five years to figure out how to do it with our CPA firm. The good news is that even if you're not to the point where your business runs without you working, it's easy to turn the income from your business into passive income for tax purposes. Here is why you would want to do this and a few simple steps for getting it done.

Turning ordinary income into passive income

As we discussed in Chapter 8, there are different types, or buckets, of income. Portfolio income, or income from investments, is always better than ordinary income. The reason Warren Buffet pays only 17 percent on his income is that most of his income is investment income.

An even better type of income is passive income. When you have passive income, you can offset your income with losses from your real estate investments. As we illustrated in Chapter 7, real estate gets such high depreciation deductions that you can have losses for your tax return even though you have positive cash flow from your real estate. The challenge is that real estate rental losses in the United States are considered to be passive losses and can only offset passive income.

So we would like to convert the ordinary income from our business into passive income. Here is how we do it. Remember Rule # 7 – It's not how much we own that matters; it's how much we control? This is the rule we're going to use to convert at least part of your business income into passive income. All we have to do is to give part of your business to a member of your family who doesn't work in the business. When we do this, their share of the income from the business is passive income. Then, we also give them a part of the real estate that has passive losses. Now, their share of the real estate losses will offset the passive income from their share of the business.

While this is simple in concept, don't do this without your tax advisor's help. There are lots of details that your tax advisor will need to be aware of so you can make this great tax strategy work for you.

Avoiding Tax Completely when Selling Your Business

In the U.S. tax law, there is a little-known provision that allows the owners of a business to completely avoid tax when the company is sold. The rule is called Section 1202 stock. Here is how it works.

First, start by forming your company as a C corporation. This can either be an LLC taxed as a C corporation or an actual corporation. Then, if the business is owned and operated for more than five years, it can be sold and there is no tax on the gain. It's actually pretty simple.

So why haven't companies used this in the past? The reason is the high corporate tax rate. Until 2018, the U.S. corporate tax rate was one of the highest in the world at 35%. Anyone who wanted to take advantage of the 1202 stock provision had to be willing to be taxed at this high rate plus pay capital gains tax on distributions.

All of this changes with the corporate tax rate reduced to 21%. Now, a business owner can form a company as a C corporation, only pay 21% on the income, and then sell the company and pay no tax on the gain. Even with a 15% tax on distributions, a successful business will pay less than 33% total tax while owning the company and avoid tax completely when the company is sold.

Chapter Nineteen

The Magic of Real Estate

"It's tangible, it's solid, it's beautiful. It's artistic, from my standpoint, and I just love real estate." – *Donald Trump*

As long as I can remember, my parents owned rental properties. They owned two duplexes and a large plot of land not too far from our house. I remember my brother-in-law planted a vegetable garden on the land and seemed to love working in the garden. My dad liked working on the real estate. Any chance he got, he wanted to be outside working on the yard or improving the property. It was a form of recreation for him.

I never understood work as a recreation until I started doing my own business and investing. Now I get it. Though my work is much different than my dad's, I understand how enjoyable it can be to do productive work that helps other people. My work is education and advice. My dad's was printing and improving his properties.

When I was young, I didn't understand all of the tax benefits my parents were receiving from their real estate. Once I earned my Masters of Professional Accounting and started working with clients who own real estate, however, I understood.

Real estate is such a good tax shelter that a serious real estate investor should NEVER have to pay tax on their cash flow or on the gain from the sale of their real estate.

Real estate is such a good tax shelter that a serious real estate investor should never have to pay tax on their cash flow or on the gain from the sale of their real estate.

RULE #16:	**The single best tax shelter in most countries is investing in rental real estate.**

We went through the magic of depreciation in detail in Chapter 7, so you understand how the cash flow from real estate can be totally sheltered from taxes via these phantom losses. Plus, you understand that rental real estate investments not only shelter cash flow from the real estate but can also shelter other income from taxes. With proper planning, rental real estate can create huge tax reductions for your business and salary income. A perfect example of how to do this is in Tax Strategy #18 at the end of the last chapter.

TAX TIP:	Since there is no tax on the sale of your residence in most countries, you may want to sell your residence and buy a new one every few years. While a personal residence is always a liability since it takes money out of your pocket, you can still make money on it if you buy and sell at the right times. Just don't get caught in the speculation trap of buying a home for the primary reason of selling it later. Buy your home because you want to live there. Any gain is just a bonus.

Like-kind exchanges

The key to building tax-free wealth in real estate, of course, is to continue buying more and more real estate. Here's why.

In our example of cost segregations in Chapter 7, you learned how to get more of your depreciation in the first several years of owning the property. Your tax basis (the purchase price of the property less all of the depreciation you have taken on the property over the years) in the property is reduced dollar by dollar for the depreciation you take. And your tax basis is important both for calculating depreciation and for calculating your gain when you sell a property.

Once your tax basis in a property goes to zero, you don't get any more depreciation. And when you sell the property, your gain is calculated as the difference between your tax basis and your sales price. This is a basic accounting principle that applies throughout the world.

In order to continue sheltering the cash flow from your real estate as well as the cash flow from your business, you need to continue buying more real estate by rolling your gains into like-kind properties through tax-free exchanges.

One of the great things about tax basis is that it includes debt. So you can buy a property with no money down and you get all of the tax basis and depreciation. The bank doesn't get any of it. Let's look at a simple example.

Suppose you buy a house for $100,000. Remember from Chapter 7 that you really purchased four types of property when you purchased the house. You purchased land, a building, land improvements, and the contents of the building. Everything except the land can be depreciated. For this example, let's assume that after you break out all of the different parts of the property, your tax preparer determines that your annual depreciation is $8,000 (this is just an estimate for purposes of this example).

Each year, you take an $8,000 depreciation deduction on your tax return. And each year, your tax basis in the property also goes down by $8,000. After the first five years, when you have fully depreciated the contents of the house, your depreciation deduction decreases to $4,000 per year.

Let's say that after seven years you decide to sell the building. By that time, you have taken depreciation deductions totaling $48,000 ($8,000 x 5 + $4,000 x 2). Now your tax basis in the property is $52,000 ($100,000 - $48,000). So, if you sell the building for $130,000, you will have a taxable gain of $78,000 ($130,000 - $52,000). Essentially, you are paying back the depreciation deduction (called depreciation recapture), plus paying tax on the increase in value of the property.

Tax Basis Example			
Purchase price of property:			$100,000
Depreciation determined by your tax preparer			
Depreciation Year 1	$8,000		
Depreciation Year 2	$8,000		
Depreciation Year 3	$8,000		
Depreciation Year 4	$8,000		
Depreciation Year 5	$8,000		
Total depreciation after 5 years	$ 40,000		
After 5 years depreciation has decreased			
Depreciation Year 6	$4,000		
Depreciation Year 7	$4,000		
Total depreciation for year 6 and 7	$ 8,000		
Total Depreciation		$ 48,000	
Tax Basis in Property		$ 52,000	

In many countries, however, you can completely avoid the gain on the sale of your property, including the depreciation recapture, simply by buying another investment property for the same price or more than the one you sold through a tax-free or like-kind exchange—also referred to as a Section 1031 exchange in the United States after the section of the Internal Revenue Code that allows this tax treatment. This means that you can sell properties that you don't want any more because they are overpriced or because you want to change your investment strategy and not have to pay any tax.

When you do a like-kind exchange, the tax basis in your new property equals the purchase price of the property, less the amount of gain you didn't have to recognize. In our example, let's say we purchased a new property for exactly the same amount as the sales price of the old property, $130,000. The new property would have a tax basis of $52,000 (the new property's purchase price of $130,000 less $78,000, the amount of gain on which we didn't pay tax). The new property is depreciated as if it were the old property. You get a depreciation deduction for the new property as a percentage of its tax basis of $52,000. The calculations get a little complicated at this point, so be sure that your tax advisor keeps really good track of your tax basis on each of your properties.

Like-kind exchanges + depreciation = zero taxes

In chapter 8, I told you how my friend, Guy Zanti, used the 1031 exchange to reduce his taxes by $20,000. Let me show you how you can use a combination of 1031 exchanges and depreciation to never again pay tax on the cash flow or the gain from the sale of your real estate.

Suppose you decide to begin your real estate investment strategy by investing in single-family homes. You buy several homes over the next few years and get comfortable buying houses that have positive cash flow while also increasing in value. After a few years, you decide that you'd like a little more cash flow and a few less properties to manage. So, you sell all of your houses and buy a couple of apartment buildings. You do this through a "qualified intermediary" and you follow all of the detailed rules of Section 1031 that your tax advisor tells you about so that your sales and purchases qualify as a like-kind exchange.

You enjoy the additional cash flow that comes from your apartment buildings for several years. You also enjoy the depreciation deductions from your apartment buildings. These deductions, as we discussed in Chapter 7, completely shelter the cash flow from income tax. Eventually, though, you decide that you want to cash in your apartment buildings for an asset that you don't have to manage at all. You notice that while apartment buildings are far easier to manage than single-family homes and produce more cash flow than single-family homes, they still require a lot of work. You look around for a building that doesn't require any work at all. What you find is a Walgreens.

Like many retail stores, Walgreens typically doesn't own properties. Instead, it finds the land, builds the building, sells the land and building to an investor, and then leases them back for 30 years. Walgreens agrees to take care of all of the maintenance and all of the expenses. All the investor has to do is pay the mortgage. You like this because Walgreens has great credit and the bank is happy to lend you the money to buy a property that has a lease guaranteed by one of the largest retail store chains in the world.

You sell all of your apartment buildings and buy your Walgreens property. Every month, Walgreens sends you a check that you deposit into your account. You can even have the check sent to your bank and directly deposited into your account and have the mortgage payment paid automatically from your account. So you don't have to do anything. You travel all over the world with the investment income from your Walgreens property till a ripe old age.

Here is the magic of the Walgreens strategy. Over the years, you took depreciation deductions on your single-family homes, then on your apartment buildings, and then on your Walgreens. This depreciation sheltered your cash flow from income taxes. Let's suppose your total depreciation deductions over the years were $4 million. You have to reduce your tax basis in your properties by all of that depreciation. Remember that tax basis is the number that is used to calculate the capital gain when you sell the property. So, if you paid $5 million for the Walgreens, and you had a total of $4 million of depreciation, then your basis would be $1 million. If you sold the property for $6 million (it's value) on the day before you died, you would pay capital gains tax on $5 million ($6 million sales price less your $1 million basis). If your capital gains tax rate is 20 percent, you would have to pay a tax of $1,000,000.

You can eliminate this capital gains tax simply by holding onto the property until you die. When you die, your basis is automatically increased to the value of the property on your date of death. This is called a basis step up. If the value is $6 million, your basis will be $6 million. Since we know that your kids are going to sell the Walgreens soon after you die so that they can have the cash, this is a great tax planning tool. You got the tax benefit from all of that depreciation while you were alive, and your children don't have to pay tax on it when you die.

	Don't Sell Real Estate Real Assets Before You Die
1.	Selling assets creates unnecessary capital gains taxes that could be avoided simply by holding onto your assets until after you die.
2.	You can always get cash from your real estate by borrowing against it and debt is tax free.

What about estate taxes? The day you die, just as we discussed in Chapter 13, the estate tax kicks in. You get an exemption, however, for a certain value of your estate. With the Walgreens now worth $6 million and assuming you have other assets including your personal residence totaling $1 million, your net estate value is $7 million. The United States has an $11 million estate tax exemption. So there won't be any estate tax on the Walgreens. (Even if the Walgreens plus your other assets total more than $11 million, there are plenty of ways to reduce or eliminate your estate tax that we discussed in Chapter 13).

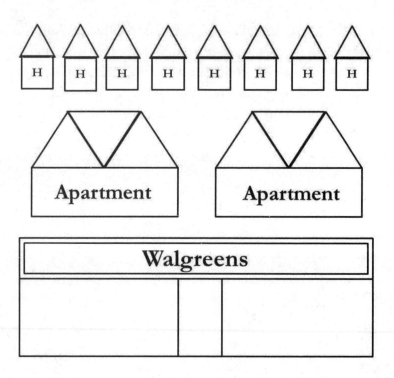

Of course, depreciation and like-kind exchanges aren't the only tax benefits from real estate. In Chapter 9, we talked about some of the tax credits you can get from real estate. There are low-income housing credits, historic structure investment credits, and other real estate tax credits. And in most countries, you don't have to pay any tax on the gains from selling your family home.

One of the biggest benefits in real estate is that loans aren't taxable. So you can borrow money from the bank through a refinance and you won't pay tax on that money. One of the arguments I hear all the time for not doing like-kind exchanges is that the taxpayer might need cash from the sale of the building. Instead of cashing out and paying tax on that cash, why not do a like-kind exchange and then later refinance the building? When you refinance, you get your cash in the form of a tax-free loan and get to keep your asset!

One of the biggest benefits in real estate is that loans aren't taxable.

If your wealth strategy includes real estate, be sure to work with your tax advisor to figure out how much depreciation you will get each year and how you can use like-kind exchanges and other tax benefits to seriously reduce or eliminate your income taxes.

Next we will move to the tax benefits of actively investing in paper assets, such as stock and option trading.

CHAPTER 19: KEY POINTS

1. Real estate investment is one of the best tax shelters.

2. A 1031 exchange (or like-kind exchange) and depreciation are key in never paying tax on the cash flow or the gain from the sale of real estate investment.

Tax Strategy #19 – Change Your Residence Every Few Years

By now, everyone knows that real estate doesn't always appreciate. So buying a house with the sole goal of selling it when it goes up in value is not a sound wealth strategy. However, this doesn't mean that you can't still have a strategy of building wealth in part by changing your residence every few years.

Most people prefer to own their own home for any number of reasons. Owning your home gives you a sense of security. It gives you a feeling of ownership. It may provide a sense of stability to you and your family. And it can also be a way to build tax-free wealth.

Let's suppose that instead of buying your dream home, you decide to buy a house that needs some fixing up. There are lots of houses like this. I have a friend who loves to find homes that are a real bargain in part because they need a lot of improvement. She has become an expert at deciding what needs to be done to a house to maximize its value. She also hates paying taxes.

So every few years she and her husband sell their house and find a new house that needs repairs and improvements. They spend evenings and weekends painting, putting in new flooring, and adding new cabinets. Did I forget to say that my friend loves interior design as well? So this is kind of a fun hobby for them. In addition, her husband is a high implementer in his Kolbe score. This means that he really likes working with his hands by using tools and building things. Why not use his hands to improve his own house?

Beyond the personal satisfaction of working together on a project, my friend and her husband enjoy tax advantages for doing this. In the United States there is no tax on the sale of a personal residence so long as you live in it two out of the past five years. My friend and her husband always live in their house until it's fully improved. Even in a bad real estate market, their improvements are enough to provide them with a tidy little gain when they sell the house. So long as their gain is not more than $500,000, the entire gain is tax-free. Then they find another house they can improve.

When they first started doing this, their goal was to own their dream home free-and-clear of any debt. They reached that goal years ago. Now they keep finding new homes that they can turn into a dream home and sell for a tax-free gain.

Of course, this strategy isn't for everyone. You have to enjoy living in a house that needs improvement. And it helps if you enjoy doing the work. Still, what a great strategy for those of you who don't mind moving every few years and would like to make money doing it—tax-free money at that.

Chapter Twenty

Stocks Can Lower Your Taxes Too

"Look at market fluctuations as your friend rather than your enemy;
profit from folly rather than participate in it."
– Warren Buffett

My first try at stock investing was a disaster. My brother, Steve, who was a professor at the Harvard Business School for many years, gave me a tip on two stocks. The first was a company nobody had heard of at the time called Berkshire Hathaway, which was run by this guy named Warren Buffett. I didn't know anything about the company except that my brother thought this Warren Buffett was a pretty smart guy. So, I bought the stock.

Steve's other recommendation was a company I knew something about called FastTax™, which processed tax returns by computer. This was 25 years ago. We used FastTax at work, and it was a pretty good program. I thought this would be a fairly safe investment.

A few years later, I needed some cash so I sold one of my stocks. I made the obvious choice. I kept the stock in the company I knew, FastTax and sold the stock in the company I didn't know, Berkshire Hathaway. You're probably laughing at me right now. If I'd kept the Berkshire Hathaway stock, it would be worth millions now. Just like most bad investing, mine was a result of a lack of education.

People who make a lot of money in the stock market are well educated about the stock market. They understand how to make money whether the market goes up, down, or sideways. They don't rely on the strategy I used for my first stock investments—buy, hold, and pray the stock goes up. Instead, they understand how to use options, futures, and other hedges to reduce their risk and increase their reward.

These same people, however, tend to be less educated when it comes to taxes. They are especially uneducated when it comes to how stock trading can produce major tax benefits with the right education...or very high taxes with the wrong—or no—education. Let's look at some of the major benefits you can have as an active stock investor, as well as some traps to watch out for.

The mutual fund tax trap

Mutual funds are the most common form of stock market investing. The problem is that mutual funds contain a tax trap that many people don't know about. Think of a mutual fund as a pass-through entity like a partnership. The income earned in a mutual fund is not taxed to the mutual fund. Instead, it's taxed to the investors. That might be okay if everyone entered a mutual fund at the same time. Everyone would simply report their share of gains and losses on the stocks sold in the mutual fund, and then they would see the value of their investment grow or decrease by those same gains and losses.

That, however, is not how it works. If you invest in mutual funds, you will likely buy into a fund that has been around for many years. Over the years, investors have come and gone while the fund has purchased many different stocks over those same years. The challenge comes when the fund goes to sell a particular stock. Let's say you decided to invest in Mutual Fund A at the beginning of the year. The fund bought Stock B for $10 per share fifteen years ago. When you joined the fund at the beginning of the year, Stock B had a market value of $50 per share. The day after you join the fund, the fund managers decided to sell the stock. So there is a gain to the fund of $40 per share on the sale of Stock B.

Who pays the tax on the $40 gain? You do, even though you just joined the fund the day before. All investors who owned shares of Mutual

Fund A on the day the mutual fund sold the stock share the gain. Doesn't seem fair, does it? It gets worse.

Suppose you paid $100 per share for Mutual Fund A when you bought it in January. At the end of the year, the stock market takes a dip in value and now your shares of Mutual Fund A are only worth $80 per share. You still have to pay tax on your share of the $40 gain from the sale of Stock B inside the mutual fund.

RULE #17:	**Mutual funds are one of the few places where you can lose money and still owe tax on your investment.**

The tax benefits of active stock investing

Let's take a look at what happens to more active investors in the stock market. Unlike the passive mutual fund investor, the active stock investor can receive many tax benefits. The most obvious is that gains in active stock investing are capital gains, and unlike mutual fund gains, you only have to pay tax on them when you sell them.

Many countries have special, lower tax rates on capital gains. In some countries, like the United States, you only get the lower tax rate when you have a long-term capital gain. Long term means that you held the asset for a time specified by your country's tax law. In several countries, including the United States, Australia, and Japan, long term is considered one year and a day. Some countries don't distinguish between long-term and short-term capital gains. In New Zealand and several other countries, there is no tax at all on capital gains.

In several countries, including the US, Australia and Japan, long term is one year and a day.

Of course, if you can have gains on an asset, you can also have losses. Losses from the sale of stock are normally considered to be capital losses. Capital losses in most countries can only offset capital gains. If you don't have enough capital gains to offset, then the capital losses carry forward to future years. In the US, however, you can use $3,000 per year in capital losses to offset other income when you don't have enough capital gains to offset.

Many countries, including the United States, also tax dividends from stocks at the lower capital gains rates. This is a fairly new phenomenon and one that could change at any time. Historically, dividends have been treated as ordinary income. Interest income is also treated as ordinary income in most countries.

For the casual investor, capital gains, dividends, and interest are the only rules you have to know. Only when you become a serious stock investor do the rules get more complicated and the benefits increase. This leads us to Rule #18.

RULE #18:	**The better the tax benefits, the more complicated the rules.**

This rule is generally true for all tax benefits and is why wealthy individuals depend so heavily on tax advisors. The reason for this rule is that the government wants to limit tax benefits to very specific circumstances. In order to define those circumstances, the rules can get a little complex. Don't worry about understanding all of the detailed rules. Just be sure your tax advisor understands the rules that apply to you.

TAX TIP:	Consider trading stocks and options in your self-directed IRA or pension account. The tax benefits can be enormous.

Tax benefits of option trading

The first complex area in paper assets is the stock and option trader rules. Remember in Chapter 6 when you learned that almost all expenses can be deductible? The way to make them deductible is to make them an ordinary and necessary business expense. This is difficult to do when you are a stock investor, since you probably aren't investing for other people and so are not technically in business.

There is an exception to the business requirement, however, for people who are in a trade. A trade includes doing work only for your own benefit so long as it is a major part of your time and wealth building activities. When you are in a trade, you get to deduct your expenses just like you would if you were in business. For stock traders, this is even better than for the typical business owner. You get to deduct your expenses as ordinary deductions, and your trading gains are capital gains—not ordinary income, which is taxed higher. If you don't meet the trader rules, then your expenses are investment expenses. Investment expenses can sometimes be deducted, depending on the amount and type of the expenses and your country's tax laws. (The U.S. recently changed its tax law so investment expenses are no longer deductible.)

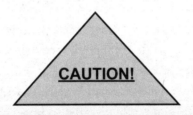

	Not All Tax Advisors Understand Stock Trading Tax Rules
1.	Whether you qualify as a stock trader is based on your facts and circumstances.
2.	The court cases are constantly changing the rules for stock trader qualification so be sure your tax advisor researches these cases each year you want to qualify as a trader.

Due to the complexity of these special rules, please be sure to work with a qualified tax advisor in your country to determine whether you qualify. Here are the rules in the United States for determining trade status.

There are three primary qualifications you must meet to be a trader. These rules are challenging because they are not specified anywhere in the actual tax code. Instead, the courts have handed them down over the years—and they keep changing. So you will have to work with your tax advisor very closely to determine whether your facts and circumstances make you a trader or to determine what changes in your activities are needed to qualify for the trader tax benefits.

The first general rule for traders relates to the volume of your trading activities. Volume means both the number of trades you make and the dollar amount of your trades. If you trade constantly throughout the day, you have a much better argument that you qualify as a trader than if you trade only a couple of times a week. Even a couple of trades a day aren't enough to make you a trader. Likewise, your trades have to be a significant dollar amount. There is no specific dollar amount that qualifies. It's just the more the better. So $1 million in trades in a week may qualify but $10,000 clearly doesn't.

The second general rule for traders relates to the amount of time you spend trading. The more time you spend trading, the more your trading looks like your primary income activity. Under the current court cases, an hour a day probably isn't enough. Even 3-to- 4 hours per day might not be enough. Whether you spend enough time to be a trader is also impacted by the third rule.

The third general rule for traders relates to the impact your trading has on your income. Is your income from trading significant when compared to your total income? If your trading income only represents 10 percent of your total income, it probably doesn't matter how much time you spend trading or how many trades you make. By definition, a trader is someone very good at trading and who makes a significant portion of their income trading.

Three Rules to Qualify as a Stock Trader	
1.	The volume of trading activities must be significant in both number of trades and dollar amount of trades.
2.	The time spent on your trading activity must be a significant part of the day.
3.	The income resulted from your trading activity must be a significant portion of your income.

Look at the general definition of a trade and you will probably do okay. You wouldn't call someone a professional bricklayer who only does the occasional project in the backyard. Nor would you call someone a professional electrician who does odd jobs for a little extra money. A true tradesman is someone who is a real professional, constantly working at and honing a trade. So once you become a truly professional trader, consistently making money and spending serious time and effort on trading, then you will likely be considered a trader for tax purposes.

Additional tax benefits for traders

There are many other benefits for serious stock and option traders as well. In the United States, certain option traders get to treat 60 percent of their income as long-term capital gains taxed at the lower rates even if all of their trades happen in less than a year. Traders in futures and foreign exchange may also qualify for this tax benefit.

Those of you who decide to become professional traders in these complex areas of finance will definitely need to work with a highly trained tax advisor who clearly understands the law. If you are interested in learning more about stock and option trading, trading in futures, and foreign exchange trading, talk to my friends at Rich Dad. They have a great program to teach people how to become professional traders. Go to taxfreewealthbook.com to find out more about their programs.

Next we will take a look at the tax benefits of investing in commodities, such as oil and gas, agriculture, and precious metals.

CHAPTER 20: KEY POINTS	
1.	Understanding the tax implications in stock trading can produce major tax benefits.
2.	The rules to qualify as a trader can be complex, work with your tax advisor to determine whether your facts and circumstances qualify for the trader tax benefits.

Tax Strategy #20 – Do Your Stock Trading inside a Self-directed Roth IRA

In Chapter 17, we discussed all the reasons why I don't like government-qualified retirement plans. One of the few times these types of plans make sense is when you trade stocks or options. And they're especially good if you don't qualify as a trader.

Remember when we talked about prohibited transactions in an IRA? One of the prohibited transactions is performing services for your IRA. An exception to this rule is directing the investments of the IRA. You are allowed, in a self-directed IRA, to direct which assets the IRA buys and which assets it sells. You can also direct when to buy and sell an asset.

When you trade stocks and options, all you're doing is directing which assets are bought and sold, and the timing of those purchases and sales. You could do this by going into your IRA administrator's website. But there is a much easier way to do it.

What if you have the IRA set up a limited liability company (LLC) that has a brokerage account? As long as you only direct the investments and don't put any money in or take any money out of the account, you can personally run the brokerage account. This gives you the access you need to buy and sell stocks or trade options on a daily basis.

Since stock and option trades are treated as short-term capital gains, if you were to trade them outside of your IRA, they would be taxed at ordinary income tax rates. So you don't give anything up by trading inside an IRA. You simply postpone paying the tax on the investment gains.

Even better is trading stocks and options inside a self-directed Roth IRA. When you do this, none of the gains are taxable—ever! How cool is that? Of course, remember that you are limited on when you can take the money out, so don't depend on the income from the stock and option trading inside your IRA while you are under 59½ years old. This is retirement income, and you should trade accordingly.

If you have money inside a 401(k) or an IRA, and your wealth strategy includes stock and option trading, consider rolling your 401(k) or IRA into a self-directed IRA and doing some of your trading inside your self-directed IRA. And consider converting your regular IRA to a Roth IRA before you start trading so that you can avoid tax on all of the gains from trading.

Chapter Twenty-One

Commodities Can Be Your Tax Friend

"Formula for success: rise early, work hard, strike oil."
– J. Paul Getty

I was earning my Masters of Professional Accounting degree at the University of Texas during the height of the 1980's oil and gas boom. Texas oil was doing so well that the Midland, Texas office one of the Big 8 (now it's the Big 4) accounting firms was hiring my program's graduates sight unseen. They wanted as many newly minted accountants as they could get.

Naturally, I decided to learn something about oil and gas. I took a class called "Oil and Gas Law." I liked that class and also took the "Real Estate Law" class. This education turned out to be particularly helpful when I graduated and took my first job at Ernst & Whinney (now Ernst Young) in Salt Lake City, Utah.

Salt Lake City was experiencing its own little natural resources boom. It boasted the largest open-pit copper mine in the world at the time (Kennecott) and was mining a lot of silver—and nearby Eastern Utah, Wyoming, and Colorado were experiencing a boom in natural gas. There was a huge natural gas find in that part of the country, and gas prices were high enough to make a lot of farmers and ranchers very wealthy, much like the ranchers in Texas got wealthy (and continue to get wealthy) from oil.

After graduation, I found that a lot of my time was spent doing tax work for mining concerns and oil developers. One of our individual tax clients owned interests in over 300 oil and gas wells. It was my job to keep track of all of the income and expenses for these wells. This was before personal computers, so we did all of it on huge spreadsheets by hand.

Soon after I was hired, the firm bought two Apple computers; one for the audit side of the practice and one for the tax side. I discovered the great benefit of using VisiCalc™, the first spreadsheet program for personal computers. I put the information from all of the clients who had oil and gas investments into a VisiCalc™ spreadsheet so that we didn't have to do it by hand any longer. What a huge time saver that was. These days, no one would ever consider doing a project like that by hand.

There was a benefit, however, to being so intimately involved in the numbers and doing them by hand. I came to really understand the tax benefits of investing in oil and gas and other minerals. In the United States, the benefits of investing in oil and gas drilling programs are enormous. Let me explain.

Oil and gas tax benefits

The United States has long held an energy policy promoting oil and gas drilling operations inside the borders of the United States to help reduce dependence on foreign oil. The government has put this into action through the tax law by providing significant tax benefits for anyone who invests in domestic (U.S.-based) oil and gas drilling operations.

In the US, oil and gas is one of the truly great tax shelters. Remember the discussion about passive income and passive losses earlier in the book? Oil and gas is the only investment that is not subject to these rules. That's right—if you invest right, you can deduct losses from oil and gas against ordinary income, even though your investment is entirely passive.

In the U.S., oil and gas is one of the truly great tax shelters.

TAX TIP: Invest in oil and gas and you can avoid passive loss rules. Oil and gas is the only investment where you aren't subject to the rules that limit losses from passive investments.

There are four types of investment in oil and gas. The first is to buy stock in an oil and gas company. This is treated like any other stock investment and has no special rules or benefits. Second, you can buy an interest in the royalties from a producing oil and gas well. This income is subject to a 15% depletion allowance, so only 85% of the income is taxed.

The other two types of investments in oil and gas are both investments in the actual drilling operation—and they provide great tax benefits. You can either invest in exploratory operations, also called "wildcat" drilling, or you can invest in development operations. Exploratory operations can be very risky, as there is no assurance that there is oil in the ground where you are drilling. Of course, with better and better technology, this risk is always decreasing with the better operators.

Development wells are drilled in established oil fields where the reserves of oil are proven. The developer may need more money to drill additional wells to get more oil out of the ground. This tends to be less risky than the exploratory drilling, though you can still lose your money. I once invested in a development well where the developer had absolute proof of huge reserves. The only problem was that we couldn't get to the oil. So, we lost our investment.

Four Types of Oil and Gas Investments		
	Type	**Tax Benefits**
1.	Buy stock in an oil and gas company.	No
2.	Buy an interest in the royalties from a producing oil and gas well.	No
3.	Invest in exploratory operations, also called "wildcat" drilling.	Yes
4.	Invest in development operations.	Yes

When a development company drills for oil and gas, it has two main categories of expense. The first is the equipment it purchases to drill. This is usually about 30 percent of the cost of drilling a well. The second is intangible drilling costs (IDC). IDC includes all of the other drilling expenses, including labor, survey work, ground clearing, drainage, fuel, and repairs.

These expenses normally would be a cost of the well and would be depreciated or amortized over the life of the well. However, Congress decided to allow people to deduct both their IDC and their equipment costs in the year they spend the money, which is usually the first year of investment in the drilling operation. That means that 100 percent of your investment is typically allowed as a deduction in the year that you make your investment in the drilling operation. If you invest $100,000, you get a deduction for $100,000 the first year. At a 40 percent tax rate, that's equivalent of the government immediately giving you $40,000 ($100,000 x 40%) for investing in the oil and gas operation.

This isn't the only tax benefit for investing in oil and gas. You also get to deduct 15 percent of the well's gross income each year. This is called depletion. It's like depreciation, only you get it every year, even after you have deducted all of the IDC and the equipment costs. Basically, it's a gift from the government. Gross income for depletion purposes includes all of the sales proceeds from the oil and gas, and isn't reduced by any expenses. So, you could have $1,000 of gross income, and expenses of $400, for net income of $600. You would then get a depletion deduction of $150 ($1,000 x 15%) and only pay tax on $450 of income ($600 less $150 depletion).

Tax Benefits for Investing in Oil and Gas	
1.	Deduction of intangible drilling cost and equipment, usually the first year of investment of drilling operations.
2.	Deduct 15% of the gross income from the well each year (called depletion).

In order to qualify for IDC, equipment and depletion deductions, you have to own a direct interest in the drilling operations. Owning stock in the drilling company or owning a royalty interest in the oil and gas doesn't qualify. Be sure to meet with your tax advisor about this before you invest in oil and gas. And one other thing, in order to get all of the IDC and equipment deductions to which you are entitled, you have to own your investment through a general partnership or sole proprietorship. You can't own it through a corporation, LLC, or limited partnership. If you live outside the United States, be sure to check on your country's tax laws to find out what tax benefits they allow.

CAUTION!

Be Careful Which Entity You Use for Oil and Gas Investments	
1.	You can lose your tax benefits from oil and gas simply by using the wrong entity.
2.	There may be a trade off between asset protection and tax benefits when investing in oil and gas.

Mining and tax benefits

Mining operations have similar tax benefits to oil and gas development. You get depletion on the gross income from selling the minerals, and there is special treatment for the mining operation development expenses, much like IDC as well as deductions for equipment. Be sure to ask your tax advisor about which mining industries in your country get special tax benefits. One country may give tax benefits to coal, while others give special treatment to oil and gas, gypsum, or other minerals.

Renewable energy tax benefits

Another type of energy that gets special tax benefits in most countries is renewable energy. Renewable energy includes wind turbines, solar energy, and electric cars. Governments love to encourage investment in new sources of energy. Tax benefits include investment tax credits for investing in wind turbines (windmills), credits for buying solar panels, and credits for buying electric cars or even for buying hybrid gas/electric cars. Some U.S. states also provide huge tax credits for investing in solar energy. And, so long as the equipment is used in business, 100% is deductible in the year it is purchased.

Agricultural tax benefits

Every country has a special interest in producing as much local food as possible. The government doesn't want to rely on importing food from other countries. And, like oil and gas, agriculture is a very risky business. To encourage investment in agriculture, the government gives special tax breaks. There are so many tax breaks for agriculture that I could write an entire book about them. Instead, let's just focus on a few of the more important tax benefits for investing in agriculture.

The most important tax benefit is the tax deduction for all of the expenses of running a farm, orchard, or ranch. This includes feed for livestock, seeds, and labor. So, you don't have to add any of these costs to your inventory (crops or livestock). You get to deduct them whenever you spend the money on them.

The depreciation rules also favor agriculture. Depending on the country, you may get to take a faster deduction for farm equipment than you do for other types of equipment. Currently in the United States, 100% of the cost of the equipment is deductible in the year you acquire it. And some of the income from your farming operations may not be taxable or can be taxable in a later year if earned through cooperatives.

Farms also get special treatment for estate tax purposes, as well. You may get to reduce the amount of estate tax you pay when you inherit a farm or may get to pay the estate tax over several years. The government wants to keep farms and ranches in business, so they give you tax breaks so that you don't have to sell the farm to pay taxes.

When you decide to invest in agriculture, be sure to look for special tax breaks for certain crops. In the United States, for example, citrus groves get specific tax breaks. Every country has its special interest groups in agriculture that get the government to provide tax breaks for a variety of farming, orchards, and ranches.

Tax Benefits for Investing in Agriculture
1. Deduction of expenses for running the farm, orchard, or ranch.
2. Depreciation deduction or full expensing for equipment.
3. Special treatment for estate tax.
4. Special tax breaks for certain crops.

Precious metal tax benefits

Another commodity that has special tax breaks in some countries is precious metals, such as gold and silver. When you own gold and silver, you probably own it as insurance against inflation. So, you're going to own it for several years. When you sell your investment in gold and silver, the gain should be treated as capital gain. Some countries, as we mentioned, don't tax capital gains, while others have special, lower rates for long-term capital gains.

United States tax policy doesn't promote ownership of gold and silver. Instead, investment in precious metals are discouraged by providing a special, higher tax rate than other long-term capital gains tax rates. At the writing of this book, the capital gains rate for gold and silver in the United States is 28 percent—almost double the rate for other capital gains. So, you may want to own your gold and silver inside your IRA or pension plan. Since you will own the metal for a long time and the tax is pretty close to ordinary tax rates, you might as well postpone the tax through a government-qualified retirement plan. And if you own it through a Roth IRA, you will never pay tax on the increase in value of your gold and silver.

In the next chapter, I'm going to show you how to properly prepare for and handle a tax audit so that you never again have to be afraid of being audited.

CHAPTER 21: KEY POINTS

1.	There are significant tax benefits in the United States for investing in oil and gas drilling operations to encourage the reduction and dependence of foreign oil.
2.	You not only get to deduct the intangible drilling cost the first year in an oil and gas drilling operation, you get to deduct 15% of the gross income from the well each year.
3.	Agriculture has special tax benefits that include 1031 exchanges, depreciation, estate tax rules and special rules for certain crops.

Tax Strategy #21 – Avoid the Passive Loss Rules on Oil and Gas Investments

Remember from Chapter 8 that when you don't actively participate in a business, the income and losses from that business are treated as passive income and passive losses. When you invest in oil and gas development, you probably won't actively participate. And in the first year, you'll share in a tax loss of 100 percent of your original investment. These losses will be passive and can only offset passive income, right? Wrong.

There is an exception to the passive loss rules for oil and gas. Even though you don't actively participate in the business, losses from oil and gas are treated as ordinary losses and you can take 100 percent of your losses against any kind of income. But in order for your losses to be ordinary, you have to be very careful about how you own your oil and gas investment.

You have to own your interest in the oil and gas development outright. You cannot own it through an LLC, LP (limited partnership), or any other entity that limits your liability. Instead, you have to rely on the developer's insurance to protect you from any lawsuits or disasters. Usually, the developer will form a partnership for the investors and everyone will be a general partner for the first year or two.

In the second or third year that you own the investment, when the well begins to produce taxable income, you can change your ownership to a limited partnership or LLC to protect you from future liability. Good oil and gas developers will automatically change your ownership from a general partner to a limited partner as soon as the investment begins earning income. So, your liability is only for the year or two that the developer is actually drilling the well.

Chapter Twenty-Two

Don't Fear the ~~Reaper~~ Audit

"The more you earn, the less you keep,
And now I lay me down to sleep.
I pray the Lord my soul to take,
If the tax collector hasn't got it before I wake."
– Ogden Nash

When I was growing up, my dad was the Scoutmaster for our local Boy Scout troop for 12 years. He was very busy running his printing business, and because of that he only took a one-week vacation each year—and that one-week vacation was taken with the Boy Scouts at summer camp.

Since this was the only vacation the family got with Dad, we'd pack up the trailer and head off to summer camp with him every year. He'd take care of the Boy Scouts while we did pretty much whatever we wanted to do. I have a lot of fond memories of our weeks at that camp.

But I have one memory that isn't so fond. It was during a week that we were at New Fork Scout Camp. I was about five years old at the time, and one night, while we were out walking, a big black bear wandered through camp. He was huge, especially to a five-year-old. I ran as fast as I could back to the trailer, my heart pounding and my eyes wide. I've never been as scared of anything in my life as I was of that bear. I thought for sure I was going to die.

As adults, we tend to be afraid of many things that seem even worse than that big black bear. For many people, the worst of these is the tax collector. In the United States, it's the dreaded Internal Revenue Service (IRS). In Canada, it's the Canada Revenue Agency (CRA). In Australia, it's the Australian Taxation Office (ATO). And in Great Britain, it's Her Majesty's Revenue & Customs (HMRC). Whatever country you're in and whatever the name of the tax collector, it's downright scary for most people to think about having their tax returns audited.

What makes us so afraid of a tax audit? Like me with the bear, we're afraid of being attacked. What could be worse than an attack by a tax auditor? They certainly can seem big and scary.

In reality, tax auditors are just normal people doing their job. Like bears, they won't attack unless provoked. And if you're well prepared before you run into them, even the toughest auditor won't scare you in the least.

RULE #19:	You can eliminate your fear of a tax audit simply by being prepared.

Let's take a look at the steps you can take to prepare for a tax audit, the best ways to handle an audit if one happens, and a few simple steps you can take to reduce your chances of an audit. This way, you'll be prepared and, unlike me with the bear, you'll have a good idea of what to do if you happen to run into a big bad auditor.

Preparing for a Tax Audit

Being prepared for a tax audit begins by deciding how you are going to handle the audit before it even comes. My challenge with the bear was that I was totally unprepared for it. So my only alternative was to run away and hope the bear didn't chase me and hope the bear couldn't get into our trailer. But hope alone is never the best option. Being prepared on all sides is best.

TAX TIP:	Purchase an audit defense plan every year. Some tax preparers offer an audit defense plan. This is a powerful way to keep a strong handle on your out-of-pocket costs and take the worry out of the cost of professional fees during an audit.

Your Tax Team

The first and most important defense against a tax audit is to have the right team in place. This begins with your tax advisor, who should also be your tax preparer. Your tax advisor is the person who should be on the front lines confronting the auditor. Imagine if I had had a big game hunter by my side when that black bear came by in the camp. I would have been a lot less frightened and in a lot less danger of attack. My hunter would have known what to do to scare off the bear and would have been prepared with the right ammunition in case the bear attacked. I could have calmly walked away while the hunter was dealing with the bear.

The same is true with a tax audit. Having a big game hunter of a tax advisor by your side, one who has seen a lot of auditors and been successful in handling many audits, is a powerful tool for reducing your stress and increasing your success on an audit. In fact, your tax advisor should be the only person directly dealing with the auditor. We will talk about how your advisor should handle the audit later on in this chapter and how to choose a great tax advisor in the next chapter.

Handling an Audit Is About Handling the Auditor	
1.	How your tax advisor works with your tax auditor will have a huge impact on the outcome of the audit.
2.	Be sure your tax advisor has good personal skills and treats all people with respect, especially government auditors.

Another team member you need on your side is a good bookkeeper. This person does not have to be your tax advisor/preparer. In fact, if your tax advisor is also doing your bookkeeping, then there is a good chance that you have a squirrel hunter on your team, not a big game hunter. Your bookkeeper is going to help you keep all of your records and documentation so you can be well prepared for the audit with accurate information. Let's talk about what documentation you are going to need for an audit.

Documentation

There are only two logical ways to prepare your documentation for an IRS or other tax audit. You can either be extremely prepared with all of the materials and documents that you need, or you can have no information whatsoever. Having no information is one way to go, because it will frustrate the tax auditor and give him or her nothing to look at. I don't recommend it. By not having the materials to support what you reported on your tax return, you're telling the auditor that you're sloppy, unorganized, and possibly lying.

The better solution is to be well prepared. And that's really not that difficult to do. It's particularly easy if you know what things you need to keep records of and how to keep those records organized. It all begins with whenever you spend or earn money. Most of the time, a tax audit is going to focus on whether you reported all of your income and whether you took only those deductions that you were allowed under the law.

Accounting Software

Step one in preparing for an audit is to record all of your income and expenses in good accounting software on your computer. There are lots of good choices. Be sure you choose software that will give you both an income statement and a balance sheet. Some software only gives you an income statement. An income statement only shows your income and your expenses. The balance sheet is what helps you be sure that your numbers are accurate. Balance sheets show your assets (what you own), your liabilities (what you owe), and your equity (the difference between your assets and your liabilities).

> *Step one in preparing for an audit is to record all of your income and expenses in good accounting software on your computer.*

If the government is auditing your business, one of the first things the auditor will ask for is your income statement and balance sheet. Having these readily available tells the auditor that you're serious about keeping good records and that you treat your business like a real business, not like a hobby.

I also advise my clients to record their personal income and expenses in the same type of accounting software. It is not only helpful for an audit but also gives you lots of good information about your income and your spending habits. Most software of this nature will also allow you to create a budget or forecast, can give you reports on where your income came from, and can compare income and expenses between years so that you know how you're doing. It's like a financial report card.

Receipts

One of the questions I get most often is about keeping receipts. The general rule is that you need receipts for any deduction you take on your return. Certain types of deductions require even more information than just a receipt. Deductions for meals and travel, for example, require a note on the receipt about who you were with, the business nature of your relationship, where you were, and what you discussed. I suggest you simply note that information on the receipt right when you get it.

There are a couple of different ways to store your receipts. My favorite is scanning the receipts into your computer. This way, you always have them at your fingertips if you need them, and they don't take up space in your office. If you want to keep the paper receipts, then just make file folders for each type of expense. Every time you spend money, you put the receipts into the proper folder. Then, when you go to prepare your tax returns, you know just where they are. You also know where they are if you're audited.

Another question I'm often asked about is how long to keep the receipts and other tax records. In the United States, the rule of thumb is seven years. In Canada, the rule is six years. Great Britain and Australia suggest you keep them for five years. I haven't found any country that suggests you keep them longer than seven years. If in doubt, check with your tax advisor.

Corporate Books

There are other documents you need to have available besides receipts and your bookkeeping records. You should always keep any contracts or other legal documents in a safe and secure place that's easily accessed. Of course, you need to keep your copy of your tax returns. And for your business, you should keep a corporate book.

Corporate books are a little like having a magic wand in an audit. You wave the magic wand and the auditor disappears. A corporate book is simply a binder that has all of the corporate records. Included in the corporate book are your articles of incorporation or organization, your by-laws, operating or partnership agreement, and minutes for any shareholder or director meetings that you hold. You should have a corporate book no matter what type of entity you own, even if it's not a corporation.

Minutes are simply notes from a meeting. You can write them in pen or record them on your computer. The notes should

Corporate books are a little like having a magic wand in an audit. You wave the magic wand and the auditor disappears.

report any major decisions that you make in your company, including the amount of dividends or other distributions you decide to pay out to your shareholders. Any big tax decisions should also go in your minutes. At my accounting firm, we send out items to be included in our clients' corporate minutes with their completed tax returns.

Tax auditors always ask for a corporate book. They're amazed when we actually give them one and it's in good order. Apparently, lots of business owners don't keep their corporate books in good order. A complete corporate book tells the auditor that you care about your business and that your records are probably complete. The real benefit of this and other good records is that the auditor will tend to believe your tax return and won't ask for as much other support for your taxes. It takes a lot less time to finish the audit, and because the auditor isn't looking as hard, they likely won't question much. That means that the auditor is likely to go away that much sooner.

Preparing for an Audit	
Step 1	Maintain organized bookkeeping records.
a.	Use good accounting software.
b.	Record your business income and expenses.
c.	Prepare income statements (timely updates).
d.	Prepare balance sheets (timely updates).
e.	Record your personal income and expenses.
f.	Create budgets and forecasts.
g.	Create reports.
h.	Compare income and expenses between years.
Step 2	Maintain and organize receipts.
a.	Keep receipts for deductions you intend to take on your tax return.
b.	Scan receipts into organized files in your computer.
c.	Or create separate paper file folders for each type of receipt.
d.	Maintain receipts for 7 years (United States), 6 years (Canada), 5 years (Great Britain and Australia).
Step 3	Be prepared with other documents.
a.	Legal contracts or agreements
b.	Copies of tax returns
c.	Corporate books (for your business) that include:
i.	Articles of Incorporation or Organization
ii.	Operating or Partnership Agreement
iii.	By-Laws
iv.	Minutes

Handling an Audit

Handling an actual tax audit is easier than you might think when you have the right tax advisor on your team. The reason for this is that you aren't going to be the one handling your audit. That's a job for your tax advisor.

> **RULE #20:** **Never try to handle a tax audit yourself. Always enlist the assistance of your tax advisor.**

There are many good reasons for you to turn over an audit to your tax advisor. First, an audit can be a pretty emotional experience if handled by you. Turning an audit over to your tax advisor will save you time and energy because you won't have to deal with the auditor. You'll still be involved, but only to gather information for your advisor.

Experienced tax advisors are comfortable working with auditors. Since it's not our money, we're less emotionally tied to it. Just like a big game hunter is not afraid of a bear, an experienced tax advisor has no fear of an auditor. That's a good thing, because *handling the auditor is the most important part of*

> *...handling the auditor is the most important part of an audit. And you can't handle an auditor well when you're emotionally involved in the audit.*

an audit. And you can't handle an auditor well when you're emotionally involved in the audit. This doesn't mean that your advisor doesn't care about the outcome. He just cares on a more professional level and less on an emotional level.

I make it a practice never to allow a client to meet the auditor. This way, if the auditor asks me a question, I can say, "I don't know." If a client is in the meeting with the auditor, it becomes a little suspicious for the client to say they don't know the answer to the question. When I'm the only person interfacing with an auditor, I can ask him to clarify what information he really needs and then give him only the information that answers his questions. I find that taxpayers who don't turn over the audit to their advisor will give the auditor much more information than is necessary. This extends the length of the audit and gives the auditor more to dig into—and to come up with more deductions to disallow.

It's critical that your tax advisor controls the audit instead of the auditor. This means controlling what information is given to the auditor as well as the pace of the audit. I find that some auditors like to drag out audits for months and months. Some audits can even go on for years. When I'm in control of the audit, I can usually speed things up, and I can narrow the scope of what the auditor is looking at.

One of the most important things I do in audits is to make the auditors feel comfortable. I want them to see that we're willing to work with them and treat them well. A couple of years ago I represented a client in an IRS audit. The auditor had first audited the client's business. The client owned only a small part of the business, so his partners' advisor handled the business audit.

In our first meeting, I tried to put the auditor at ease because she was very tense when she first walked in. I greeted her and asked how long she'd been an auditor. I then asked her how things went with the audit of the business, and she opened up to me. She said the accountant who'd handled that audit was very mean. In fact, she confided that he'd made her cry, and she was a pretty tough cookie. He must have been really harsh to make a tax auditor cry.

Clearly, that accountant took the approach that the auditor was the enemy. I took a different approach. I looked at the auditor as someone with a tough job to do, and I was going to help her get it done. The result was that the auditor was very open and honest with me about the things for which she was looking. She even told me what we needed to do in order for the audit to succeed.

In turn, I helped her. I explained the law very clearly as I understood it and showed her how it worked in the taxpayer's favor. She was very appreciative of this explanation. I had much more experience and education than she did, and my willingness to share this with her made a big impression on her. In the end, she asked me to write up her report for her explaining why the client should win the audit. Of course, I was very happy to do this.

In 30 years, I've only found two auditors who really were impossible to work with. One was not very bright, and the other was just belligerent. Still, I worked with them as a respected adversary, and the results both turned in the client's favor.

Your Tax Return Preparation

The last topic we need to discuss about getting ready for an audit is your tax return. Your tax return is the reason you're being audited in the first place. So you should make sure it's prepared well so that the audit goes more smoothly. Ideally, your tax return shouldn't raise any red flags.

> *Your tax return is the reason you are being audited. So you should make sure it's prepared well so that the audit goes more smoothly.*

A while back, I did some training with my tax staff. I asked them to list all of the things they do on a tax return to either reduce taxes or reduce the likelihood of an audit. I thought they might come up with five or six items. Instead, they came up with over 60 specific items.

I'll share just a few of the ways to reduce the chance of an audit on your tax return. One way is to look at how you name your deductions. Let's say you paid $10,000 last year to attend seminars. Seminars may or may not be deductible, depending on your business and why you took the seminar. The IRS pays close attention to this deduction. So what you call the deduction on your tax return is important. Instead of listing the expense as a seminar, why not list it as continuing education? Or, if you went primarily to network and market yourself to the other participants, why not call it a sales or marketing expense?

You're still telling the truth and reporting your seminar expense accurately. Only now you aren't raising a red flag and inviting the government to come audit you.

A good tax preparer knows all of these tricks and more. And he'll take additional time to make sure deductions and income are listed on your tax return in such a way that they won't raise a red flag to the government authorities and may actually reduce your taxes.

So I hope you now see that tax audits don't have to be that scary. You just have to remember to do three things:

1.	Prepare for the audit.
2.	Let your tax advisor handle the audit.
3.	Use a tax preparer who knows how to reduce the risk of an audit.

Another question people ask me all the time is how to find a good tax advisor and tax preparer. We'll talk about this in the next chapter, because it may be the single most important thing you can do to reduce your taxes and limit your risk of an audit.

CHAPTER 22: KEY POINTS

1.	One of the biggest fears people have is their tax authority auditing them. There is nothing to fear if you are well prepared.
2.	To be well prepared it's important to keep organized and accurate records of your spending and income as well as to utilize comprehensive accounting software.
3.	Because people are generally emotionally attached to their money, it's imperative that they allow a tax professional to handle their audit in order to eliminate the possibility of giving the auditor too much information.
4.	The best way to avoid an audit is to make sure your tax returns are prepared by a tax professional who knows how to eliminate possible red flags for an auditor.

Tax Strategy #22 – Purchasing an Audit Defense Plan

At Tax-Free Wealth Network™ firms, if we prepare your tax return, you can purchase an audit defense plan for that specific tax return. The cost is a percentage of the tax return preparation fee and covers the cost of representing you in an audit for that specific tax return. If you're audited, you don't have to pay for the time it takes us to defend your audit.

Most people don't realize that the most expensive part of an IRS audit can be the professional fees you pay to defend the audit. A typical audit can run $10,000 to $15,000 in professional fees. You may not pay any tax at all, and yet you still lose because of the cost of the professional fees.

It makes sense to be insured against the cost of the audit. You wouldn't go without car insurance. And yet, it's pretty unlikely that you will be in an automobile accident that costs more than $5,000. So why wouldn't you insure yourself against the cost of an audit that is more likely than an auto accident—and more costly?

An audit defense plan won't insure you against the taxes and interest you might owe, but it will protect you against the cost of defending yourself against the IRS. This is especially important because in an IRS audit, you are guilty until proven innocent. So you need to have the best tax advisor possible to defend you, and that means high professional fees if you don't have insurance in the form of an audit defense plan.

Chapter Twenty-Three

Choose the Right Tax Advisor and Preparer

"Day in and day out, your tax accountant can make or lose you more money than any single person in your life, with the possible exception of your kids."
-- *Harvey Mackay*

The first time I learned about the law was in my business law course in college. One of the local bankruptcy judges taught the course. He was a terrific instructor, and I loved the class. I especially loved learning about how vague the law can be. I'd learned many years earlier that something vague allowed for much more flexibility than something specific and certain. And I liked knowing that the law was flexible.

Like most children, I discovered early on how to manipulate my parents. Sometimes that meant using my mother to persuade my father to let me go somewhere he might not otherwise have allowed. Other times that meant pretending not to hear when they wanted me to do something. Most of the time it simply meant twisting the meaning of what they told me into what I wanted to hear. Then, after I did something they didn't like, I used their words to convince them they'd really allowed me to do it.

Perhaps I was always meant to study the law so that I could use it to my client's advantage. That first business law class really set me on my path to studying the tax law. I was so excited to learn the law that my junior year I signed up to take all of the tax classes available at the University of Utah School of Business. Most of my classmates were waiting to take their tax classes until their senior year, but those classes were so interesting to me that I couldn't wait. To do this, I had to push all of my other upper-division accounting classes to my senior year. I even remember taking both intermediate accounting courses the same semester so that I could fit all those upper-level classes in as a senior. All that work was worth it to me.

The "U" business school had a terrific tax professor, Professor Haney. He was a tax attorney who practiced law full time and taught tax classes on the side. He was demanding, but he understood the law well and was enthusiastic about the subject. When I was thinking about graduate school, the first person I talked to other than my wife was Professor Haney.

I asked him whether I should go to law school or get a master's degree in tax accounting. He told me that if I wanted to spend most of my time working in tax law, I would be better off practicing as a Certified Public Accountant. In his experience, CPAs spent more time doing tax work than lawyers. So on Professor Haney's advice I applied to the University of Texas Master's of Professional Accounting Program.

Since then, I have devoted my life to studying the tax law, teaching the tax law, and using the tax law to help my clients reduce their tax burdens. And taxes really are a burden. As Benjamin Franklin once said, "It would be a hard government that should tax its people one-tenth part of their income." And yet governments throughout the world now routinely take 40 to 50 percent of a person's income.

If you haven't noticed yet, I'm pretty passionate about reducing taxes. And passion is the most important element in reducing your taxes.

RULE #21: **The more passionate you and your advisor are about reducing your taxes, the lower your taxes will be.**

Every time I speak at a seminar, I'm asked the same question over and over again, "How do I find a good tax advisor?" This is one of the most important questions you can ever ask. A good tax advisor will not only help you reduce your taxes but he'll take the fear out of taxes as well. And most importantly, he'll take the fear out of a tax audit.

I'm asked the same question over and over again, "How do I find a good tax advisor?" This is one of the most important questions you can ever ask.

But being passionate about reducing your taxes is only one of the traits to look for in a good tax advisor. Another is how the advisor looks at the tax law. Is the advisor afraid of the law or does he look at it as an opportunity? Most tax accountants are afraid of the law. They won't even read it. Instead, they read an abbreviated version of the law, such as a simple tax guide. These accountants shy away from anything they don't understand, and they don't understand much.

They shy away from the law because they have never taken the time to learn the law. There is as wide a variety of education among tax advisors and tax preparers as there is among doctors, lawyers, and other professionals. Some tax preparers have only taken a few hours or a few weeks of courses to learn how to prepare tax returns. Others have some schooling, though not very much. It's only the best advisors who have graduated at the top of their classes from the best universities who really understand the tax law. The reason they attended the top schools and graduated at the top of their classes is that they wanted to learn the tax law and all of its intricacies. Like me, they crave learning about the law. The hierarchy of tax preparers is pretty simple—it's based on their level of education, both formal and practical.

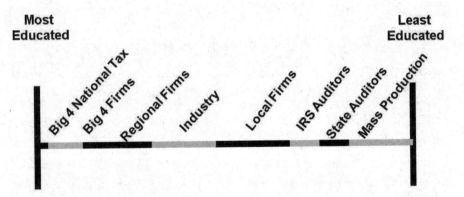

As a result, most accountants, those with less education and understanding, will only take the most obvious deductions and tax benefits when they prepare your returns. And likely you'll only talk to them once or twice a year because they don't have much to tell you. They're likely to make suggestions like maximizing your IRA, RRSP, or 401(k)

contribution. They'll tell you to prepay expenses at the end of the year. Or they'll suggest waiting until a later year to receive some income that you're owed.

What terrible advice. Did you notice how all of this advice is about saving taxes now at the cost of having to pay them later? These accountants are all about tax savings now at the cost of your future. Once, during a training meeting, I asked our staff to explain what's different about our Tax-Free Wealth Network™ firms, from other CPA firms. Our youngest staff member, right out of college, gave the most insightful answer. She said that she never expected to be working for a firm that focuses on its clients' future rather than dwelling on their past. One of the reasons most tax preparers don't focus on permanent tax savings is because they are only focused on the past and the present. They aren't taking into account your future.

Why do people hire accountants and advisors with such little understanding? Maybe it's because they don't know what to look for in a tax advisor. Or maybe it's just because these preparers and advisors tend to charge less money for their work. What a mistake to hire someone because they charge less than somebody else. The real test of an advisor is not how much they charge you, but how much they cost you.

> **RULE #22:** It's not how much your tax preparer charges you that matters; it's how much your tax preparer costs you.

Let me give you an example. One of our clients, let's call her Jill, recently reminded me about the amount of taxes we save her each year. Because of our understanding of the law, we've been able to save her $70,000 each year. Invested at 10 percent over 20 years, that amounts to about $4 million in money that she wouldn't have had if she'd stayed with her previous tax advisor. In other words, her previous advisor cost her $4 million over the previous 20 years. Yes, he charged less than my Tax-Free Wealth Network™ firm. We charged about $20,000 to do the tax planning for Jill. But that $20,000 was the best investment Jill has ever made. Her return on investment (ROI) amounts to 350 percent per year. And, since these are income taxes she is getting back, they aren't even taxable. How would you like a 350 percent tax-free return on a $20,000 investment?

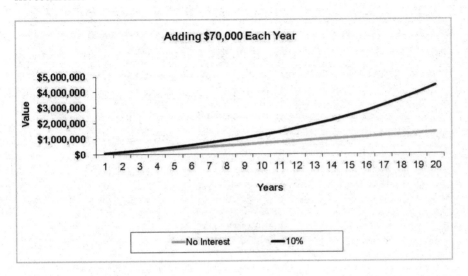

Not every client is going to save $70,000 each year in taxes. Some will save more and some will save less. And fees vary from client to client as well. The key here is to ask which accountant cost Jill more money? The one whom she paid less and who cost her $4 million, or the one whom she paid more and saved $70,000 per year? Pretty obvious, isn't it? Yet most people continue to look at how much their preparer charges rather than how much their tax preparer costs them in excess taxes.

Another tendency for tax accountants is to look at the law as if it runs in a straight line. We call these types of folks linear or left-brained thinkers. Most accountants are like this. They decided to be accountants because they like the certainty and clarity of figures. They generally don't become accountants because they like the vagueness of the law. These tax accountants do okay with routine work such as preparing an accurate tax return. What they won't do is figure out creative ways to use the law in your favor. The challenge is that accountants don't write the tax law. Good tax lawyers hired by congressmen and MPs (Members of Parliament) write the law to carry out those politicians' desires to improve the economy, encourage certain industries, and maintain government revenues. These lawyers tend to not think in a straight line. They're what we would call nonlinear or right-brained thinkers.

The tax laws aren't written in a straight line. The rules of one section of the law will impact the rules of another section of the law, and the connection isn't always obvious. On top of this, there are many interpretations of the law that come from judges in court cases. It's critical that your tax advisor looks at all of the law when figuring out how to best reduce your taxes. If he or she only looks at a single rule, he or she could easily miss out on four or five other rules that could save you money.

Not All Tax Advisors Are Created Equal	
1.	Tax advisors vary in knowledge and experience even more than health care professionals.
2.	Your tax bill will have more to do with choosing your tax advisor than anything else you do.

Of course, the most important trait for your tax advisor is that he or she cares more about you than he or she does about himself or herself. How can you know this? It's simply a matter of whether he or she spends most of the time in your interview answering your questions and talking about himself or herself and his or her services, or whether he or she is more focused on what you need. Let me share a story to illustrate this principle.

A while back, I was having lunch with one of my colleagues at a neighborhood café. I looked at the menu and found a sandwich that looked tasty. I also noticed on the menu that a pickle came with the sandwich. For those of you who enjoy eating pickles, you probably like getting one with your sandwich. But for those of us who don't like pickles, getting one with our sandwich can be devastating.

Pickles are very social. They don't stay in one place. Instead, the juice runs all over, infecting the sandwich and anything else on the plate. I'm sure this is great if you enjoy the pickle flavor. But if you don't, just having a pickle on the plate can ruin the entire meal.

Naturally, when our server took our order, I asked if she could please make sure they didn't put a pickle on my plate. "Of course," she said. "No worries." Still, I was worried. So I asked her about it again when she brought our drinks. She assured me that she'd make sure I didn't get a pickle on my plate.

A few minutes later, she brought us our orders. I looked at mine. There was a sandwich, some French fries, and a *pickle*! I was confused. Why did I get a pickle on my plate after asking twice not to get one? Was I not nice enough? (I thought I was nice enough). Did she forget? Did the cook just ignore her?

As my colleague and I sat there, we wondered what we could learn from this situation. Why did I end up with a pickle on my plate? Our conclusion was that the cook or the server must have been too busy with their normal routine to do something outside of it.

How could this tragedy have been avoided? (OK, so it wasn't *that* much of a tragedy). We thought and thought, and then it came to us. What if our server had asked me if I wanted a pickle? Would I have gotten one? Of course not. *Because that would have meant that it was in their routine to find out exactly what the customer wanted.*

The same is true when you are interviewing a tax advisor. If the tax advisor's routine is for you to ask all the questions, he will (and can) only respond to your questions. He can't find out anything you don't volunteer. If, instead, his routine is to ask you questions about your situation, you can be pretty sure that he'll be looking out for you and what you really want.

Not only that, but the tax you pay depends entirely on your facts and circumstances. Remember my saying that any expense can be deductible in the right situation? If your situation changes, then your tax will change. If your tax advisor is not asking you questions about your situation, how can he or she possibly know what the tax consequences will be to you? He or she certainly won't be able to show you how to change your situation so that you receive better tax results.

The reality is that you have all of the answers. Your advisor should have all of the questions. Don't worry about what questions you should ask your tax advisor. If you have to ask the questions, then you simply have the wrong advisor.

Don't worry about what questions you should ask your tax advisor. If you have to ask the questions, then you simply have the wrong advisor.

TAX TIP: Hire the right Tax Advisor. This doesn't just require knowing the right questions to ask a potential tax advisor. It means knowing what questions your tax advisor should be asking you.

Also, remember that only you can reduce your taxes. You have to learn enough about how the tax law applies to you so that you can use it to your benefit every minute of every day. Be sure to find a tax advisor who is willing and able to teach you the rules you need to know in order to reduce your taxes.

Many advisors don't actually want you to know the rules. They're afraid that if you know the rules, you won't need their advice. We both know that's not right. If you know the rules, you'll be more successful at reducing your taxes. When you reduce your taxes, you'll increase your cash flow. When you increase your cash flow, you'll increase your wealth. And when you increase your wealth, you're likely to need your tax advisor even more than you do now. So it's really in your advisor's best interest to take the time to teach you the rules you need to know. It's certainly in your best interest.

	Characteristics of a Good Tax Advisor
1.	Fully educated about the tax law
2.	Passionate about reducing your taxes
3.	Embraces the law as an opportunity
4.	Focuses on permanent tax savings
5.	Uses creativity in applying the law in your favor
6.	Considers the entire law when reducing taxes, not just a single rule of law
7.	Cares more about you than himself or herself
8.	Asks you questions about your specific situation
9.	Willing to teach you the tax rules

The last piece of advice I would give you here is to find a tax advisor who will also prepare your taxes. Don't use a tax preparer who isn't also your tax advisor. If you do, it can be a huge mistake. You could get great advice, and then the preparer might not know how to use this advice in preparing your tax return.

You want to be sure that your preparer isn't just accurate. He or she should also be working to reduce your taxes as he or she prepares your return, and he or she should be reducing your chances of being audited. At my firm, we look at tax return preparation as both the final step in last year's tax planning and the first step in next year's tax planning.

Take the time to look for a good tax advisor who can also prepare your tax returns. Prepare for your interview with a prospective advisor by noting the major points we've discussed in this chapter.

Technical Characteristics of a Good Tax Advisor	
1.	Must be accurate
2.	Prepares your tax returns as well as advises you on your tax strategy
3.	Reduces your taxes as he or she prepares your return
4.	Reduces your chances of being audited

Now that you have all of this knowledge about how to reduce your taxes, what are you going to do next? You should work with your tax advisor to put all of this advice to good use and reduce your taxes right away. This will immediately increase your cash flow. Just think about what you can do with all that extra money!

In the next chapter, we'll talk about how you can use that extra cash flow to massively increase your wealth.

CHAPTER 23: KEY POINTS	
1.	The tax law is intentionally vague and allows for great flexibility—if you know what it says.
2.	One of the most important things you'll ever do to protect your wealth is find not just a good but a great tax advisor and preparer.
3.	The best tax advisors have a vast understanding of the tax law, can think nonlinearly, and are passionately concerned about your needs.
4.	Never use a tax preparer that isn't also your tax advisor. You may otherwise get great advice that is never used and lose out on great tax savings.

Tax Strategy #23 – Hiring the Right Tax Advisor

Here are the top 10 things to talk about when interviewing a tax advisor:

1. What is your view of the tax law?
2. Who gets the most advantages of the tax law?
3. What made you want to become a tax advisor?
4. What would you like to know about me?
5. Tell me about your team of advisors.
6. Describe your personal business experience.
7. Tell me about your personal investment strategy.
8. Where did you earn your Masters of Tax degree?
9. Give me three examples of how to reduce the risk of an IRS audit.
10. Tell me your thoughts about asset protection.

Here are the top 10 things your prospective tax advisor should discuss with you:

1. Tell me about your dreams and goals.
2. Describe your current and projected family situation.
3. Describe your relationship with your spouse and your children.
4. Describe your current and projected investments.
5. Describe your current and projected business situation.
6. Explain your philosophy of tax reduction.
7. What would you like to learn about the tax laws?
8. How do you learn best? Auditory, visual, tactile, or kinesthetic?
9. In a perfect world, how would you like to work with your CPA?
10. Who are the other members of your team?

Are you a CPA?

Would you like to know more about Tax-Free Wealth concepts & how to incorporate them into your business?

Join our network of CPAs

Tax-Free Wealth provides a different way to look at taxes not only for the general public but for the CPA industry. So we're launching The Tax-Free Wealth Network™ to provide CPAs new & better ways to serve their clients.

Why join the network?

More Clients | Training | Community | Culture

For more information:

Text "CPA" to (480) 470-5070

United States & Canada only. Message & data rates may apply. Offer subject to change at anytime. For our privacy policy visit: https://wealthability.com/terms/

WealthAbility™

You can also contact us online:

https://wealthability.com/contact/

Chapter Twenty-Four

What Are You Going to do With All Your Extra Money?

"No one would remember the Good Samaritan if he'd only had good intentions—he had money, too."
– Former British Prime Minister Margaret Thatcher

Congratulations! You now know how the tax law works and how you can use it to reduce your taxes. Think about the great tax refund you'll get this year after you've implemented some of the strategies from this book into your everyday life.

Now, what are you going to do with all that extra money? You may be happy enough just having it in your pocket. Let's face it, refunds from the government just feel better than money that comes any other way. That's what makes tax *refunds* so much fun. It's money that you can use any way you want—all of it. The government doesn't get any of it.

Years ago I worked with a client who was so intent on the government not getting his money that I was sure he'd gladly spend two dollars to keep the government from getting one dollar. He'd do anything to save taxes because he believed the government wasted our tax dollars on needless projects. I suspect he's not the only one out there who feels this way.

I'm not recommending you spend two dollars in order to save one dollar of taxes. In fact, I'm suggesting just the opposite. I'm suggesting that you can save thousands of dollars in taxes simply by understanding the basic principles I've outlined in this book and by implementing them in your daily life, with a little help from a good tax advisor.

So what are you going to do with all that extra cash flow? Are you going to take a vacation, spend it on improving your home, or donate it to charity? Those are all worthwhile endeavors. Still, think about how much better that vacation could be, how much bigger your home could be, or how much more you could donate to charity if you took that extra cash flow and created some serious wealth.

I get it. You want to spend a little of it on yourself right away. You work hard and deserve a vacation. And if you work it right, you can deduct most or all of that vacation on this year's tax return. But what if you focus instead on building a substantial amount of wealth so that you can have better vacations, a bigger home, and do more for your favorite charity in the future? Wouldn't it be great if you didn't have to wait 20 years before you could have everything you want?

Let's look at how you can apply the extra cash flow from your tax savings to speed up the rate at which you build your wealth. The last thing you want to do after learning an entirely new way to increase your cash flow through permanent reductions of your taxes is to then invest all that money the old-fashioned way—by giving it to a mutual fund company or a traditional financial planner.

> *The last thing you want to do after learning an entirely new way to increase your cash flow through permanent reductions of your taxes is to then invest all that money the old-fashioned way—by giving it to a mutual fund company or a traditional financial planner.*

There are three concepts that you must understand in order to produce massive amounts of wealth:

1.	Compound Interest
2.	Leverage
3.	Velocity

These are the three basic principles on which all great wealth is founded.

Compound Interest

When I was growing up, I'd always heard about the magic of compound interest. When I asked what it meant, I was told that compound interest is like magic because it increases even while you sleep, and it constantly gets bigger and bigger. Here's how it works.

Let's say you deposit $10,000 into a certificate of deposit (CD) at the bank. Suppose the interest rate you earn is 5 percent. After the first year, you'll have earned $500. Now, let's say that you leave the $500 in the bank. Now you have $10,500 in the bank. The interest rate of 5 percent is applied both to the original $10,000 and to the $500 of interest you earned over the previous year. So in the second year, you'll earn $525 of interest. The extra $25 in the second year is interest you earned on the interest from the first year—*compound interest.*

Year	Amount	Interest Rate	Interest Earned	Total
1	10,000	5%	500	10,500
2	10,500	5%	525	11,025
3	11,025	5%	551.25	11,576.25
4	11,576.26	5%	578.81	12,155.07
5	12,155.07	5%	607.75	12,762.82
6	12,762.82	5%	638.14	13,400.96
7	13,400.96	5%	670.04	14,071.00
8	14,071	5%	703.55	14,774.55
9	14,774.55	5%	738.72	15,513.27
10	15,513.27	5%	775.66	16,288.93

After 10 years of this, you'll have earned $6,288 in interest. If you'd taken the interest out every year instead, you'd only have earned $5,000.

The extra $1,288 is a result of compounding. And that's the so-called "magic" of compound interest.

It's clear that compounding your interest is important. It should also be just as clear that it's a pretty slow way to build wealth. All you've effectively done is increase your earning rate from 5 percent to about 6.3 percent. And chances are that you're not even keeping up with inflation.

> It's clear that compounding your interest is important. It should also be just as clear that it's a pretty slow way to build wealth.

But what if you could increase your wealth much quicker and more substantially, all without increasing your risk? Well, you can with the real "magic" of leverage.

Leverage

Leverage is what happens when you earn interest on not just your money but also on someone else's money. This is precisely what the bank does when it borrows your money. When would a bank borrow your money? Every time you put your money in the bank, it's borrowing your money.

That's right. Banks are in the business of borrowing and lending money. When someone makes a deposit at the bank, the bank now owes that person the amount of money deposited. The bank also has the right to use that money so long as it's eventually paid back to you. That's why when you deposit money into the bank it's "credited" to your account. From the bank's point of view, it has just borrowed that much money from you, and the bank is liable to you. The bank's liabilities to its depositors are recorded as credits on its balance sheet.

Now what does the bank do with your money? It lends it out to someone else at a higher interest rate than what it pays you. This is called leverage. Let's look at the $10,000 you loaned the bank by putting it into the CD. The bank pays you 5 percent. Let's say the bank lends that money to a business owner at 8 percent. The bank now is earning 8 percent on your money and is paying you 5 percent. So the bank makes a net of 3 percent on money that doesn't even belong to it.

Step 1: You make a deposit

Bank's Balance Sheet

Assets		Liabilities	The bank pays you 5%.
Cash*	+ $10,000	Deposits	+ $10,000
	+ $10,000		+ $10,000

For simplicity's sake, required federal reserves are not included in the example.

Step 2: The bank lends out your money to a business owner

Bank's Balance Sheet

Assets		Liabilities	
Cash	$10,000	Deposits	+ $20,000
Loans	+ $ 10,000	Your Deposit $10,000	
The bank loans out your money at 8%.		*Business Owner's Deposit $10,000	
	$20,000		+ $20,000

In this example, assume that once the borrower (business owner) receives his loan he then deposits the borrowed money into his business account that he has with this same bank.

Sometimes I hear people talking about debt as though it's something extremely risky. This isn't necessarily the case. Nobody would think of a bank being in a particularly risky business so long as it keeps to its primary strategy of lending to low-risk borrowers. The bank does a lot of investigation of someone who wants to borrow money from it before making a loan. That investigation reduces their risk. Another term for an investigation is simply gathering information or education. Education reduces risk.

CAUTION!

Debt is Dangerous for the Uneducated	
1.	Debt is leverage and can speed up your downfall just as fast as it can speed up your wealth.
2.	Before using debt to build wealth, get educated. One of the best ways is by playing Rich Dad's *CASHFLOW* game and taking Rich Dad classes.

By lending out your $10,000, the bank will make $300 per year. No wonder it's willing to pay you interest on your deposit. This is why banks do so much advertising to entice depositors into their bank. The more money they have in deposits, the more they can lend out at higher interest rates.

Parties Involved	Amount	Interest Rate	Result
You Earn	$10,000	5%	$500
The Business Owner Pays	$10,000	8%	$800
The Bank Makes	$800 interest from business owner - $500 interest paid to you = Net $300		

So how can you use this principle of leverage to increase your wealth? You just do what the bank does. You simply entice someone else to lend you the money that you then invest in something that pays you a better rate than what you are paying on your loan.

Who is going to want to lend you money? Banks.

That's right. The same bank where you might otherwise deposit (or lend) your money is also willing to lend you money for the right investment. Banks will lend you money to invest in a business or real estate. (Of course, they'll also lend you money for personal reasons, such as a vacation, but they'll charge very high rates of interest for this. It's called a credit card.)

Notice that banks like to lend money to people on the right side of the CASHFLOW Quadrant—business owners and investors. That's because there's less risk on the right side of the CASHFLOW Quadrant. And banks will only lend to business owners and investors who have the knowledge to be successful so that they will likely pay back the loan.

Let's say you borrow $100,000 from the bank for your business. The bank may charge you 8 percent interest on this loan. You take this $100,000 and buy equipment and inventory that will create income of $12,000 per year. You pay the bank 8 percent, or $8,000, and your net income from borrowing this money is $4,000. You have just used leverage in much the same way as the bank.

Leveraging Money			
Step 1		Step 2	
Borrow	$100,000	Purchase Equipment and Inventory	$100,000
Multiplied by Interest Rate	8%	Multiplied by Return	12%
Equals Cost to You	$ 8,000	Equals Income of	$ 12,000
$12,000 income - $8,000 interest paid = $4,000 net income to you.			

Go back to the $10,000 you deposited in the bank. Instead of putting it into the bank, suppose you put it into your business along with the $100,000 the bank loaned you. You end up earning 12 percent on your $10,000 plus 4 percent on the bank's money. In total, after the first year, you have earned $5,200 ($10,000 x 12% plus $100,000 x 4%). Compare that to the $500 that you would've earned if you'd only put your money into the bank's CD. That's the magic of leverage!

Velocity

When I think of velocity I always think of a racecar. How fast can I go? A few years ago, my partner, Ann, gave me a gift certificate for Christmas to race a Formula-1-style racecar at Phoenix International Raceway. I was very excited to do this because I love to drive fast. Who doesn't? And this time I could do it legally.

When I got to the track, I found out I wasn't the only person who liked going fast. There were about 20 other people at the track with the same idea. The first thing the instructors did was put us all in a small room to teach us about the cars we'd be driving and the raceway. Then they gave us coveralls, a helmet, and goggles so that we'd be somewhat protected in case of a crash. From there, we went out to the track, and they walked us through how to drive the racecars.

They then put us all in a van and drove around the track. This was to show us where to go on the track in order to maximize our speed and reduce the chance of an accident. I was amazed at how fast the van drivers were able to take their big vans around the racetrack. They were clearly practiced and excellent drivers. Finally, we were allowed into our cars. The first time around the track, they had us go pretty slow. They wanted us to get a feel for the car and for the track. At last, after that first lap, they let us rip and go as fast as we wanted.

At first, I was a little tentative. I slowed down as I took the curves and then sped up on the straight-aways. But after I went around the track a few times, I started to use my brakes less and to hold my speed through the curves. After a few more times, I discovered that I could hold my gas pedal to the floor throughout the entire track without being in danger of losing control. It felt great to maintain my velocity throughout the entire race.

These exact same principles apply to the velocity of money. Just as with a car, the key to going as fast as possible without losing control is to gain knowledge and experience quickly and apply that knowledge and experience to the race. In the case of money, the race is to reach your dream. The faster you can gain knowledge and experience, the sooner you'll reach your dream.

The key to financial velocity is to keep your money moving. Think about your compound interest with the bank. All you did was leave your money sitting in the bank. It wasn't moving. So while it earned a small amount of interest, it took 10 years just to earn $6,288. Then think about what happened when you added leverage. You earned almost the same amount in the first year that it would have taken 10 years to earn relying solely on compound interest.

You could've earned still more by using the principle of velocity. Think about it this way. Leverage is really just compound interest using someone else's money. Velocity is a way to increase your leverage. Here's how it works.

> *The key to financial velocity is to keep your money moving.*

Let's say you borrow the $100,000 from the bank to add to your $10,000 to invest in your business. One of the reasons the bank has agreed to lend to you is that you have put some of your own money into the business. This is called having skin in the game.

After the first year, you have earned a total of $13,200 on that money at 12 percent. You have to pay the bank its interest of $8,000, so you are left with just over $5,000. Now if the bank was willing to lend you $100,000 so long as you put in $10,000, then the bank should be willing to lend you another $50,000 because you now have another $5,000 invested of your own money in the business. This is true even though that $5,000 came from business earnings. Banks like to see you leave earnings in the business. These are called "retained" earnings because you retain them in the business.

Compound Interest, Leverage, and Velocity Creating Retained Earnings Year 1	
Borrowed Money ($100,000) plus your money ($10,000)	= $110,000
Multiplied by investment earnings ($110,000 X 12%) =	$ 13,200
Minus cost of borrowing ($100,000 X 8%)	- $ 8,000
Equals retained earnings of	= $ 5,200

With the additional $50,000, plus the $5,000 you have from your first-year earnings, you can earn another 12 percent. You still have the original $110,000, so you earn 12 percent on that money, too. In the second year, you will now earn $19,800 ($165,000 x 12%). You have to pay the bank its interest of 8 percent on the total loan of $150,000, or $12,000. This leaves you with net earnings in the second year of almost $8,000. That's $3,000 more than you earned the first year.

Compound Interest, Leverage, and Velocity Creating Retained Earnings Year 2	
Borrowed Money ($150,000) plus your original $10,000 plus retained earnings of $5,200	= $165,200
Multiplied by investment earnings ($165,200 X 12%) =	$ 19,824
Minus cost of borrowing ($150,000 X 8%)	- $ 12,000
Equals retained earnings of	= $ 7,824

The additional earnings are the result of using all three of our core wealth principles: compound interest, leverage, and velocity. You earned compound interest on all of the money. You leveraged your initial $10,000 investment by borrowing $100,000 from the bank. Instead of being content with the earnings on the $110,000, you decided to leverage again with the earnings from the first year. This is where you borrowed the additional $50,000. Leveraging your first year's earned interest is called velocity. You're simply moving your money into additional leverage so that you can continue gaining speed in building your wealth. By doing this you would earn a total $13,000 after just two years.

Compare this to the $1,025 you would've earned had you just put your $10,000 into a bank CD earning 5 percent or the $11,000 you would have earned if you hadn't re-leveraged your first-year interest by borrowing the additional $50,000. And the longer you go and the more velocity you gain, the faster and faster you build your wealth.

It's all about momentum. The more you leverage and the faster you re-employ your money, the faster you will build your wealth. Just remember the lessons at the speedway:

- Start by getting a proper education from experts who know what they're doing.

- Then take some practice runs with the experts. When you do start investing or building your business on your own, start slowly and get used to the feel of the track (the investing or the business).

- After a few turns around the track, you can pick up speed and move faster and faster until, before you know it, you'll be moving at a very fast speed and won't even have to slow down for the curves in the road.

WEALTH TIP:	Use my simple formula to create massive passive income. Start with earned income, invest in growth assets, create a huge amount of capital from your growth assets, and then invest in assets that generate passive income. With a substantial amount of capital, even investments with modest returns result in massive passive income.

And that's when it really gets fun. It's where I am now with my business. I started by learning from the experts as an employee. I looked at it as my internship. Eventually, I went out on my own, starting slow at first, without any employees. Then I added a few employees, and I eventually added partners.

Now I'm moving at breakneck speed. I no longer spend hours and hours at the office doing the work. I train others to do the work and employ tried and true systems to make sure they do what they've been trained to do. I can now re-employ my personal capital and leverage with other people. It's not just money I can leverage. I can leverage other people's time, talents, and even their personal contacts.

> *The more you leverage and the faster you re-employ your money, the faster you will build your wealth.*

This is the only way to safely build long-term wealth very quickly. Get-rich-quick schemes never work in the long run. They are like winning the lottery—very risky, and even when you do win you don't know what to do with your winnings and soon lose them.

Using compound interest, leverage, and velocity will work every time when you follow the rules I've outlined here. And you don't even have to use your savings. Just use the money you saved by permanently reducing your taxes.

CHAPTER 24: KEY POINTS

1.	Tax savings are exciting, but the most exciting part of tax savings is using that money to increase your wealth.
2.	The three foundations of wealth building are compound interest, leverage, and velocity.
3.	Compound interest by itself is a very slow way to build wealth, but combined with leverage and velocity, it's a powerful wealth-building tool.
4.	The only way to actually save money in taxes is to first start implementing the strategies found in this book. Find a great tax advisor and get started today!

Tax Strategy #24 – Build Massive Passive Income through Your Tax Savings

Throughout Chapter 24, we used the example of investing $10,000 to generate wealth through compounding, leverage, and velocity. Now, let's look at what happens when you add the tax benefits from all of the lessons in the previous twenty-three chapters. In our example in this chapter, with leverage and velocity, you increased your earnings on $10,000 investment from just over $1,000 to over $13,000 in two years. What happens when you add your tax benefits?

Let's suppose that your tax strategy produces tax savings of $20,000 per year. You can take that $20,000, add leverage (say $80,000) and buy an additional investment for $100,000. That $100,000 produces income at 12 percent, or $12,000. You pay 8 percent to the bank on your $80,000 loan or $6,400, leaving you with additional earnings of $5,600. The second year, you earn 12 percent on $105,600 ($100,000 plus $5,600 earned in the first year) for a total earnings of $12,672. You pay interest on your $80,000 loan of $6,400, leaving you with additional earnings of $6,272. Plus, you have another $20,000 of tax savings, since your tax strategy produces $20,000 of tax savings every year. So, you invest this along with another $80,000 bank loan, producing net income of $5,600 from this investment. Now, after two years, you have added $11,872 of investment earnings to your original $13,024 for a total of $24,896 of investment earnings over just two years on a single investment of $10,000, plus investing your tax savings from your tax strategy. Compare this to your $1,025 of earnings from putting $10,000 in the bank without any leverage, velocity, or tax planning. You increased your earnings by over 23 times in just two years by changing how you think about money. And this doesn't even include the $40,000 you have in additional equity because of your two years of saving $20,000 in taxes.

Compound Interest Earnings Year 1 and 2	
Year 1 Interest =	$500
Year 2 Interest =	<u>$525</u>
Total =	$1,025

Leverage and Velocity Earnings Year 1 and 2	
Year 1 Investment Earnings =	$5,200
Year 2 Investment Earnings =	<u>$7,824</u>
Total =	$13,024

Leverage, Velocity and Tax Benefits Investment Earnings Year 1	
Tax Strategy produces $20,000 in tax savings + use $80,000 in Leverage (borrow) to purchase an investment =	$100,000
Multiplied by investment earnings ($100,000 X 12%)	$ 12,000
Minus cost of borrowing ($80,000 X 8%)	– $ <u>6,400</u>
Equals investment earnings of =	$ 5,600

Leverage, Velocity and Tax Benefits Investment Earnings Year 2	
Investment ($100,000) plus year 1 earnings ($5,600) =	$105,600
Multiplied by investment earnings ($105,600 X 12%)	$ 12,672
Minus cost of borrowing ($80,000 X 8%)	– $ 6,400
Equals investment earnings of =	$ 6,272

Invest Tax Benefits from $20,000 Tax Savings Year 1 and 2	
Year 1 Investment Earnings =	$5,600
Year 2 Investment Earnings =	$6,272
Total =	$11,872

Total Earnings from a Single Investment Plus Tax Savings Leverage, Velocity and Tax Benefits	
Leverage and Velocity Investment Earnings =	$13,024
Tax Investment Earnings =	$11,872
Total =	$24,896
Return on Investment =	125%

Are you beginning to see the amazing benefits of adding tax savings to your wealth strategy? You almost doubled your investment earnings in just two years simply by investing your tax savings from your tax strategy. Of course, this is just an example. Your tax savings could be more or less than $20,000 per year, depending on the level of your income and the quality of your tax advisor. No matter what, you are better off using a combination of compounding, leverage, velocity, and tax savings to build your wealth.

Tax-Free Wealth:
A Few Final Thoughts

You've learned a lot about permanently reducing your taxes and building wealth in this book. Don't stop here. Be sure to take the time to sit down with your team to build your own tax and wealth strategy. You now have lots of ammunition for creating a tax strategy and Chapter 24 gave you a few insights into building a wealth strategy. The real key to your wealth is to combine your tax strategy with your wealth strategy. Begin by looking at your key team members—your tax strategist (tax advisor) and your wealth strategist. At the end of Chapter 23, I gave you a few hints on how to find your tax strategist.

But what about your wealth strategist? Wouldn't a team member who understands all of your situation, understands how to build massive passive income, and understands how to build a team be crucial to your wealth? Of course. Where do you find this person? The answer is simple. Your wealth strategist should be your tax strategist. Building wealth is a fairly simple formula. Compound interest plus leverage plus velocity plus tax reduction. The most complex part of this formula is your tax reduction. So why not have a wealth strategist who understands this complex area and already knows your entire situation—your tax advisor?

Now you have additional ammunition to attack your wealth. You have someone on your team who understands you, how to build wealth, and how to reduce your taxes. Then make the effort to implement everything you have learned, using all of the concepts we've discussed so that you can enjoy tax-free wealth. Never forget that a good strategy starts with a dream, a dream to reduce your taxes and then using those tax savings to build permanent wealth.

Yes, it's going to take time and effort. Begin by making a conscious decision to reduce your taxes and increase your wealth now. The longer you postpone doing it, the more taxes you'll pay and the longer it will take to reach your dream. The great thing about reducing your taxes is that you really can start doing so today simply by applying the concepts you've learned in this book.

And think about how much fun you're going to have building your wealth when you stop relying solely on compound interest and start using leverage and velocity instead. After all, it's much more fun driving a fast racecar than it is walking around the block. And you'll get to your destination much quicker.

My favorite part of the business is helping others reach their dreams. Please be sure to visit wealthability.com for additional resources to achieve your tax-free wealth goals. It's been a pleasure sharing this information with you. I hope to meet you in person sometime soon at a Rich Dad seminar or in our offices in Tempe, Arizona.

About the Author
Tom Wheelwright, CPA

Tom Wheelwright, CPA, is the creative force behind WealthAbility, the world's premier Tax-Free Wealth movement serving entrepreneurs and investors worldwide. As the founder and CEO, Tom has been responsible for innovating new tax, business and wealth consulting and strategy services for premium clientele for the past 22 years.

Tom is a leading expert and published author on partnerships and corporation tax strategies, a well-known platform speaker and a wealth education innovator. Donald Trump selected Tom to contribute to his Wealth Builders Program, calling Tom "the best of the best." Robert Kiyosaki, bestselling author of *Rich Dad Poor Dad*, calls Tom "a team player that anyone who wants to be rich needs to add to his team." In Robert Kiyosaki's book, "The Real Book of Real Estate," Tom, himself, authored Chapters 1 and 18 of this book. Tom also contributed to Robert Kiyosaki's *Rich Dad's Success Stories. Who Took My Money?*, *Unfair Advantage* and was Robert adjuvant for *Why the Rich Are Getting Richer.*

Tom has written several articles for publication in major professional journals and online resources and has spoken to thousands throughout the United States, Canada, Mexico, Asia, South America, Africa, Europe and Australia.

For more than 35 years, Tom has devised innovative tax, business and wealth strategies for sophisticated investors and business owners in the manufacturing, real estate and high-tech fields. His passion is teaching these innovative strategies to the thousands who come to hear him speak. He has participated as a keynote speaker and panelist in multiple roundtables, and led ground-breaking tax discussions challenging the status quo in terms of tax strategies.

Tom has a wide variety of professional experience, ranging from Big 4 accounting, where he managed and led professional training for thousands of CPAs at Ernst & Young's National Tax Department in Washington,

D.C., to in-house tax advisor for Pinnacle West Capital Corporation, at the time a Fortune 1000 company. Tom also served as an adjunct professor in the Masters of Tax program at Arizona State University for 14 years where he created the course for teaching multi-state tax planning techniques and taught hundreds of graduate students. He currently teaches his Tax and Asset Protection class with fellow Rich Dad Advisor, Garrett Sutton.

Tom has his Master's of Professional Accounting degree from the University of Texas at Austin and his Bachelor of Arts degree from the University of Utah.

Sign up for Tom's FREE Weekly Report!
Text "JOIN" to (480) 470-5070

United States & Canada only. Message & data rates may apply.
Offer subject to change at anytime.

For more tools & resources visit Tom at:
wealthability.com

References and Resources

For additional information, the following websites are suggested:

Books and Information for Investors and Entrepreneurs
www.RDAPress.com

Real Estate
www.Ken.Mcelroy.com
www.mccompanies.com

Asset Protection and LLC Formation
www.sutlaw.com
www.corporatedirect.com

Tax Planning
www.wealthability.com

Sales Strategies
www.salesdogs.com

The Rich Dad Company
www.RichDad.com

WealthAbility™

Recommended Reading
- *Unfair Advantage* by Robert Kiyosaki
- *The Real Book of Real Estate* by Robert Kiyosaki with 22 of His Trusted Real Estate Experts
- *SalesDogs* by Blair Singer
- *Team Code of Honor* by Blair Singer
- *Start Your Own Corporation* by Garrett Sutton, Esq.
- *Writing Winning Business Plans* by Garrett Sutton, Esq.
- *The ABCs of Real Estate Investing* by Ken McElroy
- *401(k)aos* by Andy Tanner
- *The Corruption of Capitalism* by Richard Duncan
- *Creature from Jekyll Island* by G. Edward Griffin

Team Players
- The Rich Dad Company: richdad.com
- Rich Dad Education: richdadeducation.com
- Rich Dad Coaching: richdadcoaching.com
- Blair Singer: blairsinger.com
- Andy Tanner: 401kaos.com
- Garrett Sutton, Esq.: sutlaw.com
- Ken McElroy: kenmcelroy.com

Websites
- RichDadAdvisors.com
- wealthability.com
- facebook.com/Tom.Wheelwright.CPA
- facebook.com/TaxFreeWealthBook
- richdad.com

Contact Us
- wealthability.com
- 888–801–8944

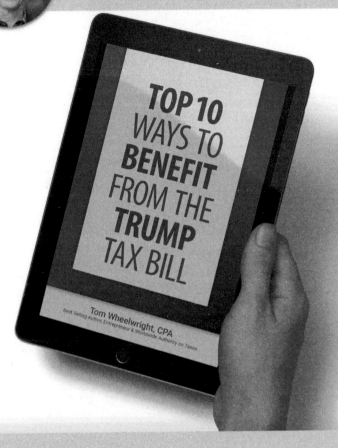

Notes

RICH DAD ADVISORS

The Rich Dad Advisors series of books was created to deliver the how-to content to support Robert Kiyosaki's series of international bestsellers: *Rich Dad Poor Dad* and the Rich Dad series of books. In *Rich Dad Poor Dad*—the #1 Personal Finance Book of all Time—Robert presented the foundation for the Rich Dad principles and philosophies and set the stage for his context-changing messages that have changed the way the world thinks about money, business and investing.

The Rich Dad Advisors series of books has sold more than 2 million copies worldwide and RDA Press, exclusive publisher of the Rich Dad Advisor series and the licensor of International Rights for the series, will be releasing several new titles that will expand both the scope and depth of the series.

Rich Dad Poor Dad represents the most successful book on personal finance in our generation. Over the last 15 years, its messages have inspired millions of people and impacted tens of millions of lives in over 100 countries around the world. The Rich Dad books have continued to international bestseller lists because their messages continue to resonate with readers of all ages. *Rich Dad Poor Dad* has succeeded in lifting the veil of confusion, fear, and frustration around money and replacing it with clarity, truth, and hope for every person who is willing to commit to the process of becoming financially educated.

In order to make good on the promise of financial literacy and ultimate freedom, Robert Kiyosaki assembled his own team of personal and trusted advisors, proven experts in their respective fields, to deliver the only complete 'how-to' series of books and programs that takes the messages of Rich Dad to the streets of the world and gives each reader the step-by-step processes to achieve wealth and income in business, investing, and entrepreneurship.

RDA Press is driven by several of Kiyosaki's actual Advisors who have committed to take the messages of Rich Dad, convert them to practical applications and make sure those processes are put in the hands of those who seek financial literacy and financial freedom around the world. The series gives practical, proven processes to succeed in the areas of finance, tax, entrepreneurship, investing, property, debt, sales, wealth management and both business and personal development. Three of these trusted and accomplished Advisors—Blair Singer, Garrett Sutton, and Ken McElroy— are the driving forces behind RDA Press.

RDA Press is proud to assume the role of publisher of the Rich Dad Advisor series and perpetuate a series of books that has sold millions of copies worldwide and, more importantly, supported tens of millions in their journey toward financial freedom.

Best-Selling Books in the
Rich Dad Advisors Series

BY BLAIR SINGER

Sales Dogs
You Don't Have to Be an Attack Dog to Explode Your Income

Team Code of Honor
The Secrets of Champions in Business and in Life

Summit Leadership
Taking Your Team to the Top

BY GARRETT SUTTON, ESQ.

Start Your Own Corporation
Why the Rich Own their Own Companies and Everyone Else Works for Them

Writing Winning Business Plans
How to Prepare a Business Plan that Investors will Want to Read and Invest In

Buying and Selling a Business
How You Can Win in the Business Quadrant

The ABCs of Getting Out of Debt
Turn Bad Debt into Good Debt and Bad Credit into Good Credit

Run Your Own Corporation
How to Legally Operate and Properly Maintain Your Company into the Future

The Loopholes of Real Estate
Secrets of Successful Real Estate Investing

Scam-Proof Your Assets
Guarding Against Widespread Deception

Piercing the Corporate Veil
When LLCs and Corporations Fail

BY KEN MCELROY

The ABCs of Real Estate Investing
The Secrets of Finding Hidden Profits Most Investors Miss

The ABCs of Property Management
What You Need to Know to Maximize Your Money Now

The Advanced Guide to Real Estate Investing
How to Identify the Hottest Markets and Secure the Best Deals

ABCs of Buying Rental Property
How You Can Achieve Financial Freedom in Five Years

Notes

How Can I Protect My Personal, Business and Real Estate Assets?

For information on forming corporations, limited liability companies and limited partnerships to protect your personal, business and real estate holdings in all 50 states visit the Corporate Direct website at

www.CorporateDirect.com

or

call toll-free: 1-800-600-1760

Mention this book and receive a discount on your basic formation fee.

A BRIGHTER FUTURE STARTS WITH ONE STEP

WHY THE RICH ARE GETTING RICHER

What Is Financial Education ...Really?

ROBERT T. KIYOSAKI

Author of the International Bestseller *Rich Dad Poor Dad*

TOM WHEELWRIGHT, CPA • ADJUVANT